The Outer Banks Cookbook

The OUTER BANKS COOKBOOK

Recipes and Traditions from North Carolina's Barrier Islands

ELIZABETH WIEGAND

ThreeForks™

GUILFORD, CONNECTICUT
HELENA, MONTANA

AN IMPRINT OF THE GLOBE PEQUOT PRESS

Text design by Nancy Freeborn

Photos.com: shell border throughout, p. ii, p. vii, p. 22, p. 23, p. 33, p. 61, p. 63, p. 78, p. 79, pp. 86–87, p. 103, p. 115, pp. 126–27, p. 137, pp. 142–43, p. 156, p. 159, p.161, p. 163, p. 164, p. 171, p. 173, pp. 214–15, p. 227, p. 233, p. 245, p. 249, pp. 250–51, p. 255, pp. 264–65, p. 281, pp. 283–84, p. 289, p. 293, p. 315, p. 316

Clipart.com: p. 19, p. 20, p. 31, p. 37, pp. 39–41, pp. 44–45, p. 52, p. 54, p. 57, p. 62, p. 65, p. 66, pp. 68–69, pp. 70–71, p. 73, p. 75, p. 81, p. 85, p. 96, pp. 98–99, p. 101, p. 102, p. 108, p. 116, p. 119, p. 121, p. 128, p. 131, p. 133, p. 135, p. 139, p. 141, p. 146, p. 153, p. 154, p. 157, p. 169, p. 172, p. 183, p. 195, p. 197, p. 207, p. 209, p. 210, p. 213, p. 217, p. 225, p. 229, p. 236, p. 241, p. 242, p. 267, p. 268, p. 271, p. 277, p. 293, p. 305, p. 310, p. 313, p. 317, p. 320

Library of Congress Cataloging-in-Publication Data is available.

ISBN 978-0-7627-4601-9

Printed in the United States of America

10 9 8 7 6 5 4 3

This book is dedicated to the wonderful people of the Outer Banks,

especially Della Basnight,

a true "Banker" even if she is from "Maddeo" (Manteo),

as the folks down Hatteras Island would say.

contents

Photo on facing
page courtesy of
Island Photography

Acknowledgments

I would like to thank all those wonderful home cooks and professional chefs who so willingly shared with me their food, stories, and recipes:

Della Basnight, a true friend who opened so many doors to her friends, family, and restaurants up and down the Banks; Peggy Snead, for the secret to her marvelous cake; Helen and Luther Daniels, Frank White, John Gaskill, Natalie Gould Mandell, Ivadean Priest, Tom and Alice Skinner, John Gillam, Missy and Tommy Manning, Dale Mutro, Dennis Williams, and Jeanie Williams, who shared what life was like on the Outer Banks when they were young, along with their recipes; Lynne and Ernie Foster, for their connections on Hatteras and their recipes; Denise Selby Daniels, with the marvelous Wanchese Watermen calendar; and these chefs: Annie Davis of The Great Gut Deli, Bud Gruninger of Basnight's Lone Cedar Café, Carlen Pearl of The Colington Café, Dolly Gray Jones of Sam and Omie's, Leonard Logan of Elizabeth's Café, Wes Stepp of Red Sky Café, Forrest Paddock of The Salty Gourmet, Tom Sloate and Lee Miller of Penquin Isle, Jane Oden of Breakwater, Rob Robinson of The Bad Bean Taqueria, Ruth Toth of Café Atlantic, Daphne Bennink of The Back Porch, Jomi Price and Anna Merrill of Mack Daddy's, Tom Lozupone of Stripers Bar & Grille, Michael Kelly of Kelly's, Jerry Smith or "Chef Dirt," Sam McGann of The Blue Point, and Rhett Elliott, Christine Zambito, and Kevin Wirt of The Sanderling Resort & Spa.

And a very special thanks to Allie Hawkins of Island Photography, who graciously provided photos. Her approach to photography is to look for the emotions and true expressions of people, events, and places, and it shows in all of Mike and Allie's beautiful images. Thanks also to my friend, Lisa M. Stroud, for capturing my best image.

And a heartfelt thanks to those who provide me with the best of life—their love and support—especially my husband, Steve; our three daughters, Kate, Em, and Bec; and my dear friends who went that extra mile to test my recipes and listen to me whine.

Introduction

When most people think of the Outer Banks, they conjure up visions of white sandy beaches, pounding surf, the smell of suntan lotion, and hours spent lounging with the sand between their toes and the sun on their brows. Maybe they recall the wild horses roaming up near Corolla or down in Ocracoke, or the hang gliders at Jockey's Ridge, or the miles of undeveloped, pristine ocean and sand along the Cape Hatteras National Seashore.

The Outer Banks as a destination continues to win awards, like the recent "Best Beach in the whole country" or "among the Ten Most Romantic Escapes in the U.S." So many fall in love with and on the Outer Banks, then return to be married here, that wedding planning and photography are a huge business. Honeymooners share the playground of the Outer Banks with college buddies, family reunions, hang gliders, surfers, and kite boarders, with big dreams of catching big waves, feeling hot sand, and tasting the salt.

Not me. I go to the Outer Banks to eat. My mouth salivates at the thought of eating crisply fried oysters from Rose Bay, soft-shell crabs shed on Colington Island on the full moon of May, or fresh yellowfin tuna brought into Hatteras Village Harbor, grilled rare and served with a mouth-burning wasabi sauce. Or maybe warming up with some classic Outer Banks clam chowder, or firing up the grill for bacon-wrapped scallops, or peeling green-tailed shrimp, fresh and succulent from the waters of Pamlico Sound. My husband, on the other hand, dreams of reeling in a big striper from the beach, or snagging some dolphinfish out in the Gulf Stream, which he can proudly bring back to our kitchen.

Wild horses believed to be descendants of Spanish Mustangs at Corolla and Ocracoke. Photo courtesy of Island Photography

So much seafood, too many choices. Eat in, or choose from dozens of restaurants that dazzle the tastebuds. Now, that's my kind of trip to the Outer Banks.

The Weather and Sea Fare

Seen from above or on a map, the Outer Banks look like a long, skinny finger extending from the Virginia border, cut through by an inlet or two, and extending past Cape Hatteras, then making a sudden turn west toward the mainland. Not all of the Outer Banks are islands; technically, the northern reaches are part of a sandy spit. But they might as well be an island, cut off from the rest of the world with no road leading north, save the beach at low tide.

The sandy ridges of the Outer Banks are a barrier, protecting the largest estuarine area of connecting sounds in the country from the potentially raging Atlantic Ocean. At many points, you can see both ocean and sound, and really feel how fragile this environment is.

The weather is always a factor on the Outer Banks, for it can affect mobility and safety, and the chances of bringing in seafood. Too much rain or not enough increases or decreases the chance for shrimp to thrive, the salinity oysters need to grow, or whether larvae can feed. Flooding from the mainland can float pollutants into the marshes where fish, oysters, and clams spawn and develop. Wind-driven tides remove vegetation needed for crabs to molt, or fish to feed. Hurricanes can destroy homes for humans and sea creatures alike.

The availability of shellfish and finfish is affected by this sometimes wild weather. But the good news is that it most always bounces back within a season or two. It's the human factors, pollution, development, and overharvest-

The Outer Banks has been named as one of the most romantic destinations in the country, and weddings are frequently held on the beach. Photo courtesy of Island Photography

ing, that are creating havoc with oysters, clams, and some fish. Watermen along the Outer Banks are searching for ways to cope and continue to bring quality seafood to the table.

The Mouthwatering Effects of Tourism

The Outer Banks draws seven million visitors each year to its 100-plus miles of sandy shores. Most come during the summer, renting huge McMansions lining the beaches from Corolla to Hatteras, with the Cape Hatteras National Seashore in between. Others play in the surf, sleep in motels, and eat at the many restaurants lining both the beach roads and the Bypass. The lucky few continue generations of family traditions, opening their own cottages to hordes of visiting family during the warmer months for stays that can last weeks at a time.

Clams, crabs, oysters, and more await at this fresh seafood market in the Duck of today. E F Wiegand

Tourists have always been an influencing factor, especially on Outer Banks menus. What is cooked and served today reflects flavors from around the world, yet surprisingly, the old, traditional foods remain. Thank Heavens.

To understand how the Outer Banks cuisine developed, take a look at its history. We'll start with who was here first—the Native Americans.

The First Outer Banks Tourists

The very first tourists on the Outer Banks were Native Americans from the mainland who came to fish, much like today's anglers. The Algonquians had a large settlement on Roanoke Island, and evidence points to one permanent Indian settlement on the barrier islands, near Buxton on Hatteras. So these locals also saw traffic, albeit via canoes, headed to the beaches.

Other coastal tribes near the Outer Banks included the Machapungas or Mattamuskeets on the mainland between Albemarle Sound and the Pamlico River, and the Poteskeets, on the mainland opposite Currituck Banks. They and other Indian tribes from farther inland traveled to the Outer Banks during the early summer or late fall, before and after their harvests, to fish and hunt and thus supplement their food supply. They didn't stay, just visited the sandy banks long enough to make their catches to take back home.

With hooks and line, arrows and spears, and a series of weirs or impoundments, they caught mullet, flounder, trout, channel bass, and other fish. Sometimes they built fires in the middle of their canoes at night to blind the fish, which they would then spear with the sharpened end of their oar. They barbecued their catch, then flaked the fish into pieces to further dry in the sun so that they could transport the fish back home. Skate, oysters, and clams were opened and then dried on a gridiron of canes.

The woods on the soundsides of Hatteras Island, at Collington, and up in Duck, provided the Indians with small deer, raccoons, and other game, and they hunted or trapped migrating ducks and geese from the marshlands. Later, early colonists would object to hunting by the Poteskeets, who lived on the mainland opposite of Duck, because they were raising cattle that roamed freely on the island. The Indians pressed their case with the North Carolina Council in 1715, and were awarded the right to continue to hunt.

Blackberries and grapes grew on some of the sandy hammocks, providing welcome treats. Otherwise, these barrier islands offered little vegetation to eat. Fortunately during their travels, the Indians carried ground cornmeal in pouches to mix with water to fry into corn pones, as well as dried egg yolks to enrich their meat stews.

These visiting Indians were the first to enjoy a seasonal visit to the Outer Banks, taking home their catch and undoubtedly good memories, just as today's tourists do.

Native Americans on Roanoke Island

Roanoke Island has always served as a base for the rest of the Outer Banks. The Algonquians who lived there permanently were a peaceful and generous people. During the era of the first European contact, two of their chiefdoms existed: that of Wingina, who first welcomed the Englishmen Barlowe and Armadas; and of Wanchese, who traveled back to England with them. They were also part of the Croatan Algonquian tribe near Buxton Woods on Hatteras. Their villages had streets, buildings, storage sheds for grains, longhouses, fenced fields, and tall palisades.

On Roanoke, they grew tobacco, which they used in their prayers and as a medicine. Maize, or corn, was the primary crop, which they planted three times during the growing season, after the wild fruit began to ripen so that the birds would leave their seed alone. Both men and women took care of the communal cornfields.

Between the mounds of corn they planted beans and peas, which they cooked into a mush and then made into a bread. Potatoes, melons, gourds, and pumpkins were grown in small garden patches near their huts, as painted by the Lost Colony's Governor and artist, John White. Sunflower seeds were cooked to make a broth and bread. On Roanoke, they grew an herb whose ashes were used to season their food.

The Algonquians also picked wild berries, such as elder, black, dew, and huckleberries; grapes, persimmons, and pawpaw; walnuts and acorns; and the seeds of sea oats growing on the dunes. In the wooded areas, they hunted with bows and arrows for bears, deer, rabbits, and other small game, and in the marsh, ducks and geese.

Fishing was a fine art, for they used reeds to build weirs, not unlike present-day pound nets, for channeling fish into impoundments. Spears and harpoons, using sharp points probably made from horseshoe crabs and large fish bones, helped them snare a variety of fish, from mullet, flounder, trout, rays, and even porpoises. Mounds of oyster shells indicate they enjoyed oyster roasts. Likewise with clams. Coastal

Indians cooked their fish, even shellfish, on grids made of reeds over hot coals.

They were superstitious about their ability to land their catches, too. Legend has it that a young hunter or fisherman would never allow himself to eat his first kill or catch, because that would kill his ability to catch forever. Neither was a "big-bellied woman" allowed to eat the first fish caught with a brand-new weir, for fear that the weir would never catch much fish after that.

The Outer Banks Welcome

Three days after Captains Philip Amadas and Arthur Barlowe finally found their way through an inlet in the Outer Banks and anchored in Pamlico Sound in July 1584, they were greeted by three Indians onshore. The Englishmen rowed over and, assured that no one on either side meant any harm, rowed back to one boat with one of the Indians, who accepted some wine and meat, and a hat and shirt as gifts. Not to be outdone, the Indian left, fetched his canoe, and began to fish by their boats, filling his dugout till it overflowed with his catch. He paddled ashore and divided the fish into two piles on the beach, then pointed to each ship before leaving. The next day, another greeting party appeared. Among them was Granganimeo (the brother of their chief, Wingina), who tried to use sign language to make the Englishmen feel welcome. Some of the Indians came aboard and traded furs for tin breastplates, copper kettles, and knives. For several days, Granganimeo kept the men fed, sending them venison, hares, fish, root crops, fruit, and corn.

Then Barlowe and seven others followed the Indians twenty miles or so up the sound to the island they called Roanoke, where there was a village of nine cedar houses inside a palisade. Barlowe wrote about this encounter, but historians have questioned whether he exaggerated

Endurance Seafood specializes in soft-shell crabs. E F Wiegand

this story in order to present a more enticing image of this Brave New World.

He claims that at the landing was the wife of Granganimeo, who ordered the villagers to pull their boats ashore. She led them to her five-room house, sat them before a big fire, and ordered their clothes off, which she then washed and hung to dry. Then she led them to an inner room, where she had laid out boiled venison, fish, melons, root vegetables of all kinds, a wheat porridge, and some fruit. They were served wine, which Barlowe noted was only available while the grapes lasted for lack of casks for storage, and also tea flavored with sassafras, black cinnamon, and ginger.

The Englishmen refused to stay the night, out of fear. So this generous woman sent them on their way with more food for their supper, pots and all, then sent out mats to cover them from the rain while they slept in their rowboats out in the sound. Men and women from the village sat on the banks all night to make sure they were okay.

The rest of that summer was spent trading with these Algonquians and exploring the waters around Roanoke. They returned to England with rosy reports, which some claim were overly positive in order to persuade the Queen to continue her support of their explorations.

They also took back two fine specimens of Wingandacon—Manteo and Wanchese, each leaders of tribes on Roanoke Island. They were present when Queen Elizabeth knighted Walter Raleigh and gave permission for a permanent settlement in this New World called Virginia in her honor. After Wanchese returned from his visit to England, he could not understand why the colonists would not trade or share more of the riches of their island, and things soured between the natives and the English.

The Lost Colonists

The story has been told often, most eloquently by North Carolina native Paul Green's long-running play, *The Lost Colony,* of how Governor John White brought settlers from England searching for a better life to Roanoke Island; of how he left them to return to England for more supplies and support, but got waylaid and did not return for three long years, only to find them gone. Lost.

No matter how bountiful the waters seemed to be, life was hard for all coastal Native Americans who lived there at that time, compared to those who lived in the interior. Although the Algonquians were able to nourish themselves by what nature provided, it was basically subsistence living. With the Lost Colonists, the Indians did not offer much food, even for trade. Reportedly, the friendly Croatans told John White before he left for his return voyage seeking more supplies, that they did not have enough resources to sustain his colonists because of an ongoing drought. They could coax only a meager amount of food from this relatively infertile land, because rather than replenishing nutrients back into the soil when they planted corn, they would move on to a new patch of land, slashing and burning to make their garden plots. Perhaps they ran out of room on Roanoke.

There were other significant threats. Northeasters and hurricanes ravaged the islands like they do today. There were the hostile and more sophisticated Tuscaroras in the interior, and later, an increasing number of European settlers and their guns. By the time explorer and historian John Lawson arrived at Hatteras in 1700, the coastal Indians had all but disappeared, merging with other tribes on the mainland, migrating to more fertile lands, dying from disease, or being killed by their enemies.

Pirates, Pilots, and Permanent Settlers

Colington Island, near Kill Devil Hills, was "given" to Sir John Colleton as a land grant. He never set foot there, but his agents established a plantation in 1664 on its rolling, sandy hills, hoping to establish cattle production. That was the beginning of cattle roaming all up and down the Outer Banks, until roads and cars and tourists drove them away. Cattle ranching was the biggest commercial enterprise, not fishing, well into the 1900s.

During the late 1700s and early 1800s, pirates had a good time looting and pillaging along the shores of the Outer Banks. The most famous, of course, was Blackbeard, who had several hideouts along North Carolina's coast. But it was at Ocracoke that he lost his head, in 1718.

Ocracoke was the only navigable inlet back in those days, and as it is now, is a treacherous port to enter. So local watermen, pilots, would help guide the schooners laden with goods for the mainland through the inlet and up the sounds. Residents and visitors benefited from this traffic, with taverns and imported food more easily available. Along the rest of the Outer Banks, settlers moved into the maritime forests, where they could coax vegetables from backyard gardens, fish from the sound and ocean, and hunt waterfowl from the marshes. They built wooden cottages with outdoor kitchens. Most wandered the beaches in search of what washed ashore, and many of those cot-

Ocracoke was home to pirates and pilots, both of whom dealt with the dangerous waters surrounding the island.
E F Wiegand

tages were constructed from lumber salvaged from shipwrecks. Their lives were largely self-sufficient, not needing much from the outside world, and it's a good thing, because of their isolation.

For centuries, the Outer Banks methods of cooking remained simple—boiling fish or one-pot chowders, and baking fish and shellfish in fireplaces and later ovens, or frying in heavy, cast-iron skillets. Bay leaves, native to the Banks, and onions were the main seasonings. Biscuits and cornbread were made daily, or "pie bread" or cornmeal dumplings were added to boiled crabs, chicken stew, or fish chowders. Dairy foods, like butter and fresh milk, were scarce, so pork fat was used as the grease, and cans of evaporated milk were kept in the pantry. Early Bankers didn't eat deep-water fish like grouper or dolphinfish, but rather fish from the sounds, like drum and mullet, and they had ample supplies of oysters, clams, and crabs. They considered shrimp a nuisance, a "bug," which they traded on the mainland as fertilizer for sacks of corn. Figs and blackberries provided the means for sweets.

The Outer Banks traditional diet was simple, but relatively healthy and most certainly delicious, too.

Nags Head, the Unpainted Aristocracy

The ducks, geese, and other waterfowl that migrated to the sounds of the Outer Banks brought huge numbers of hunters during the colder months during the late 1800s and early 1900s. Folks from up North caught a train to Norfolk, then a steamer, and stayed in hotels at Manteo or Nags Head or at private hunting lodges built on the tiny islands dotting the sounds. Local guides took them out hunting, while local cooks made sure they were well fed.

For many of the same reasons that tourists flock to the Outer Banks today, wealthy planters from the mainland came to Nags Head where access was a bit easier and closer than Duck or Hatteras. They came to escape the heat and drudgery, and to enjoy the fresh sea air and fresh breezes. They could also escape the malaria prevalent in the coastal plains where many lived year round.

After crossing the more northern Albermarle, then Croatan, and finally the Roanoke Sounds from the inland cities of Edenton or Elizabeth City, folks landed on the soundside, the western edge of the Banks, at the original village of Nags Head. There was a hotel or two, a few shops, Midgette's grocery, and a pavilion. Because the sound was so shallow, larger boats couldn't make it all the way into shore. So a boardwalk was built that extended way out into the water so people and their cargo could offload.

But, like today, tourists were drawn to the beach. Hot sand made the mile trek a scorching feat. So another boardwalk was built, this time to the oceanfront.

By 1855, the first oceanfront cottage was built. The new owner, forced to buy hundreds of acres, convinced his neighbors and friends back on the mainland to make the summertime trek to Nags Head and sold them lots for one dollar. By 1885, there were the original thirteen cottages—the Unpainted Aristocracy, as the editor of the state capital's newspaper christened them almost a half century later. They were simple cottages, made of shingles and scavenged wood, with hip-roofed porches, wide benches, and propped shuttered windows sited to capture summertime's prevailing southwest breeze. Only a few had fireplaces or woodstoves, so most families left on Labor Day.

These summering families needed fresh vegetables, ice, canned goods, and fish for their servants to prepare their meals. So the locals provided and prospered from them. Although everyone was cordial, there was little social mixing between the island's isolated, hardworking families and the wealthier summer people.

The village of Nags Head was located on the sound, where shallow water required extended piers to offload passengers and cargo. Photo courtesy of the David Stick Collection, The Outer Banks History Center

First in Flight

On a December day in 1903, Wilbur and Orville Wright made history with a hop into the air with their flying machine. Della Basnight recalls hearing her grandfather talk of transporting "the boys" over on his ferry, listening to their animated conversation about the weather and their tests, yet how quickly they got quiet when he asked what was in all those cloth sacks. He later claimed to have been the first "aircraft carrier."

The Wright brothers were in Nags Head during the winter, which can be cold, windy, wet, and downright inhospitable. From what they wrote home to their sister, you'd have thought they just about starved to death while trying to get their machine to fly on the sand. "Our pantry in its most depleted state would be a mammoth affair compared with the Kitty Hawk stores," wrote Orville.

Outer Bankers were used to fishing, hunting, or growing their foods, relying on few store-bought items. Not the Wright brothers. They needed to purchase their food, but could only find a few canned goods, eggs, and tomatoes, with biscuits and sandwiches made for them by Mattie Twiford Midgette, who opened a grocery store with her husband, Jethro Sr. (The Midgettes were among the original Banks settlers, descended from three brothers from Scotland or a shipwrecked Frenchman, depending on whom you talk to. Today you'll find many descendants with names that are variations of Midyet, Midgett, or Midgette.)

Only occasionally would Orville or Wilbur have bacon or eggs, butter or milk. "I have just stopped a minute to eat a spoonful of condensed milk.

Cottage Row on the beach at Nags Head. Note the low, flat sand, with no big sand dunes to protect the cottages from the surf. Photo courtesy of the David Stick Collection, The Outer Banks History Center

No one down here has any regular milk. The poor cows have such a hard time scraping up a living that they don't have any time for making milk. You never saw such pitiable looking creatures as the horses, hogs, and cows are down here. The only things that grow fat are the bedbugs, mosquitoes, and wood ticks. . . ."

Although they found the folks at Nags Head and Kitty Hawk hospitable, Wilbur wrote, "There is little wealth and no luxurious living. They are friendly and neighborly and I think there is rarely any real suffering among them." If they had come during the warmer months, there would have been little wind, but they would have found better living conditions, especially among the summer families at Nags Head.

Summers at Nags Head

For over a century, some of the Unpainted Aristocracy along Cottage Row witnessed more than salt spray. There were the Union troops that marched up and down the beach and used the hotel as headquarters, and the All Saint's Chapel for runaway slaves. Their windows were darkened when German submarines and ships hovered and burned just off the coast. Nor'easters, like the Ash Wednesday storm of 1962, and hurricanes, particularly those in 1899, 1933, 1944, and again during recent years, with Isabel in 2003, flooded their floorboards with water and sand, causing several of them to be moved, some up to four times, away from the ocean swells.

Some still stand and continue to welcome descendants of the original families back each summer.

Tom Skinner was four years old when his family first started coming to Nags Head for the summer in 1926. It was already a family tradition, for he is a descendant of Francis Nixon, the wealthy Perquimans County plantation owner who started the trend in the early 1830s of bringing families to the Outer Banks to escape summertime heat and the threat of malaria.

One of the older cottages on the beach at Nags Head. Note the extended rooms added to the back, and the servant quarters at the end. E F Wiegand

His childhood summers there with his family were wonderful, he recalls. After Memorial Day, they caught the *Trenton* at the wharf at Elizabeth City and, along with cows, horses, carts, chickens, a cook and boxes of food, were ferried over on the steamer to the soundside of Nags Head, where his grandparents had built a cottage in 1867 to take advantage of the "good air." His father built their own cottage on the beach in 1933, after the "Big Storm," and after the bridges were built. The house was positioned, like others along Cottage Row, with porches and windows to catch the southwest breeze. It had a water pump on the back porch, and the kitchen was part of the house, not a separate entity like those in older homes.

When all the summer neighbors had arrived, the ritual was to dig a deep pit on the beach for a huge bonfire, and ten to fifteen families would gather at night to roast hot dogs and marshmallows.

His father liked to have fried fish for breakfast, and the cook had the big meal of the day, "dinner," ready by midday. "Everybody brought chickens and had the chicken coops set up in the backyard. After they were gone, fish was a staple," he recalls. Cattle and pigs were allowed to roam all over the island, and he remembers some cows chasing him and his buddies up Engagement Hill, a big sand dune near the sound.

Sometimes they found whole boxes of oranges and apples washed up on the shore, fallen from passing ships. Watermelons and cantaloupes sent from the Currituck mainland were tasty, he remembers. Figs were really good in August, too. But the biggest treat was a cold Coca-Cola or Pepsi, for a nickel, from the Midgettes' store across the street.

In 1914, Jethro Midgette built the cedar-shingled, two-story grocery store, which he called "Peach," on the soundside where the ferry docked and most locals lived. Mattie Twiford Midgette, his wife, stocked the shelves and kept the ledgers while Jethro fished or delivered ice and groceries. After the horrible flooding from the storm of 1933 and the completion of the new bridge, the Midgettes sensed there would be a shift from the village on the sound to the Cottage Row on Beach Road.

So Peach was placed on timbers and rolled to the ocean side of the island, across the street from where the oldest beachfront cottages in Nags Head were already situated or were being built. A house for the Midgette family was built behind the store. The Midgettes later turned the second floor into The Last Resort, a rooming house for tourists, especially the musicians who played at the Casino up the beach.

As with most old-time groceries, steady customers were given credit, their purchases noted in a ledger and paid for at the end of the summer. One page records the largest single entry, uniquely marked PAID, for flour, yeast, cheese, coffee, cream, and sugar by the Buchanan family, who hosted a luncheon for President Franklin Roosevelt the next day, in 1937.

Midgette's Store remained the only place to get groceries, pick up mail, and make phone calls in Nags Head until the 1960s. (Closed in the early 1970s, the store became the home of the Midgettes' daughter, Nellie Myrtle Pridgen, a recluse and avid beachcomber. Today, it's a museum that houses thousands of artifacts she found on her daily beach walks.)

Tom Skinner earned his nickels and dimes delivering groceries for Jethro Midgette for 25 cents per day. He'd take the groceries into each house and set the box on the table or in the icebox. Jethro, as everyone called him, also delivered ice from the ice plant that used to be where the Roanoke Island Festival Park is now located. Jethro also pulled his dory onto the beach about three times a week, and put out a net 200 yards or so in the surf during the early evening. The next afternoon, neighbors and children, Tom Skinner among them, would help him pull in the net and capture the harvest, which ranged from hundreds of spots, croakers, sea trout, and bluefish to a pitiful handful at times. Jethro sold the excess to the cooks along Cottage Row.

Those idyllic summer days lasted for the Skinner family until Labor Day, when everyone went home and the beach was deserted. "Only every tenth house had a fireplace or woodstove," Skinner recalls. "Even when we came down at Thanksgiving in 1970, folks thought we were nuts." After a long legal career, he and his wife, Alice, retired to Nags Head permanently in 2003.

Isolated Life on the Banks

While development continued at Nags Head, the rest of the Banks remained isolated, almost cut off from the rest of the world. The water continued to be the primary means of carrying cargo and catches of seafood until the advent of cars and bridges from Nags Head in the late 1930s. Schooners, sloops, sailboats, and steamers plied the sounds and ocean, making lighthouses very necessary beacons to help navigate the treacherous waters surrounding the Outer Banks, known as The Graveyard of the Atlantic.

John Gaskill of Wanchese spent the summers of his youth during the 1920s and '30s at Bodie Island Lighthouse, where his father was a "keeper" for twenty years. Tall, handsome, and spry despite his ninety-one years, he loves to tell stories of his long life on the water, whether as Navy engineer, or ferry captain, or young "investigator" of the shores of Bodie Island. Asked how he has lived for so long, he replies, "drinking and cussing."

As a lighthouse keeper, his father shared the duties of keeping the oil lantern burning from sundown to sunup with one other keeper year round. His family joined him

Bodie Island Lighthouse is the third to stand in this location. The gift shop is located in the former lighthouse keeper's quarters, where John Gaskill lived as a young man. Photo courtesy of Island Photography

when the children were not in school, during the summer and holidays. It was John's duty as an older boy to climb the nine flights of stairs—214 steps, to be exact, he says—to extinguish the light just as the tip of the sun rose from the eastern horizon.

John and his brother had the beach to themselves, with the nearest neighbors a hunting club on one side and the lifesaving station on the other, both an eight-minute walk through briars and burrs. Many of his free hours were spent gathering the family dinner.

He remembers collecting oysters from the beds in "front" of the lighthouse, on the soundside, where they would recycle their old shells to keep the oysters coming. He was fond of the tiny pea or oyster crabs they'd find inside some oysters. When there was a strong north wind that would blow the water from the sound, he would look out his second-story window for the telltale signs of crabs—the holes that pockmarked the shoals—so that he could beat out the seagulls. He preferred the soft-shells, so when he would find one still working its way out of its old shell, he'd cover it with seaweed and mark the spot with a stake, then move on to others and catch the new soft-shell on his way back.

"Our diet wasn't very good," he recalls. With little or no vegetables grown during the summer, they had mostly canned goods to eat. "The Elizabeth City boat brought groceries and ice, and took fish back," he says. A cistern collected rainwater. He remembers during the Depression hunting swans, which he could sell for a whole dollar apiece. His family "got by" in the winter by eating ducks he hunted with his trusty best friend, his Chesapeake Bay retriever, and goose for holiday dinners. They ate a lot of boiled drum, or channel bass, served with boiled potatoes and cabbage, and for lunch, bacon gravy biscuits. The brambles near the marshes produced really nice blackberries. And he remembers the cows that were put out to pasture there, eventually rounded up because they ate so much of the vegetation.

John says he would climb the tower and wistfully watch the ships going by, promising himself that one day, he, too, would sail away.

The Evolution of Outer Banks Cuisine Today

During the 1950s and '60s, cars and another bridge allowed visitors to come down from Virginia and the Washington, D.C., area, and from North Carolina's inland cities, for a shorter week's vacation at the beach. Most stayed around Nags Head, Kill Devil Hills, and

Kitty Hawk. Only a few ventured north on the sandy road up to Duck, and hardly anyone went to the wilds of Corolla or to the sandy villages of Rodanthe or Avon down the Banks. Only sport fishermen landed in Hatteras to charter boats.

Then came the huge influx of tourists during the 1970s and '80s that has continued into the twenty-first century. As elsewhere in desirable locations around the country, the area has experienced a huge building boom, with new "cottages" with six to ten bedrooms built from the sound to the ocean, thrusting through the sand north of Corolla and any available space all the way down to Hatteras. Markets, gift stores, fast-food joints, and restaurants line the bypass and one-lane roads, all with heavy traffic during the warmer months. Today the driving force behind the economy is no longer fishing, but tourism.

What effect has that had on the cuisine of the Outer Banks?

Traditional fried foods, baked fish, steamed oysters, and boiled shrimp continue to satisfy—and delight—the appetites of both locals and tourists alike. But with more affluent visitors, the area's chefs have responded with more contemporary, cutting-edge dishes using fresh, local ingredients that would delight the most sophisticated and experienced palates.

So you don't have just fried soft-shells, although they are heavenly. Instead, you get soft-shells served with a roasted peanut sauce or a tangy aioli. Tuna is served rare, carpaccio-style, not just turned into tuna salad. Dolphinfish is served with crabmeat fromage, or grilled for tacos.

It's a marvelous juxtaposition, this blending of old and new, of flavors and methods of cooking and food presentation. And that makes eating on the Outer Banks today an exciting and delicious experience.

Della's Wine Recommendations

Della Basnight grew up in Manteo, then lived in Manhattan, Los Angeles, and Raleigh before returning to the same street where she was born. She's worked in the wine business, selling higher-end, fine wines to restaurants and markets, for the last twenty-three years. Each year she has visited the wineries of California, or France, Italy, Spain, Portugal, Switzerland, and Venezuela. While in Raleigh, she served as chair of The American Institute of Wine and Food, co-founded the Triangle Wine Experience, helped set up the Pinehurst Wine Festival, and was the Traveling Sommelier for Opus One.

She teaches waitstaff at Outer Banks restaurants about pairing wine with food, so that they are better able to serve their patrons. She made some delicious recommendations here, in a range of prices and styles.

Fish

- For spicier dishes, such as the Spanish-Style Dolphinfish or Gremolata Flounder, try a Spanish rioja made with the tempranillo grape, or a shiraz or syrah.
- For grilled fish served with a spicy salsa, try a riesling, like that produced by Hogue in Washington State, Gainey in Santa Barbara, California, or J. Lohr in Monterey, California; or indulge yourself with a Weinbach, from Alsace, France.
- For baked fish with milder flavorings, try an un-oaked chardonnay, such as the one from Iron Horse from the Sonoma Valley in California, or the less expensive Estancia chardonnay.

Clams

- For non-spicy clam dishes, try a sparkling wine, such as the lovely version from North Carolina's Biltmore Estate, or a non-vintage champagne such as Perrier Jouet (not the Fleur).
- For clam dishes that feature bacon, Della recommends a light pinot noir, such as that from Four Graces or Ponzi in Oregon's Willamette Valley.

Crab

- For sweet or delicate crab dishes, choose a sancerre from France such as Delaporte's; or a less-acidic sauvignon blanc, such as the less expensive but excellent Woodbridge sauvignon blanc from Robert Mondavi in California; or a fumé blanc, such as that from California's Ferrari-Carano; or a pouilly fumé from Pascal Jolivet in France.
- For spicier crab dishes, try a riesling, like that from Hogue in Washington State, Gainey in Santa Barbara, or J. Lohr in Monterey, California; or a Weinbach from Alsace, France.

Soft-shell Crabs

Della says the uniqueness of a just-shed soft-shell deserves celebration with a champagne, or a sparkling wine, like Mumm's Cuvée M Napa, or Roderer Estate; or try a crisp and clean sauvignon blanc, such as that from Napa Valley's Girard or Robert Mondavi.

Shrimp

- For spicy shrimp dishes, try a Spanish rioja, like Marques de Riscal, or Matchbook Tempranillo, a Californian version of the rioja grape. Other appropriate reds include shiraz or syrah.
- If you prefer white wine with shrimp, try a riesling, like that from Hogue in Washington State, Gainey in Santa Barbara, or J. Lohr in Monterey, California; or a Weinbach from Alsace, France. Tablas Creek Cote Du Tablas Blanc is a nice California blend of white Rhone varietals.

Oysters

There's nothing like pairing oysters with sparkling wine, Della says, such as that from North Carolina's Biltmore Estate Brut, done in the time-honored "methode champenoise." Or, try a non-vintage champagne, such as Perrier Jouet Brut (not the Fleur).

Scallops

- For creamy scallop dishes, Della recommends a classic chardonnay with good acid that will hold up to the cream, like Iron Horse from California's Sonoma Valley; or a pinot gris, like that from Four Graces in Oregon's Willamette Valley, Erath from the Dundee Hills of Willamette, or Hugel's pinot gris from California.
- For scallops with lime or lemon, try a sauvignon blanc from New Zealand or from Woodbridge in California.

Tuna

For tuna, Della recommends a pinot noir, like the inexpensive Talus; or try a very light merlot, like that by Cypress from California's coast; or a more complex beaujolais, such as any Louis Latour Beaujolais Village made with the gamay grape.

Chicken and Duck

- For duck, two wines from California to try are Chalone's Monterey pinot noir and Ferrari-Carano Siena, a blend of sangiovese, malbec, and zinfandel from Sonoma County.
- For the Bourbon Pecan Chicken recipe, Della suggests the Napa Valley chardonnay from Franciscan Oakville.
- With the Chicken aux Pêches, a good pairing is the Sonoma-Cutrer Russian River Ranches chardonnay or Hogue's riesling from Washington State.

drinks and cocktails

DRINKS AND COCKTAILS

The original thirteen Nags Head cottages, christened "the Unpainted Aristocracy" by *Raleigh News & Observer* editor Jonathan Daniels in 1929, were situated to catch the best of summer's southwest prevailing winds. The nine left standing today feature benches built into the deck of the southwestern corner of the house, as an extension of the beach-facing porch.

That's where the cocktail hour was, to catch the breeze, catch the sunset, and catch up with neighbors. Lots of these early-evening social hours were spent roving from one cottage to the next, folks having a drink or two before dispersing to their own cottages for a light supper, for the heavy meal of the day was at "dinner," at noon or early afternoon. For most, the cocktail hour was the entertainment of the day.

Today we have Happy Hour, that time of day when you wind down and watch the sunset over the sound. It's a tradition in the Outer Banks, no matter what you call it.

Nags Head Bloody Mary

Like many fortunate eastern North Carolinians, Missy Taylor Manning grew up spending weeks at a time at the 1855 Outlaw Cottage, Nags Head's oldest, which belonged to a relative. When she married into the Manning clan of Raleigh, she and Tommy also gathered with his brothers at their cottage on the Neuse River in Oriental, known as the sailing capital of North Carolina. It was there that this recipe was developed by her brother-in-law, Howdy, now the esteemed North Carolina Superior Court Judge Howard Manning, Jr. This Bloody Mary migrated back to Nags Head, where it was served at brunch from a silver or crystal pitcher as "the hair of the dog what bit ya."

What's a glug? Turn an opened bottle over your intended mixture for a second or two, then turn it back upright before repeating.

1 large (46-ounce) can tomato juice

1 pint premium vodka, plus 2 jiggers

4 lemons, quartered, with juice squeezed

4 limes, quartered, with juice squeezed

Freshly ground black pepper to cover surface completely

2 heaping tablespoons prepared horseradish

8 glugs Tabasco (more to taste)

10 glugs Lea & Perrins Worcestershire sauce

½ teaspoon celery seed

1 teaspoon garlic salt

10 celery stalks with leaves

10 large green olives

1. Mix all ingredients together in large pitcher or jar. Stir well; let stand 1 hour or overnight in fridge. Stir again before serving.

2. Decant mixture to a silver or crystal pitcher.

3. Serve over ice in tall glasses. Garnish each drink with a celery stalk and an olive.

YIELD: *10 or more servings*

Sam & Omie's

Sam & Omie's is known as the place to go for breakfast, whether you're headed out early to fish on the pier across the street or on a charter boat, or have enjoyed a lazy morning sleeping in. According to most of its patrons, Sam & Omie's serves the very best Bloody Mary on the beach.

The place got its start feeding the commercial fishermen back in the 1930s, when Sambo Tillet, a bit of a gruff, would take orders for eggs fried or scrambled, with or without bacon or sausages, then go to the back and cook up a big batch of scrambled eggs and meats, and set it on the table. "Here you go boys," he'd bellow. "That's it." Forget about individual orders.

Service is a bit different today. Their she-crab soup has quite a reputation, and the bar becomes quite lively at night.

Sam & Omie's has been serving breakfast, especially to fishermen, for over seventy years.
E F Wiegand

Bourbon Rabbit Run

Back in the 1960s, it is said that some of the more adventure-seeking waitstaff at The Arlington and the Parkinson Hotels on the beach at Nags Head would awaken at four a.m. and together make "The Rabbit Run." They headed to Oregon Inlet to see the boys off, the local guys heading out as crew on the big fishing charter boats.

Why was it called The Rabbit Run? Because every time they saw a rabbit darting about the road or dunes, they'd take a swig of bourbon. (Please note this is a practice that is not recommended by anyone these days, especially after noting the number of rabbits observed on the Outer Banks.)

Shake all ingredients together, then pour over ice. Garnish with sliced orange.

PER DRINK:

1½ ounces bourbon

1 ounce Triple Sec

4 ounces fresh orange juice

Thinly sliced orange

Dirty Boogie Cocktail

During the heyday of the Nags Head Casino, this dance hall featured big names, like Fats Domino, The Platters, The Temptations, and even Louis Armstrong, as well as The Drifters, Maurice Williams and the Zodiacs, and other more local bands every weekend night during the season. Known as the "Barefoot Bar," the hall required that shoes be left at the door in a big trough so as not to mess up the giant waxed wooden floor. Locals and tourists packed in to listen to the music, but especially to do the Jitterbug, Bop, Twist, Shag—whatever the hottest dance was at the time.

Dancing would just get wild at times, going beyond what the movie *Dirty Dancing* portrayed. "We were known for our Dirty Boogie," says native Della Basnight, who as a teen would watch and imitate every move. Beer was the only alcohol served at the Casino, which served as the social center for the Outer Banks from 1938 until a nor'easter eventually brought it down in 1976.

Mix all ingredients together, then add ice. Garnish with the cherry.

PER DRINK:

1½ ounces Chivas Regal

4 ounces club soda

Splash of cherry juice

1 maraschino cherry

Bourbon Slush

Café Atlantic on Ocracoke is not allowed to serve any alcohol other than wine, so this recipe from co-owner Ruth Toth is only for their private celebrations. She notes it keeps a long time in the freezer.

9 cups water

3 cups bourbon or whiskey

1 12-ounce can frozen concentrated orange juice, thawed

1 12-ounce can frozen concentrated lemonade, thawed

1 cup sugar, more or less to taste

1 tablespoon instant tea

1 large (64-ounce) bottle lime-flavored soda, chilled

1. In a large container, mix all ingredients. Divide among four plastic containers, and freeze until firm.

2. When ready to serve, remove from freezer, and add enough chilled lime-flavored soda to make it slushy.

YIELD: *about 24 servings*

Ocracoke's Meal Wine

Ocracokers of old made do with what they had, especially when it came to making wine. On the mainland, they'd trade fish for corn. After the corn was ground, they mixed the cornmeal, or "meal," with sugar, raisins, and yeast, and allowed it to ferment in glass jugs, adding more sugar every four days. Later generations continued the tradition using plastic trash cans. One recipe calls for allowing the mixture to brew for "two weeks or 14 days, whichever comes first."

A portside scene in Ocracoke Village. E F Wiegand

Hurricane Cocktail

Made famous in New Orleans' French Quarter at Pat O'Brien's bar, this is also a fitting drink in homage to the strength and fury of hurricanes that have terrorized the Outer Banks over the years. Invented during World War II, it was first poured into a glass that had the shape of a hurricane lamp. Which is what some Outer Bankers need when the storm hits—both the lamp and the drink!

1. Mix all ingredients well in a shaker with ice.
2. Strain mixture over ice into tall glass.
3. Garnish with orange slice and cherries.

PER DRINK:

2 ounces dark rum

2 ounces light rum

2 ounces passion fruit juice

1 ounce orange juice

1 ounce fresh lime juice

1 tablespoon grenadine

Ice cubes

1 slice orange

2 cherries

East Lake Rye

One of the first boats bought in 1933 by Captain Will Etheridge to use for his fledgling seafood company in Wanchese was *Carrie.* She had been used during the Prohibition to run East Lake Rye, a moonshine made in the swamps (crossed by Highway 64 today) to larger boats waiting out in the ocean. Captain Will also took charters out to fish during the tourist season, and during the off months used *Carrie* to catch fish. The Etheridge Seafood Company is now a multimillion-dollar business, one of the state's largest.

Peacharina

PER DRINK:

1 half fresh peach

1 teaspoon sugar

4 ounces bourbon, separated

Peaches and whiskey have long been a favorite mix in the South. Southern Comfort is a blend that began by steeping peaches in a rough whiskey, down in New Orleans.

Tom Sullivan, eighty-four, now retired and living at Nags Head, shared this recipe with a warning: This drink is strong. He recalls how in the early 1940s, he took his new bride to Nags Head to visit with his aunt, Mrs. Fannie Skinner Turner, who lived in one of the oldest cottages on the beach. During cocktail hour, she served him his first Peacharina. It was so good he had another, and when asked to say the blessing at supper, proceeded with, "Now I lay me down to sleep . . . "! He claims he "was more embarrassed than ever."

1. In a bowl, cut the peach into chunks, and sprinkle with the sugar. Smush the peach with a fork (or potato masher if doing a large quantity). Pour 2 ounces of bourbon on top.

2. Cover and refrigerate overnight. When ready to serve, add the remaining 2 ounces of bourbon. Mix thoroughly.

3. Serve in old-fashioned glass over ice. You may add a little water, if desired.

A Dip, a Nip, and a Nap

The Arlington and Parkinson Hotels on the beach at Nags Head were the premier places to stay during the early tourist years. Many would come on Memorial Day and stay for the whole summer. Cocktail hour on the beautiful verandas was what most patrons looked forward to each day. Della Basnight remembers one elderly gentleman who came with his ailing wife and their servant. "He always said his day was made if he got 'a nip, a dip and a nap.'" He always enjoyed talking with the "summer girls" who worked at the hotel, and it was a special privilege to be invited to join him for cocktails. Drinks were served from silver and crystal by waiters in black ties and tails. "You had to dress up, too," Della recalls, which was a big thing for the summer girls.

The
Mother
Vineyard

A huge, knobby set of trunks, twisted and deformed, entwine under a massive maze of trellises that support the oldest cultivated grapevine in the United States. Believed to be over four hundred years old, this Mother Vineyard, as it is known, is now surrounded by quiet suburban homes on a back street of Manteo near Shallowbag Bay.

Sir Walter Raleigh's explorers reported in 1584 that muscadine vines on Roanoke Island "covered every shrub and climbed the tops of high cedars. In all the world, a similar abundance was not to be found." Who planted the vines that make up the Mother Vineyard an equal distance apart? The earliest settlers reported that the Croatan tribe of Algonquians made and enjoyed wine, and we now know they had enough agricultural knowledge to produce hybrids, use natural fertilizers, and use scaffolding to protect their other crops. Or did the Lost Colonists, using their planter's knowledge, cultivate the wild vines growing on the island?

The Mother Vineyard is a rare albino muscadine that produces white grapes, similar to the bronze muscadine, or Scuppernong, which thrives all over the hot, humid coastal plain of North Carolina and is used for jellies, pies, and cakes as well as wine.

Kinnakeeters, Yaupon Eaters

The village of Avon used to be known as Kinnakeet, which was named for the Algonquian who was chief of Hatteras Island when explorer and historian John Lawson arrived in 1701. Lawson found natives with blue eyes and freckles and a copy of the English Bible. Were they descendants of the Lost Colony or of shipwrecked sailors?

Because this crook of the island was at one time full of red cedars, Kinnakeeters learned to fashion boats from this perfect natural resource and became sought-after boatbuilders. They bartered these skills for goods needed from the mainland.

And particularly during the Revolutionary War when tea was scarce, they bartered another natural resource, yaupon. The Algonquians had taught them how to make the "black drink" by drying the tender leaves and bark, then steeping them in water to make a strong, pungent tea, which they used as a ceremonial beverage and as a cure for kidney stones, diabetes, and alcoholism. But there was another use for *Ilex vomitoria*. When preparing for battle, Indian braves would make the tea with the berries included, which would cause them to vomit, thus cleansing their bodies and souls.

Yaupon tea—made without the berries—smelled good to the European settlers but tasted inferior to the real thing. But it was better than no tea at all. So Kinnakeeters harvested and dried the abundant yaupon growing among the dunes, then traded it for fresh produce from the mainland.

Neighboring villages teased them about being "Kinnakeeters, Yaupon Eaters." In 1873 the post office changed the village name to Avon, after the river in England, but the derogatory chant kept up for years.

Yaupon grows wild on the Outer Banks and was used by Indians and settlers for tea. Here, a hedge has been trimmed in the Elizabethan Gardens on Roanoke Island.
E F Wiegand.

appetizers

APPETIZERS

Start big and knock their socks off, I learned at several cooking schools. What guests remember the most is the first thing you serve them, and the last. That means the appetizer must impress, and open their taste buds. Several professional chefs told me that when they go out to eat at another restaurant, they frequently order several appetizers rather than one with an entree, so chefs tend to knock themselves out to impress with that first course.

Restaurants along the Outer Banks seem to follow that rule, too.

Here you'll find some very impressive appetizers that chefs have shared, and some nice finger foods and dips to soothe hungry appetites while you wait for the sun to set at cocktail hour.

You will also find more recipes among the shrimp, clam, and other shellfish chapters that can be served either as first-course appetizers or entrees.

Dare Deviled Eggs

No Southern picnic or Sunday gathering would be complete without a special serving plate of golden deviled eggs. Here's a version that includes either shrimp or crabmeat, two of Dare County's bounties from the sea.

You would think it a simple matter to boil an egg, but there are many ways to accomplish that. I've found the method used here works best if you need to shell the eggs without marring the white. If you unintentionally dismember too many whites of the eggs, just make an egg salad. And as I heard Julia Child exclaim once, during a cooking class I was attending, "Never, ever admit a mistake. That's what parsley's for!"

12 eggs, room temperature

2 tablespoons mayonnaise

1 teaspoon Dijon mustard

1 tablespoon finely cut chives

½ teaspoon salt

Freshly ground pepper, to taste

¼ cup steamed shrimp, chopped fine, or backfin crabmeat

1 teaspoon Old Bay seasoning, or sweet paprika (optional)

1. Place eggs in a large pot and cover with cold water. Gently bring to a boil over medium heat. Watch pot carefully, and immediately remove the pot from the heat when the bubbles begin. Cover the pot, and let it stand for about 15 minutes.

2. Drain water from pot, and run cold water over the eggs until water remains cold, about 2 minutes.

3. Peel the eggs. The best method is to tap them all over on the countertop. Starting at the big end where there is usually an air pocket, carefully slide the shell away from the whites. Rinse each egg quickly in cold water if needed to remove any pieces of shell.

4. Slice each egg in two lengthwise, and carefully pop or scoop out the yolk into a mixing bowl.

5. Mash the yolks with a fork, then add mayonnaise, mustard, chives, salt, and pepper and mix thoroughly. Then gently fold in either shrimp or crabmeat.

6. Stuff the middle of each egg white with the yolk mixture, and arrange on a serving plate or platter. Sprinkle the tops with either Old Bay or paprika, if desired.

YIELD: *24 stuffed eggs (if you're lucky!)*

Velveeta Pimento Cheese

1 pound Velveeta, grated

1 pound Jalapeño Velveeta, grated

12 ounces sharp cheddar, grated

2 tablespoons horseradish

2 bunches green onion, chopped

2 tablespoons mustard

1 quart mayonnaise

2 large jars pimentos (Spanish pimentos), diced and drained well

My friend Missy shared this recipe that her family has used for decades. She makes up a batch for the crowd when they're headed to their annual August beach trip to Nags Head. For generations, Missy's family frequented the Outlaw Cottage, one of the remaining "Unpainted Aristocracy," as the quaint, historical beachfront homes are called.

This pimento cheese can be used for sandwiches or heated as a dip for tortilla chips, and keeps well in the refrigerator for weeks. Missy prefers the texture with the cheese grated by hand rather than using a food processor.

Mix all ingredients together.

YIELD: *8 cups*

Traditional Pimento Cheese

1 pound sharp cheddar, grated

1 4-ounce jar pimentos, chopped with juices

Ground pepper and salt to taste

A few cloves of garlic, crushed; 2 tablespoons diced pickle relish; 2 hard-boiled eggs, diced; and/or 2 tablespoons diced pickled jalapeño peppers (optional)

About 1 cup mayonnaise

Pimento cheese is a Southern thing. And, like all things Southern, you can argue for ages about the real recipe. Included below are "traditional" options various cooks use. Whatever your preference, nothing beats celery sticks stuffed with pimento cheese, or a pimento cheese sandwich made with toasted bread—or a grilled P.C., sandwich, as we say in the South.

Mix all ingredients together except for the mayonnaise, which you will add gradually until you have the texture you desire.

YIELD: *3 cups*

Spicy Toasted Pecans

Pecans grow very well on Roanoke Island, where every island home tried to have a couple of trees growing in the yard. Seven different varieties reportedly grow within the village of Wanchese.

These pecans are wonderful additions to Happy Hour on the beach.

1. Preheat oven to 375 degrees.

2. Melt butter in a large saucepan over medium heat. Add seasoned salt and pepper, and Tabasco or Texas Pete sauce if desired.

3. Remove pan from heat, and add pecans, stirring until well coated. Spread pecans in a shallow baking pan and bake until toasted, 8 to 10 minutes.

4. Cool completely before storing.

YIELD: *2½ cups*

3 tablespoons butter

½ teaspoon Tabasco or Texas Pete sauce, added to melted butter (optional)

1 teaspoon seasoned salt and pepper

2½ cups pecan halves

Figs and Cheese

Figs are the only fruit trees that grow profusely on Hatteras Island. Resident Lynne Foster, writer, former marketing executive, and manager of the Albatross Fleet, describes her backyard figs as "honeyed fruits with the flavor of ambrosia," and uses the abundance in her backyard to produce these delectable appetizers.

Look for figs that are plump and tender but not mushy. Take a whiff, too—they should smell sweet and not sour. Highly perishable, fresh figs should be eaten or "put up" quickly. Store at room temp.

Figs with Rosemary and Brie

About 8 figs, depending on size

1 tablespoon chopped fresh rosemary, or more to taste

4 ounces Brie cheese, cut into 8 cubes

Ground black pepper, to taste

1. Preheat oven to 350 degrees.
2. Wash and stem figs. Using a sharp knife, make an **X**-cut into the top of each fig, cutting two-thirds of the way through. Or, cut figs in half.
3. Place a cube of cheese into each cut fig. Sprinkle with the chopped rosemary, and grind black pepper over to taste.
4. Place figs in a baking dish, and bake for about 7 minutes, until cheese is melting and figs are heated through. Serve warm.

YIELD: *4 appetizers*

Figs with Gorgonzola and Walnuts

About 8 figs, depending on size

4–6 ounces Gorgonzola cheese, divided into 16 chunks

16 whole walnut halves

Salt and pepper to taste

1. Preheat broiler. Cover a baking sheet with foil.
2. Wash, stem, and halve figs. Place on prepared sheet.
3. Press a walnut half into the center of each fig. Cover with a chunk of cheese. Sprinkle with salt and pepper to taste.
4. Place under broiler until cheese almost melts and figs are warmed through, about 3 to 5 minutes.
5. Serve warm.

YIELD: *4 appetizers, or 8 cocktail servings*

Fig Preserves Crostini

A lovely hors d'oeuvre using fig preserves. Be sure to pick up several jars of this local treat from Ocracoke or Hatteras Islands, or make your own, following recipe on page 305 in Desserts chapter

Spread crostini with softened goat cheese. Top with a dollop of fig preserves. Serve within a couple of hours.

YIELD: *24 or more servings*

1 package (6–8 ounces) crostini or toasted bread, or crackers

1 log (5–8 ounces) chèvre (goat cheese), plain, softened

1 small jar (6–8 ounces) fig preserves

Della's Figs

Della Basnight was the youngest girl of the Basnight brood that grew up on Agona Street in Manteo. She and her older sisters would collect figs from all the yards up and down the street and place them in paper bags with the plan to sell them. Her sisters had jobs as the Running Board Girls, who would hop onto the old cars' running boards and direct tourists to their desired locations in town. So Della was enlisted as the fig salesman. At five years of age, she desperately wanted to exchange a trip to the beach to go swimming, which her sisters promised her if she would man her little red wagon filled with bags of figs. She stood in front of the drugstore downtown, trying her best to remember how to make change.

Della continues in sales to this day, selling fine wines to restaurants and markets on the Outer Banks.

Figs with Prosciutto and Goat Cheese

Sweet, honey-flavored figs are perfect for pairing with salty cured country ham or the Italian version, prosciutto.

8 fresh figs (or more, depending on size)

8 slices thinly sliced prosciutto (or a matching number to figs), halved lengthwise

4 ounces goat cheese, plain or flavored with herbs (optional)

1. Preheat grill or broiler.

2. Wash, dry, and stem figs. Halve the figs, then wrap each half with a slice of prosciutto.

3. Grill (or broil) until prosciutto begins to crisp and the fig is warmed through, about 4 to 6 minutes.

4. If desired, add goat cheese. Instead of halving the figs, make an X-cut from the top, two-thirds through the fig. Squeeze the bottom of the fig to make it "open," and place a chunk of the goat cheese inside. Then wrap with prosciutto and grill until meat is crispy and cheese is soft.

5. Serve warm as "finger food" if size permits, or serve on a backdrop of dressed greens.

YIELD: *4 appetizers, or 8 single hors d'oeuvres servings*

Figs with Country Ham and Green Salad

This is a variation of a classic Italian salad that's perfect for the Outer Banks with its abundance of figs during the summer and the availability of country ham from North Carolina's coastal plain.

1. Have four salad plates chilled.

2. Wash and stem figs, then quarter. Season with salt and pepper.

3. In a small saucepan, heat balsamic vinegar to boiling, then reduce heat and simmer until vinegar is reduced by half, about 3 to 4 minutes. Remove from heat and add olive oil. Let cool slightly.

4. On each salad plate, divide greens. Salt and pepper. Add quartered figs, then sprinkle slivers of ham over figs, especially, and the greens.

5. Drizzle the vinegar and oil mixture over greens and figs.

6. Using a vegetable peeler, shave off strips of the Parmigiano-Reggiano cheese over the top of each plate. Serve immediately.

YIELD: *4 appetizers or lunch plates*

8 fresh, ripe figs

Salt and pepper, to taste

6 tablespoons high-quality balsamic vinegar

4–5 tablespoons extra-virgin olive oil

1 6-ounce bag or 3 cups baby greens or arugula

2–3 ounces thinly sliced country ham, slivered

2 ounces hard Parmigiano-Reggiano cheese

Angels on Horseback

This appetizer is so named because of how the oyster curls against the bacon when cooked. A traditional savory from England, where "rashers" wrapped around oysters are served on toast points, it's also known as Oysters en Brochette in New Orleans.

Since oysters are plentiful in the sounds surrounding the Outer Banks, Angels on Horseback give tribute to the artistic, life-size Winged Horses you'll find exhibited in front of restaurants, businesses, and homes that have helped raise money for Corolla's wild horses and a new monument to flight. See the accompanying sidebar on page 43.

These appetizers are good served individually with toothpicks, or on buttered toast points, or on top of lightly dressed fresh spinach.

12 slices bacon, divided in half

1 pint shucked oysters, or 2 dozen raw, in shell, plus reserved juice

1 tablespoon lemon juice

⅛ teaspoon cayenne pepper or
    ½ teaspoon hot sauce, like Tabasco
    or Texas Pete

½ teaspoon salt

1 clove garlic, minced

2 dozen buttered toast points or
    6 ounces baby spinach with
    1 tablespoon lemon juice and
    2 tablespoons olive oil, optional

Toothpicks or skewers (for serving)

1. In a large skillet, lightly cook bacon over medium heat until just translucent, about 3 to 4 minutes. (Partially cooking the bacon will help keep the oysters from overcooking.)

2. Drain shucked oysters; or if using raw oysters, open them, retaining juice and shells.

3. In a small bowl, combine lemon juice, cayenne pepper or hot sauce, salt, garlic, and oyster juice from shells. Add the oysters and toss to coat. Marinate for 10 minutes.

4. Preheat broiler.

5. If using pre-shucked oysters, line a baking sheet with foil, then place metal rack on top. If you have the shells, rinse and settle the largest half-shells in crumpled foil on baking sheet.

6. Roll each halved bacon slice around an oyster. Secure each with a toothpick or skewer, and place on the rack or on a shell.

7. Place under broiler, and cook until bacon is crisp and the edges of the oysters have curled, turning once to cook both sides evenly. Serve immediately on toast points or fresh spinach dressed lightly with lemon and olive oil.

YIELD: *6–8 appetizers; makes 24*

Winged Horse Extravaganza

Those absolutely wild horses you'll see in front of restaurants, businesses, and a few cottages along the Outer Banks are winged, life-size works of art from the 2003 celebration of the Centennial of Flight, designed to raise money for the Corolla Wild Horse Fund and the Monument to a Century of Flight. Sponsors purchased ninety-nine fiberglass horses with aluminum aircraft wings, then commissioned artists to decorate them in a fanciful manner. CitiArtFX, a not-for-profit division of Outer Banks Press, chose winged horses as an icon to represent both the wild ponies that roamed these barrier islands and the significance of the Wrights brothers' achievements here.

Singer Jimmy Buffett sponsored Captain Sipster, a takeoff on pirates and rum libations; Chillin'Out, decked in black and white, now stands guard at Penguin Isle Soundside Grill & Bar; and others with playful names such as Stampede, covered with postal stamps, and Peg-leg-asus, a Blackbeard Buckaneer, were auctioned off or kept for display by sponsors. You can order posters and pictorial books of the Winged Horse Extravaganza from Outer Banks Press.

You'll find splendidly decorated statues of winged horses all over the Outer Banks, decorated by artists to raise money for the Corolla Wild Horse Fund and the Monument to a Century of Flight. E F Wiegand

Bar-B-Que Shrimp from Elizabeth's Café

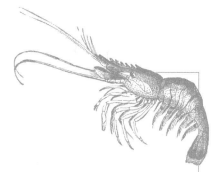

Extra-jumbo shrimp, 16/20 count, about ¼ to ½ pound per person

Bottled barbecue sauce, Kansas City or Texas-style with tomato base

Mango chutney sauce (Major Grey's Indian mango sauce)

A renowned wine expert, Logan says this dish pairs nicely with an Alsace-style pinot blanc.

The owner of Elizabeth's Café & Winery in Duck, Leonard Logan, has always had a hand into cooking. During his college days at Duke University, and later in law school, he earned his spending money by taking care of the food duties for fraternities or other campus organizations, basically catering his way through school. Later he worked as an attorney for the state, based in Manteo but living in Wanchese, where he nosed his way into the kitchens of several older women to learn the traditional ways of preparing local foods. He and an ex-wife started Elizabeth's Café, which she ran while he continued his work as a lawyer. But then his wife left, and he decided to give up his day job.

Logan laughs when he remembers his days at Duke University, when he always took along these barbecued shrimp on any picnic dates with fellow coeds. It was a guaranteed way to impress, he recalls. Today, these shrimp on the menu still impress diners of Elizabeth's Café & Winery. They're very easy to make as an appetizer when the grill is fired up, he says. At the Café, they make their own barbecue and mango sauces, but he says that's not worth the time for home cooks.

Don't overcook, Logan warns. "There is a magic moment when the shrimp will be perfectly done—tender but not rubbery. Experiment, for it depends on the grill heat and the temperature of the shrimp when placed on the grill." This will get your grill dirty with baked-on barbecue sauce

1. Preheat a grill. Peel and devein the shrimp, leaving the tails on to use as a handle.

2. Place shrimp in a bowl, and brush or pour barbecue sauce over, dredging the shrimp in sauce.

3. Place the shrimp directly on a lightly oiled grill and cook, turning only once. A total cooking time of 3 to 4 minutes should be sufficient.

4. Serve with mango chutney sauce on the side or as a dip.

Hot Spinach and Artichoke Dip

You'll frequently find a dish similar to this listed on many Outer Banks appetizer menus. This is a spicier version. Serve with raw vegetables, crostini, or baked pita chips.

1. In a large sauté pan, heat olive oil, then add onions. Sauté for about 3 minutes, then add spinach, handfuls at a time, stirring until spinach is wilted.

2. Add the garlic, and stir for 1 minute, then add artichokes. Continue to stir until heated through. Season with salt, pepper, and cayenne to taste, and set aside.

3. In a blender or food processor, or in a large bowl, blend together the cream cheese, mayonnaise, and cheeses.

4. Mix artichoke/spinach mixture with the cream cheese mixture. Taste, and season if necessary. Dip may be stored in the refrigerator until ready to use.

5. Preheat oven to 350 degrees. Spray or grease a baking dish, and spread the dip inside. Bake for 15 to 20 minutes, or until the top is browned and bubbling.

6. Serve the dip hot with crostini or raw vegetables.

YIELD: *about 1 quart*

1 tablespoon olive oil

1 cup chopped onions

1 10-ounce bag fresh spinach, or ½ cup frozen spinach, thawed and squeezed dry

1 tablespoon minced garlic

1 14-ounce can artichoke hearts, drained and coarsely chopped

Salt and pepper to taste

Cayenne to taste

1 8-ounce package cream cheese, room temperature

¼ cup mayonnaise

¼ cup grated Parmesan cheese

½ cup grated pepper jack cheese

Roasted Red Pepper Hummus with **Belgian Endive**

1 cup garbanzo beans

2 cloves garlic, degermed

2 tablespoons extra-virgin olive oil

2 tablespoon lemon juice

¼ cup roasted red peppers

1 teaspoon toasted sesame seed oil

Salt and pepper to taste

Belgian endive leaves, trimmed

Easy yet elegant and healthy, this delicious appetizer reflects the atmosphere of The Sanderling Resort & Spa. Executive chef Christine Zambito, herself the mother of two young ones, understands the need for simplicity, and that's why she suggested this recipe for cocktail hour. You may roast a red pepper yourself, or purchase bottled roasted peppers, found on most grocery store shelves.

1. In a small food processor, mix together all ingredients except Belgian endive.
2. Put mixture, now hummus, into a pastry bag with a straight tip, or, use a plastic resealable bag, snipping diagonally across one corner.
3. Pipe hummus into bottom half of each endive leaf.
4. Serve within 2 hours.

YIELD: *8–10 appetizers*

Grilled Bruschetta with Assorted Toppings

An easy first course or lunch, especially if you purchase the tapenade spread and the vinaigrette when you gather the greens and bread from the market. This delightful recipe comes from Christine Zambito, executive chef at The Sanderling in Duck.

1. Preheat grill, grill pan, or oven to 500 degrees.

2. Slice bread diagonally about ¼ inch thick.

3. Brush each slice with olive oil.

4. Toast each piece of bread on grill or oven until lightly charred and crispy on each side.

5. Spread desired topping on each toasted bread.

6. Mix together field greens and vinaigrette.

7. Serve with a small mound of field greens in the center of each plate and 2 to 3 bruschetta on each plate.

YIELD: *4–6 appetizers*

1 loaf crusty Italian bread

¼ cup extra-virgin olive oil

Purchased tapenade and/or fresh tomato salsa

2 cups field greens

2 tablespoons champagne vinaigrette (or another light vinaigrette)

Bruschetta is a lovely hors d'oeuvre for a wedding reception or Happy Hour on the beach. Photo courtesy of Island Photography

Clams Casino from Café Atlantic

24 medium-size, or topneck, clams

½ cup (1 stick) softened butter

2 tablespoons finely minced fresh garlic

Cracker meal (made from crunching 12 saltine crackers with a rolling pin)

8 slices Swiss cheese

6 cooked slices of bacon, cut into quarters

Co-owner and chef Ruth Toth is so fond of Ocracoke clams because of their salty taste. Here's her helpful hint: Freeze the fresh clams in their shell for about 2 hours, then thaw them briefly in cold water, and they will be much easier to open.

Cracker meal is an old-fashioned, Outer Banks topping used to give a crunchy "crust" to some seafood dishes.

1. Preheat oven to 450 degrees.

2. Shuck the clams, and loosen the meat from the bottom shell. Leave the clam open-face on its bottom shell and place in a shallow baking pan.

3. In a small bowl, mix together the softened butter and minced garlic.

4. Sprinkle the clams lightly with cracker meal, then dab each with ½ teaspoon of garlic butter. Top with a slice of Swiss cheese cut to the size of the clam, and ¼ slice of cooked bacon.

5. Place clams in oven and bake for approximately 8 minutes or until the clams are bubbly and hot.

YIELD: *4 appetizers*

"Hot" Crab Dip

"A zinger" was what Chef and Director of Operations Tom Lozupone of Stripers Bar & Grille wanted when he developed the recipe for this appetizer. At the restaurant it's served with toasted French rolls, but crackers or toasted pita bread are also good.

1. Preheat oven to 425 degrees. Grease a shallow 1- to 2-quart baking dish.

2. Place all ingredients except for the crabmeat in a large mixing bowl, and blend until smooth.

3. Gently fold in crabmeat.

4. Place mixture in prepared baking dish and spread evenly.

5. Bake until bubbly and slightly browned, approximately 15 minutes.

6. Remove and let cool for 5 minutes. Serve with toasted French bread or rolls, toast points, crackers, or tortilla chips.

YIELD: *about 3–4 cups*

1 pound (2 8-ounce packages) cream cheese, softened

1/3 cup horseradish (some prefer less)

1/4 cup mayonnaise

1/3 cup sour cream

1 teaspoon blackening spice (see page 261)

1/3 cup Parmesan cheese

1/4 cup hot sauce

Juice of 1 lime

1 pound crabmeat, cartilage picked out

French bread or rolls, toast points, crackers, or tortilla chips

Blue crabs await their fate in bushel baskets, in which they'll be shipped north and to area restaurants. E F Wiegand

Artichoke and Crab Dip

We've always called the usual artichoke dip "Fish Eye," perhaps because a child once exclaimed, "Eeew, it's got fish eyes in it!" With crabmeat added, it's even more delicious.

1 tablespoon garlic, minced

1 14-ounce can artichoke hearts, drained and chopped

1 cup grated Parmesan cheese

8 ounces cream cheese, room temperature

½ cup mayonnaise

1 tablespoon chopped fresh dill

1 teaspoon prepared horseradish (or to taste)

½ pound backfin crabmeat (or up to a pound, if preferred)

Crackers, crostini, or celery sticks

1. In a medium bowl, thoroughly mix together all ingredients except for crabmeat.

2. Place mixture in a medium saucepan, and cook over low heat, stirring, until cheeses are melted.

3. Add crabmeat, and gently stir until heated through. Pour into a serving dish, or into a chafing dish over a low heat source.

4. Serve with crackers, crostini, or celery sticks.

YIELD: *about 4 cups*

"Bankers" Before "Outer Banks"

It wasn't until the cottage-building boom to accommodate the desired hordes of tourists began in earnest that the term "Outer Banks" was really used, and it was a PR ploy. Those who lived on these banks of sand that kept the ocean and sounds from abutting simply called themselves "Bankers" who lived either up the Banks or down the Banks.

There's a story of how some Bankers went to Baltimore to shop and see the sights during the late 1930s. As was the custom of the day, they dressed in their finest when traveling. When asked by merchants and innkeepers who they were, they replied "Bankers." Then it was rumored they were financial wizards there to invest big sums of money, and so the town of Baltimore treated them to dinners and other freebies to woo their business.

Crab Remick

There really are two Penguin Islands—Big and Little—just off the soundside of Nags Head, near where the old pier and harbor were located. Maybe it was a cold winter's day when they received their names, for no real penguins are found anywhere near!

At the Penguin Isle Soundside Grill & Bar, at Milepost 16 on the Bypass, this dish has always been a popular appetizer. Chef Lee Miller says the sauce is also good for topping oysters on the half-shell. For an entree, serve over seasoned rice.

28-ounce can tomatoes, chopped

½ sweet bell pepper, red or green, chopped small

¼ onion, chopped small

¼ cup light brown sugar

¼ cup cider vinegar

1 teaspoon red pepper flakes

1½ cups mayonnaise

¼ cup prepared horseradish

1 pound jumbo lump crabmeat

2 tablespoons butter

2 tablespoons lemon juice

Salt and pepper to taste

4 thin slices Swiss cheese

1. Combine tomatoes, bell pepper, onion, brown sugar, vinegar, and red pepper flakes in a medium sauce pot. Simmer over medium heat until vegetables are tender, not dry, for about 25 to 30 minutes. (Chef Miller says, Do not burn!)

2. Cool for about 15 minutes, then strain through a sieve. Save the vegetable mixture and discard the juice. Refrigerate until chilled, about 1 hour.

3. Preheat oven to 425 degrees.

4. Add mayonnaise and horseradish and mix thoroughly. You now have Remick sauce.

5. Divide crabmeat among four ramekins. Melt butter, then pour evenly over the ramekins. Sprinkle each with lemon juice, then salt and pepper to taste.

6. Top each with ½ cup of the Remick sauce, then with a slice of Swiss cheese.

7. Bake until bubbly hot and slightly golden brown, about 5 to 8 minutes.

8. Serve immediately.

YIELD: *4 appetizers, or 4 entrees when served with rice*

Crabmeat Canapés

During the summer when crabmeat is in season, I just can't seem to get enough of this marvelous treat. With jumbo lump crabmeat, you don't want to do much to detract from its lovely, inherent taste. Having a "container," whether it's a pastry shell or toast point, helps to present crabmeat for a lovely appetizer.

1 package mini pastry shells, or crostini or crackers

½ pound jumbo lump crabmeat

Juice of ½ lemon or lime

1 tablespoon finely chopped fresh chives or parsley, or combination

1 teaspoon Old Bay seasoning, plus sprinkling

2 tablespoons mayonnaise

Chive strips or parsley sprigs

1. If using frozen mini pastry shells, cook according to the package directions. Place shells on serving platter.

2. Pick over crabmeat to remove any cartilage. In a mixing bowl, gently combine crabmeat, lemon or lime juice, chives and/or parsley, Old Bay seasoning, and mayonnaise.

3. Stuff each pastry shell with mixture, and sprinkle very lightly with Old Bay. Place a chive strip or parsley sprig on top of each.

4. Serve immediately, as shells will not remain crisp.

YIELD: *about 2 dozen canapés*

Crabmeat Pâté

This is a fantastic appetizer. It's tasty, and, it can be made ahead, which allows me to enjoy the sunset and my guests.

Use a crab, fish, or beach-themed mold. Once the pâté is well chilled, it can be turned out onto a serving plate garnished with fresh herbs, lemons, or lettuce.

1. Pick though crabmeat and discard any pieces of cartilage. Set aside.

2. In a large mixing bowl, using a mixer or whisk, combine butter and lemon juice. Add mayonnaise, mustard, and horseradish.

3. Slice eggs in two. Mash yolks with a fork, then place in bowl with mayonnaise mixture. Add cheese, garlic, chives, parsley, salt, and pepper.

4. Finely chop the egg whites and add to the mixture, then the crabmeat. Using a flexible spatula, gently mix ingredients well.

5. Place in a 3–4-cup mold and chill for at least 2 hours or overnight.

6. Unmold onto serving platter, and serve with crostini, pita chips, crackers, or a crusty baguette.

YIELD: *about 3 cups*

1 cup (8-ounces) backfin crabmeat

½ cup (1 stick) butter, softened

2 tablespoons lemon juice

½ cup mayonnaise

1 tablespoon Dijon mustard

1 tablespoon prepared horseradish

½ cup freshly grated Parmesan cheese

3 boiled eggs, yolks and eggs separated

1 teaspoon minced garlic

2 tablespoons minced fresh chives or scallions

3 tablespoons minced fresh parsley

1 teaspoon salt

½ teaspoon freshly ground black pepper

Crostini, pita chips, crackers, or crusty baguette

Crabs and Goats Cocktail Spread

1 cup backfin crabmeat

¼ cup bottled cocktail sauce with horseradish

⅓ cup chevre

Juice from 1 lime

1 tablespoon chopped chives

Salt and freshly ground pepper, to taste

Crackers, crostini, or toast points

Sitting on the beach one late spring evening, we could see that it was going to be a gorgeous sunset. So we ran inside and gathered the makings for our Happy Hour drinks. I found a partial container of backfin crabmeat in the fridge. Hurry, my husband said, the sun is setting. So I quickly dumped some bottled cocktail sauce in with the crab, added a mound of lovely goat cheese, squeezed a little lime left from our drinks, chopped a few stems of chives, and added some salt and pepper, then mixed it all together. I ran down to the beach with some crispy crackers and the crab, and we toasted to a day well spent with the sand between our toes.

Mix all ingredients together. Spread on crackers, crostini, or toast points.

YIELD: *4 appetizer servings*

Crab-Stuffed Mushroom Caps

These make delightful finger food appetizers, or a filling meal served on spinach softened in butter with garlic.

1. Preheat oven to 325 degrees. Spray a shallow ovenproof casserole dish with nonstick cooking spray.

2. Rinse mushrooms and pat dry. With a knife, remove stems so that there is a deep well. Salt and pepper to taste, and place in the prepared dish.

3. In a mixing bowl, beat egg slightly, then add crabmeat, chives, parsley, and 2 tablespoons of the cheese, the salt, and Old Bay. Gently stir to combine.

4. Stuff each mushroom cap with the mixture. Sprinkle the tops with the remaining tablespoon of cheese.

5. Place in oven and bake for about 20 minutes, or until mushrooms are tender. Serve immediately.

YIELD: *12 appetizers, or 3 entrees*

12 large white mushrooms

Salt and pepper to taste

1 egg

1 cup (about ½ pound) backfin crabmeat

1 tablespoon finely chopped chives (or onions)

2 tablespoons finely chopped parsley

3 tablespoons freshly grated Parmesan cheese, divided

½ teaspoon salt

1 teaspoon Old Bay seasoning

Native vs. Local

"On the Banks, 'natives' are people born here. 'Locals' are those who have moved and lived here for decades. 'Visitors' are those who have bought houses here and stayed for a couple of years but the natives and locals don't know if they're really staying yet," says Della Basnight, who was born in the house two doors down from where she lives now. And, she adds, how they cook and what they eat depends on where they're from or how long they've been here.

Crab and Avocado

The creaminess of the avocado and the sweetness of the crab make an awesome pairing. Serve immediately after preparing to prevent discoloration of the avocado. This looks pretty served in large, flat scallop shells available in cookware stores.

2 firm, ripened avocados

3 tablespoons lemon juice, divided

2 tablespoons sesame oil

½ pound lump crabmeat

1 teaspoon flat parsley, finely chopped

1 teaspoon Old Bay seasoning

Salt and pepper to taste

1. Slice avocados in half and remove the pits. Peel off the skin without marring the meat of the avocados, keeping the halves intact. Immediately sprinkle the peeled avocados with 2 tablespoons lemon juice to prevent discoloring. Thinly slice each half, then fan slices out on serving dish. Repeat with other halves.

2. Whisk sesame oil and 1 tablespoon lemon juice together, and add salt and pepper to taste. Drizzle over the fanned avocado halves.

3. Pick over crabmeat to remove any cartilage, then gently mix with parsley and Old Bay. Season to taste with salt and pepper. Spoon crabmeat onto the fanned avocado.

YIELD: *4 appetizers*

Blue crabs in crates. E F Wiegand

Crabmeat with Avocado Salsa

Less expensive backfin crabmeat is dressed up when mixed with this tangy salsa. Serve the crabmeat scooped into endive leaves, or on bruschetta or crostini.

1. Slice avocado in half lengthwise, and twist to separate the two halves. With the sharp edge of the cutting knife, hit the stone and pull up. The stone should come out with the knife blade. Dice the avocado with this easy method: Make cross-hatch cuts into avocado, then gently invert the skin. The pieces of avocado should fall out, or scrape them from the skin into a mixing bowl. Sprinkle with lime juice immediately.

2. Add vinegar, tomato, bell pepper, onion, jalapeño pepper, olive oil, salt, and pepper to the avocado. Stir gently to mix.

3. Add the crabmeat and gently stir until mixture is combined well. Taste for seasonings.

4. Scoop spoonfuls of the crabmeat mixture into the endive leaves or onto the bruschetta or crostini.

YIELD: *8 appetizers*

1 large ripe avocado

1 tablespoon lime juice

1 tablespoon red wine vinegar

1 medium tomato, peeled, seeded and chopped

1/3 cup finely chopped red bell pepper

1/3 cup finely chopped red onion

1 tablespoon finely chopped jalapeño pepper

2 tablespoons olive oil

1/2 teaspoon salt

Several grinds black pepper

1/2 pound (8 ounces) backfin crabmeat

1 head endive, cleaned, or a dozen-plus bruschetta or crostini

Crab-Stuffed Shrimp

An elegant appetizer served over fresh spinach greens with tomato-red pepper relish, or as an entree served over rice seasoned with sun-dried tomatoes and spices.

1 pound extra-large shrimp

2 tablespoons finely chopped sweet onion

1 tablespoon finely chopped chives

1 egg, beaten

1 teaspoon Tabasco sauce

1 tablespoon seasoned bread crumbs (I like Old Bay's)

2 tablespoons mayonnaise

½ teaspoon salt

¼ teaspoon freshly ground pepper

½ pound backfin crabmeat

Sweet paprika or Old Bay seasoning

1. Preheat oven to 400 degrees. Coat a baking sheet with nonstick spray.
2. Shell shrimp, leaving tail on. Carefully butterfly by splitting each shrimp lengthwise until almost cut through, then spread apart.
3. Pick through crabmeat and remove any cartilage.
4. In a mixing bowl, combine all ingredients except for crabmeat and paprika or Old Bay. Gently stir crabmeat in.
5. Stuff each butterflied shrimp with the mixture and place on prepared baking sheet. Lightly sprinkle tops with paprika or Old Bay, your preference.
6. Bake for about 10 minutes, until the crabmeat stuffing is lightly browned and the shrimp are pink. Serve immediately.

YIELD: *6–8 appetizers, or entree for 4*

Fresh crabs are brought to Endurance Seafood on Colington Island, where they are shipped to Fulton Fish Market in New York City and to area restaurants. E F Wiegand

Clam Fritters

Folks in Kinnakeet and down Hatteras Island call these pancake-like delicacies fritters, and enjoy them by the plateful served hot off the stove, usually along with their meal. However, during lean times, they were also a "seafood pancake dinner" served with applesauce or coleslaw.

These fritters make a great appetizer served with a dollop of softened cream cheese or sour cream topped with fresh chives.

1. Drain clams, and reserve the juice. Chop clams by hand or preferably in a blender. Drain chopped clams again, reserving any juice

2. Stir together the egg, salt, and pepper. Add as much flour as needed to hold the mixture together. If needed, reserved clam juice can also thin the batter. Stir in clams.

3. Heat oil over medium-high heat in large frying pan. When hot, drop batter by large spoonfuls to form 2- to 3-inch circles.

4. Flip fritters as soon as bottom side begins to turn a golden color, and brown on the other side.

5. Serve with softened butter or softened cream cheese flavored with chives or parsley.

YIELD: *6 appetizers (about 18 fritters)*

1 pint (2 cups) clams, chopped and drained

1 egg, beaten

½ teaspoon salt

½ teaspoon pepper

About ½ cup flour

¼ cup canola or corn oil

Bacon-Wrapped Scallops

An elegant appetizer frequently served at wedding receptions held on the beach, this is very easy to do, either on the grill or under the broiler.

1 pound fresh large sea scallops

2 tablespoons lemon juice

2 tablespoons melted butter

2 tablespoons olive oil

1 pound thinly sliced smoked bacon

Freshly ground pepper

2 tablespoons finely chopped fresh parsley

1. Preheat oven to 350 degrees. Line a lipped baking sheet with foil.

2. Rinse the sea scallops and pat dry. Place in a bowl.

3. Mix together the lemon juice, butter, and oil. Pour over the scallops, and place in the refrigerator for about 30 minutes. If grilling, soak 2 dozen or so long toothpicks or short wooden skewers in water for 30 minutes.

4. Meanwhile, partially cook the bacon by separating slices onto the foil on the baking sheet and placing in oven for about 5 minutes, just until bacon is beginning to cook but still limp.

5. Preheat grill, if using, or broiler. Wrap bacon around the edge of each scallop, cutting bacon when it begins to overlap (should be about half a slice). Use 2 wooden skewers to secure the bacon to each scallop, or toothpicks if broiling. Grind pepper over all wrapped scallops.

6. Grill for about 3 minutes per side, or 3 to 4 minutes under the broiler. Watch carefully and do not burn, but allow bacon to become crisp and scallops cooked through. You may need to turn the scallops a few times to ensure even cooking.

7. Remove from heat, and place on serving dish. Sprinkle with chopped parsley and serve immediately while hot.

YIELD: *about 1 dozen appetizers*

chowders and soups

CHOWDERS AND SOUPS

The Outer Banks is famous for its chowder, made without milk or cream, chock full of onions and flavor. You'll be surprised how well the taste of clams comes through, and how filling it is.

Soups and chowders are not just meant for cold winter days. Even during the heat of the summer, they can be a filling meal on their own, but also make terrific starters. Because of these options, yields for the following recipes are given in approximate one bowl–size servings.

Hatteras Clam Chowder

This chowder from Basnight's Lone Cedar Café is adapted from a recipe handed down five generations of the Basnight family, originally from Dolly Midgett, born in 1826 on Hatteras Island. Note the traditional absence of cream or milk.

1. Bring the water to boil in a large pot. Add littleneck clams, and steam, removing clams as they open. When all clams are opened, strain the cooking water (stock) through cheesecloth and reserve. Remove clams from shells and set aside.

2. In the same large pot, render or sauté the bacon until it is softly crisp. Drain on paper towels, and chop into small pieces.

3. Remove half of bacon fat, than add onions. Cover and cook over low heat for 5 minutes, or until onions are soft. Add reserved clam stock and simmer for 15 minutes.

4. Add potatoes, littleneck clams, sea salt and pepper, and simmer for another 15 minutes. Serve very warm.

YIELD: *8 servings*

100 littleneck clams, cleaned, or 4 cups chopped clams

1 quart (4 cups) water

2 medium onions, medium dice

4–5 potatoes, peeled, medium dice (about 5 cups)

½ pound smoky bacon, sliced thin

Sea salt and white pepper to taste

Wanchese Seafood Chowder

4 tablespoons olive oil or bacon
  drippings

2 onions, chopped

3 cloves garlic, minced

1 large green pepper, chopped

2–3 stalks celery, chopped

4 carrots, sliced

1 package Polish sausage or smoked
  sausage, chopped

1 large can chopped tomatoes

1 large can tomato sauce

2 cups frozen okra

2 cups frozen corn or mixed vegetables

6 potatoes, diced

32 ounces chicken broth

2 teaspoons salt

½ teaspoon pepper

1–2 pounds seafood, cooked or raw
  (fresh peeled shrimp, scallops,
  crabmeat, fish chunks, or any
  leftover seafood you may have
  on hand)

Denise Selby Daniels is married to one of the eleven Daniels brothers that have continued fishing and operating the family seafood business out of Wanchese for generations. Well aware of how weather, water, changes in governmental regulations, and increasing development continue to threaten their way of life, Denise and her friend Robin Daniels launched the first Wanchese Watermen calendar in 2007, which they hope will bring attention to the hardworking fishermen who bring in fresh seafood for our tables. Besides lovely photographs, the calendar also features a recipe for each month.

This stew came into being, Denise says, because of all the leftovers she constantly deals with helping to run Graybeard's Seafood. Leftovers should always be so good!

1. Heat the olive oil over medium heat in a large soup pot. Add onions, garlic, green pepper, celery, and carrots and sauté until vegetables are tender.

2. Add the sausage and cook 5 more minutes.

3. Add all remaining ingredients except seafood. Make sure there is enough liquid in the pot to cover all vegetables. If not, add more chicken broth or water to cover. Cook for 30 minutes.

4. Add the seafood and cook until seafood is cooked through. Taste for seasoning, and add more salt and pepper if necessary.

YIELD: *8 servings*

Making Do
with Spam Stew

When the Great Atlantic Hurricane of 1944 hit Hatteras Island, more than one hundred buildings were swept off their foundations between the villages of Hatteras and Avon. Afterward, the entire village of Kinnakeet, now known as Avon, had to relocate several miles south of where their houses once stood.

Jeanie Williams, a lovely and spry ninety-four-year-old, was a "Kinnakeeter" who along with her three sisters relocated to Manteo after they married, living in houses side by side. Jeanie recalls that she was in Elizabeth City having her second child when the storm hit. "Everything was completely cut off down to Avon," she said. "My mother-in-law made this Spam Stew, because she had no fresh meat. Their garden was ruined, but they pulled up a few scraggly carrots and had some potatoes and onions on hand." The Spam was cut into chunks, then simmered with the vegetables. When the potatoes were half done, the traditional Outer Banks "pie bread" or pastry strips were added during the last 15 minutes of simmering. This Spam Stew became a family favorite.

"We learned early to make do with what we had," she says, her blue eyes gleaming. She pauses, then laughs.

During a terrible nor'easter in May 2007, the road on Hatteras Island was washed over and filled with sand, stranding the film crew of *A Night in Rodanthe* based on the novel by best-selling novelist Nicholas Sparks, who makes his home farther south near the coast in New Bern. You have to wonder if co-stars Richard Gere and Diane Lane had to make do with Spam Stew.

Breakwater Restaurant's Winning Chowder

4 slices applewood-smoked bacon, chopped and cooked

1 tablespoon sherry

1 tablespoon apple cider vinegar

1 tablespoon Old Bay seasoning

1 tablespoon Cajun seasoning

4 cups (32 ounces) seafood stock

1 pint heavy cream

1 pint half-and-half

1 pound red potatoes, chopped, skin on

4 leeks, white part only, diced

1 cup fresh corn

1 ½ pounds fillets of tilefish, grouper, dolphinfish, wahoo, or other white-fleshed fish, bloodline removed, and cut into chunks

1 pound backfin crabmeat

Salt and fresh ground black pepper to taste

Breakwater Restaurant sits at the edge of Oden's Dock in Hatteras Village. Jane Oden runs the front of the house, while son Don mans the kitchen, sending out delectable local seafood, such as crab cakes rolled in potato chips and tuna tortillas. This recipe won the yearly Day-at-the-Docks Chowder competition.

1. Combine bacon, sherry, vinegar, seasonings, and seafood stock in a heavy stockpot. Start cooking on low heat, slowly adding cream and half-and-half.

2. Add potatoes and leeks to pot. Keep on low.

3. When potatoes are about halfway done, add corn. When potatoes are three-quarters done, add fish.

4. Add crab at the very end and salt and pepper to taste.

YIELD: *at least 8 servings*

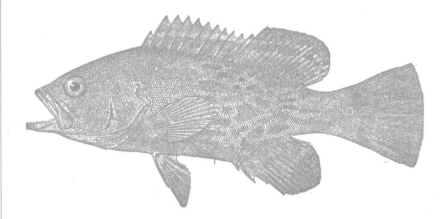

Crab pots wait during the winter to be baited and thrown back into the sounds surrounding the Outer Banks as soon as the water warms during late spring. E F Wiegand

Day at the Docks:
a Celebration of Hatteras Island Watermen

Discover what life is like for Hatteras fishermen, past and present, during a celebration in September. The Spirit of Hatteras Weekend includes a Day at the Docks, where beach dories, mullet skiffs, modern commercial fishing vessels, and charter boats are on display along the waterfront of Hatteras Village harbor. Talk with the men who use pound nets, set crab pots, haul in gill nets, or help reel in big fish. Watch them compete to be the fastest to don survival suits or rig baits. Cast your vote for the tastiest chowder on Hatteras Island, then join all of the fishing community in prayer for the Blessing of the Fleet as workboats of all sorts parade by.

This outstanding community event came about because of Hurricane Isabel, which in 2003 carved a breach in the island, creating a new inlet and thereby isolating Hatteras Village. It was the watermen who were able to help the village cope and were the first to get back to work.

The village celebrated with music and a dessert feast when Highway 12 was quickly rebuilt. A year later, they decided to do it again, and honored the spirit of Hatteras on the anniversary of Isabel by adding a Blessing of the Fleet. The next year's celebration included honoring the watermen of Hatteras Island with A Day at the Docks.

Corn, Chorizo, and Clam Chowder

Forrest and Jennifer Paddock operate The Salty Gourmet in Hatteras Village, which offers a marvelous selection of cookware, gourmet foods, wine, coffee, and microbrews. Forrest, who has worked as a chef in several Outer Banks restaurants, offered this favorite recipe.

2 tablespoons butter

2 tablespoons olive oil

4 ounces chopped spicy Spanish chorizo

1 cup diced yellow onion

½ cup each diced green and red bell pepper

2 tablespoons minced garlic

1 tablespoon Pimenton de la Vera (smoked Spanish paprika)

3 tablespoons all-purpose flour

1 cup clam juice

1 cup water

1 cup heavy cream

2 cups shoepeg corn

2 cups chopped fresh clams

1 tablespoon fresh thyme

1 tablespoon fresh parsley

1. In a large, heavy-bottom pot, melt butter with the olive oil over medium heat.

2. Add chorizo, and fry till crisp. Turn heat down to medium-low, and add onions and peppers and sauté until they just begin to take on color.

3. Add garlic and smoked paprika and sauté till fragrant, about 1 minute.

4. Add flour and cook stirring until the flour takes on a tan color. Add clam juice, water, and cream; bring to a boil and simmer for 20 minutes.

5. Add the corn, clams, and fresh herbs, and simmer for 5 more minutes.

6. Serve in deep bowls with lots of bread for dipping.

YIELD: *8–10 servings*

Café Atlantic Creamy Clam Chowder

Ruth Toth, co-owner of this charming restaurant just round the bend from Silver Lake on Ocracoke, says she has tweaked this recipe for years. She uses fresh Ocracoke clams, which are dug from the shallow waters surrounding the island. Ruth likes their salty taste.

1. Shuck and chop clams, saving the juice.
2. Heat oil in a large frying pan, and add celery, peppers, garlic, and onions. Sauté until vegetables are softened, about 5 minutes.
3. Finely slice bacon (I find cutting strips with kitchen shears is quick). In a small sauté pan, fry bacon until crisp. Set aside, making sure to reserve the bacon fat.
4. In a large pot, combine water, clam juice, potatoes, Worcestershire sauce, hot sauce, and pepper. Cook over medium-high heat until potatoes are tender.
5. Add vegetables, bacon, and bacon fat. Add chopped clams and bring to a boil.
6. Remove from heat and stir in half-and-half or cream. Salt to taste.

YIELD: *6–8 servings*

About 25 large fresh clams

2 tablespoons oil

3 stalks celery, coarsely chopped

1 green pepper, coarsely chopped

1½ teaspoons minced garlic

1 large onion, coarsely chopped

3 strips bacon

6 cups water

6–8 medium red bliss potatoes, diced

1½ teaspoons Worcestershire sauce

1 teaspoon hot sauce

½ teaspoon pepper

1 cup half-and-half or cream

Sam & Omie's Clam Chowder

If you want to feed a crowd, here's a good way to start. Dolly Gray Jones, the cook at Sam & Omie's, makes this fresh daily to feed the crowds that come through the screen doors at this timeless Nags Head establishment. Bikers, beachgoers, fishermen from the pier across the Beach Road, all know they can get a delicious taste of the Outer Banks here, although this recipe breaks from the traditional style by adding carrots and garlic.

1 pound bacon, chopped

2 cups chopped onion

2 cups chopped celery

2 cups chopped carrots

Salt and pepper, to taste

2–3 tablespoons Italian seasoning, to taste

1 tablespoon minced fresh garlic

3 46-ounce cans clam juice

2 bags frozen hashed brown potatoes

2 51-ounce cans chopped clams

1. In a large sauté pan, brown the bacon. Drain the grease.

2. In a very large pot or kettle, add all the rest of the ingredients, and the bacon.

3. Bring to a boil, then turn to a simmer and cook until the vegetables are tender.

4. Taste and season.

YIELD: *as Dolly says, "a lot."*

Soups Out of Favor

Sea turtles, especially loggerheads, were once fished in waters of the Outer Banks. It was a cruel catch, requiring spearing and beating, which sometimes rendered them unsellable. Some learned to catch the 50-pounders by hand, diving into the water to grab their shells and wrestle them to shore. Turtles were sold to make soup and stews, considered by many to be a delicacy.

Diamondback terrapin soup was a Northern specialty. These terrapins grew in abundance in the brackish water of the marshlands surrounding Pamlico and Currituck Sounds, where Bankers considered them pests that fouled their fishing nets. But one of the keepers of the Bodie Island lighthouse devised a dredge in 1849 that allowed him to catch thousands sleeping during the winter in the muddy muck. He took his huge catch to Norfolk where he was so well paid that he came home and dragged his dredge for another couple of thousand, which again brought him very good money. Other Bankers joined in, and it wasn't long before the diamondback terrapin was almost exterminated.

Spicy Stripers Oyster Stew

Chef Tom Lozupone of Stripers Bar & Grille in Manteo prepares a spicy version of Oyster Stew, enhanced by a dollop of chimichurri sauce, a Latin American blend traditionally made with parsley, onion, and pepper and spiced up with vinegar. .

If you want more than four servings, the broth can easily be doubled. There should be enough chimichurri for the doubled recipe.

On April 1, the restaurant hosts an Oyster Fools eating contest. Past winners consumed the likes of fifty-two raw oysters in seventy seconds.

12 raw oysters per serving (4 dozen oysters for 4 servings)

Oyster Stew

4 cups (2 pints) heavy cream

2 cups whole milk

½ cup (4 ounces) clam juice

1½ teaspoons kosher salt

¾ teaspoon white pepper

½ teaspoon cayenne pepper

Chimichurri Sauce

½ cup cilantro, packed

2–4 green onions, coarsely chopped (1 ounce or about 2 tablespoons)

2 large cloves garlic (½ ounce or 1 tablespoon minced)

1–2 whole jalapeños, stems removed (½ ounce, or 1 tablespoon minced)

1 teaspoon kosher salt

1 teaspoon coarsely ground black pepper

2 cups olive oil

For the oyster stew:

1. Place all ingredients except oysters in a stockpot and bring to a boil.
2. May be refrigerated for up to 5 days.

YIELD: *4 servings*

For Chef Lozupone's variation of Chimichurri Sauce:

1. Place all ingredients in a blender and blend on low until well pureed.
2. Refrigerate for up to 3 weeks.

YIELD: *3 cups*

Prepare the oyster stew with oysters and chimichurri:

1. Shuck oysters. Allow 12 per serving.
2. Preheat a large saucepan. Place oysters in the pan, and shake the pan to stir the oysters around. When oysters begin to "curl" around the edges, add 1½ cups (12 ounces) per serving of the oyster stew broth. Bring to a boil.
3. Place the stew in individual serving bowls, and top with 2 tablespoons of the chimichurri.

YIELD: *4 servings*

Ocracoke Oyster Stew and Grits

"Scalloped oysters" and oyster stew are favorite ways to cook oysters on Hatteras and Ocracoke Islands. Soda crackers, the saltines we now know, are crumbled and layered among oysters, then saturated with milk and butter, then baked.

This is an adaptation of that traditional preparation, using stone-ground grits as an additional layer of flavor.

1. Drain oysters, reserving juice in a large, heavy-bottomed saucepan. Bring to a boil, and boil until somewhat reduced, about 10 minutes. Strain through a fine-meshed sieve or through cheesecloth to remove any sand. Set aside.

2. In the same large saucepan, melt butter over medium heat, and add celery and onion. Stir constantly, cooking for about 2 to 3 minutes, or until vegetables are tender. Add the strained oyster juice, and bring just to a boil again. Add oysters, Tabasco sauce, and salt and pepper. Lower heat, and simmer until edges of oysters begin to curl. Add enough cream, depending on how liquid oysters are, to make a thick broth, and stir until mixture is warmed through. Do not boil. Taste and add more salt and pepper or Tabasco sauce if needed.

3. Serve immediately over individual bowls of grits. Sprinkle with chives, scallions, or parsley.

YIELD: *4 servings*

1 quart shucked oysters, with juice

4 tablespoons butter

¼ cup finely chopped celery

¼ cup finely chopped onion

1 teaspoon Tabasco sauce

1 teaspoon salt

½ teaspoon freshly ground pepper

1–1½ cups heavy cream

1 batch cooked grits, kept warm (see page 234)

2 tablespoons thinly chopped fresh chives, scallions, or parsley

Newport Clam Chowder

Chef Tom Lozupone has served this popular version of clam chowder at all the restaurants he's worked at on the Outer Banks, including Chilli Peppers and Stripers Bar & Grille. He cautions that you must stir frequently to prevent the chowder from scorching.

Every October, Stripers hosts a contest to see who can eat the most steamed clams in a minute.

2 sticks butter (½ pound)

½ pound Spanish onion, chopped (about 1 cup)

4 stalks celery, chopped

8 cups (2 quarts) red potatoes, medium dice

6 cups (1½ quarts) heavy cream

2 8-ounce packages (1 pound) cream cheese, softened

3 cups (24 ounces) chopped clams with juice

1 tablespoon fresh chopped dill

2 teaspoons white pepper

1. In a large pot or stock pan, melt the butter over medium heat. Add the onion and celery and sauté until soft.

2. Add the potatoes to the pan, and cook, stirring frequently, until potatoes turn opaque in color.

3. Stir in the heavy cream. Add the softened cream cheese, and stir to incorporate. Turn the heat to high and bring to a rapid boil.

4. When soup is boiling, add the clams and clam juice. Bring to the boil again, and add the dill and white pepper.

5. Continue to boil, stirring constantly, for another 2 minutes, Turn off the heat and allow the chowder to sit for 15 minutes.

6. Stir, then serve in individual bowls. Garnish with crackers or croutons. May be stored in the refrigerator for up to 5 days.

YIELD: *8 servings*

Corn and Crab Soup

Fresh, sweet corn from the farm stands and fresh, sweet crab from the sounds—you can't get any better than that on the Outer Banks. Here's to early summer! The less expensive backfin crabmeat is perfect for soups. Just make sure to pick through the crab to discard that undesirable cartilage. My family is lactose-intolerant, and finds this soup "creamy" enough with just the corn's "milk."

1. Prepare corn by cutting kernels from ears with a sharp knife. Run the non-sharp side of the knife down the trimmed ear to "milk" the juice from the remainders of the cob. Reserve kernels and juice.

2. In a large soup pot, heat butter over medium-low heat. Add onions and cook slowly until wilted and translucent, about 5 minutes. Add red pepper and stir for 2 to 3 minutes. Add garlic, stirring constantly for 1 minute.

3. Add chicken broth and water. Bring just to a boil, then add corn and its milk. Add more water, if necessary, to reach your desired consistency. Turn heat to low and cook for about 8 to 10 minutes, or until corn is tender.

4. Add crabmeat, and if desired, heavy cream. Stir, and gently heat until warm. Season with salt and pepper.

5. Garnish each bowl with basil or parsley before serving.

YIELD: *6 servings*

4–6 fresh ears of sweet corn or 3 cups frozen sweet white corn

2 tablespoons butter

1 onion, finely chopped

¼ cup red pepper, finely chopped

2 small cloves garlic, finely chopped

2 cups chicken broth

1 cup water

½ cup heavy cream (optional)

1 pound backfin crabmeat

Salt and pepper to taste

Shredded fresh basil leaves or chopped parsley

She-Crab Soup

Associated more with Charleston and South Carolina's Low Country, she-crab soup also has a history on the Outer Banks. It was the Scots who loved their soups and chowders, and they settled in North Carolina as well.

These days female crabs whose roe (eggs) are showing must be tossed back into the water. Occasionally you'll open a crab and still find some roe, and since it's too late to toss her back in, you can enjoy that additional treat. As a substitute for the roe's color and texture, cooks use hard-boiled egg yolks. But there is no substitute for the glug of sherry added at the end.

4 tablespoons butter

1 rib celery, minced

¼ cup minced onion

3 tablespoons flour

2 cups milk

2 cups heavy cream

1 pound crabmeat, picked over for cartilage

1 teaspoon finely grated lemon zest

¼ teaspoon nutmeg

½ teaspoon white ground pepper

1 teaspoon salt

4 yolks of hard-boiled eggs

¼ cup dry sherry

1 teaspoon paprika, divided

1. Press the yolks through a sieve and set aside.

2. In a heavy-bottomed pot, melt butter over medium-low heat. Add celery and onion, and stir. Cook until vegetables are soft, about 4 minutes.

3. Add the flour, and stirring constantly, cook for about 2 minutes, until mixture is smooth and bubbling. While stirring, slowly pour in milk, then cream and cook until mixture is smooth and comes to a boil.

4. Add crabmeat, lemon zest, nutmeg, pepper, and salt. Turn heat to low, and stir gently until crabmeat is heated through. Add half of the egg yolks, the sherry, and $\frac{1}{2}$ teaspoon paprika. Stir gently and heat through.

5. To serve, place soup in individual bowls. Divide the remaining pieces of egg yolk among the bowls, sprinkled on top. Dust with remaining paprika. Serve immediately.

YIELD: *6 servings*

Shrimp Bisque

Use the shrimp shells to make a quick stock, which will give this soup a more intense flavor.

1. In a large pot, melt butter over medium heat. Add onion and celery and cook for about 5 minutes, or until soft. Add garlic, and stir for 1 minute.

2. Add shrimp stock, Tabasco sauce, salt, pepper, and bay leaf. Bring to a boil, then simmer for about 15 minutes.

3. Raise the heat and allow the mixture to almost come to a boil, then add shrimp. Stir, and cook until shrimp are thoroughly cooked, about 3 to 5 minutes.

4. Lower the heat, and stir in cream. Taste for seasoning and add more salt and pepper if necessary. Continue to cook until thoroughly warm.

5. Remove the bay leaf. Ladle the soup into bowls, and sprinkle with paprika or Old Bay, if desired.

YIELD: *4 generous servings*

2 tablespoons butter

½ cup chopped onion

½ cup chopped celery

1 tablespoon minced garlic

3 cups shrimp stock, chicken stock, or water

1 teaspoon Tabasco sauce

1 teaspoon salt

½ teaspoon freshly ground pepper

1 bay leaf

½ pound (2 cups) small shrimp, peeled and deveined, chopped in half

1 cup heavy cream

Sprinkle of paprika or Old Bay seasoning

Shrimp Stock

Anytime you have to peel shrimp, save the shells in the freezer until you have a big bag full. Then make a simple stock: place the shells in a large pot, add 1 or 2 stalks of celery chopped up, about 2 carrots, and a small chopped onion. Cover with water, and bring to boil. Reduce heat and simmer for about 30 minutes. Strain, and you have a delicious base for soups or to make grits for that classic shrimp and grits.

clams

CLAMS

Native Americans up and down the East Coast used clamshells to make strings of beads, which they used as wampum, or money—thus the native quahog's Latin name, *Mercenaria mercenaria*.

Because of the large estuarine system along Pamlico and Albermarle Sounds, clams are naturally plentiful most years. However, because they are filter-feeders, they are highly susceptible to polluted waters, and sometimes runoff from development or hurricanes can close some areas to shellfish harvesting.

Clams are also being farm-raised in Pamlico Sound. Tiny clams are hatched in a nursery, stocked onto waters leased from the state, then grown in pens, trays, or bottom nets. When they are at least 1 inch wide, they can be harvested. Most littlenecks, the smallest clams, that are sold in Outer Banks markets have been farm-raised. The larger cherrystone and topnecks are less tender, and are best chopped up for chowder or fritters.

You'll see clammers out in shallow water or on a shoal with an incoming tide and a long-handled clam rake with strong prongs that are 1 inch apart, which happens to be the minimum legal size allowed. Most string along a floating net or bucket to hold their finds.

You can dig them yourself, even with your hands or toes. Just make sure your wampum is in unpolluted water. Watch for governmental warning signs.

Clam Tips

- Fresh clams can be stored for several days by placing them immediately on ice and maintaining their temp at 35 to 40 degrees Fahrenheit.

- Some Outer Bankers use this method for dealing with "gritty" clams: If you have dug them yourself, brush off sand and debris and then soak them in salt water, with about 1 cup of added cornmeal. This will help the clams purge themselves of sand. Then you can refrigerate or freeze them.

- Do not rinse, store, or transport clams in fresh water.

- Shells should stay tightly closed or close up when tapped. Discard any broken shells.

- You may freeze clams in their shells, in resealable plastic freezer bags, for up to 6 months.

- Shucked clams can be frozen in their own juice for up to 6 months.

- To make it easier to open clamshells, place them in the freezer for about 2 hours.

- For frying clams, please see the Primer on Frying Seafood on page 161.

Deviled Clams

2 dozen (or more) large cherrystone clams, retain clamshells

½ cup crumbled Ritz crackers

½ medium onion, chopped fine

2 hard-boiled eggs, chopped fine

4 tablespoons melted butter

¼–½ teaspoon Tabasco sauce

1 teaspoon Worcestershire sauce

½ cup evaporated milk

Salt and pepper to taste

Luther Daniels, who is eighty-six years old, recalls getting three-quarters of a cent for each clam he'd catch when a teenager. It was spending money, says this retired marine engineer, who served on the first nuclear merchant ship, the NS *Savannah*.

His wife, Helen, is an intuitive cook. "I've only owned one cookbook in the sixty-four years we've been married," she says. Her aunt taught her to cook "by taste."

For this recipe, she uses about one large clam per filled half-shell, and counts on two half-shells per person for one serving.

1. Clean clamshells. Place in a shallow pan or cookie sheet.

2. Preheat oven to 425 degrees.

3. Chop clams, but be careful not to make them too mushy.

4. In a large bowl, crumble Ritz crackers. Add chopped clams and half of the accumulated juice.

5. Add onion, eggs, melted butter, Tabasco and Worcestershire sauces. Stir. Add enough of the evaporated milk to moisten and allow mixture to stick together.

6. Place equal scoops of clam mixture into clamshells. Bake until browned on top, for about 20 to 25 minutes.

YIELD: *6 appetizers or 2 entrees*

Clam Factory in Ocracoke

Ocracoke has always laid claim to having the best clams, prized for their saltiness and texture. Back in 1897, Henry Doxsee from Long Island, New York, set sail on a schooner loaded with canning equipment for the Outer Banks. He was in search of good clams, for the clam factory his father owned up north faced a dwindling supply of clams from local waters. Doxsee set up a factory on the southwest side of Silver Lake and hired local young women to pick out and can steamed clams. They were paid $3.60 a week, and worked from six in the morning to six every evening, six days a week. Boats brought clams from around Ocracoke and other parts of the Outer Banks. The factory closed when Henry died in 1905.

Steamed Clams

These are best served in individual serving bowls, but you may use one large bowl instead. Just be prepared to keep count of empty shells to ensure your fair share! Have a bowl for empty shells ready on the table.

If you'd like to make this for dinner, rather than as an appetizer, serve over linguine.

1. Place olive oil in large pot with fitted lid, and turn heat to medium-high. When oil is warm, add onion, and stir constantly for 2 minutes. Add garlic, and stir for an additional minute.

2. Add wine and water, and bring to a bubbling boil.

3. Add clams, and cover. Cook until clams open, about 4 to 6 minutes or longer. You may remove clams as soon as they open to individual serving bowls so they will not get tough.

4. When all clams have been opened and removed, add butter to cooking liquid. When butter is melted, stir in the parsley.

5. Divide the liquid evenly among the clam bowls. Or, if some stubborn clams took too long to open and the other clams have gotten too cold, you may place the clams back into the cooking liquid to heat them up. Serve immediately. Or, if you prefer, place cooked linguine in the bottom of the bowls before adding clams and liquid.

YIELD: *2–4 appetizer servings or 4 entrees with linguine*

1 tablespoon olive oil

¼ cup minced onion

1 large clove garlic, minced

½ cup dry white wine

½ cup water

2–4 dozen littleneck clams

2 tablespoons butter

1 tablespoon chopped parsley

Baguette for dipping into cooking liquid (optional)

8 ounces linguine, cooked and drained (optional)

Country Ham and Clam Linguine

Salty and sweet, both ham and clams, these two combine to make a savory pasta topping. For a hearty meal, count on a dozen littleneck clams per person.

2 tablespoons butter

2 tablespoons olive oil

2 tablespoons green onions, including tops, chopped

1 generous tablespoon minced garlic, or to taste

½ teaspoon dried crushed red pepper

1 bottle (8 ounces) clam juice

1 pound dried linguine

4 dozen littleneck clams, scrubbed

4 ounces country ham, diced, about ½ cup

1 large ripe tomato, peeled, seeded and chopped

1 teaspoon chopped fresh Greek oregano

1 tablespoon chopped fresh thyme

1 tablespoon chopped fresh parsley

1. In a large, heavy pot over medium heat, melt butter with olive oil. Add green onions, garlic, and red pepper and stir for 1 to 2 minutes. Do not allow garlic to burn.

2. Add clam juice and bring to a boil, then reduce heat and simmer until slightly reduced, about 8 minutes.

3. Meanwhile, cook linguine in a large pot of salted water for 8 minutes. Drain and set aside.

4. Add clams, country ham, tomato, oregano, and thyme, and cover. Steam until clams begin to open, removing them as soon as they open to a large bowl, about 3 to 8 minutes.

5. When all clams are opened and removed, turn heat on high and cook liquids until slightly reduced, about 5 minutes. Return all clams and any collected juice back to the pot, cover, and cook for just a minute to warm clams up.

6. Divide clams and sauce evenly over linguine. Sprinkle each serving with parsley.

YIELD: *4 servings*

Scavengers

Residents of the Outer Banks have always had to make do with they could find, and most times the sea provided them with plenty to eat. But often more than food washed up on shore.

When ships wrecked, they were quickly scavenged for anything and everything, from the bounty onboard to the planks and nails. In fact, there's a legend that Nags Head got its name from the pirates who tried to lure ships to the sandbars offshore by placing a lantern on the necks of horses, or old nags, to resemble another ship bobbing safely at sea.

But it wasn't just the pirates who did the scavenging. Linens, china, silver, and furniture plucked from the surf became prized heirlooms and stories for many families. Della Basnight, who lives in Manteo today, recalls that much of what graced her family's table were items gathered from shipwrecks.

Helen Daniels, eighty-four, grew up on the north end of Roanoke Island, and remembers a huge bunch of green bananas found over on the beach that her father hung up in their dairy house to ripen. A young child, she got into trouble for trying to get one down with a stick, bruising them all in her efforts. Boxes of apples and oranges would also wash ashore.

Helen's father also salvaged timber from a shipwreck on the beach at Nags Head, which he dragged behind a horse across the sand dunes, loaded onto a raft, and floated over to Roanoke Island to build their house. "We were like pirates," says Helen. "We'd go and strip the wrecks of everything."

crabs

CRABS

Callinects sapidus, the scientific name for the blue crab found in North Carolina, means "beautiful swimmers." One bite of the luscious, steamed meat from a Beautiful Swimmer can send me floating into ecstasy.

Most of North Carolina's blue crabs are found in Albermarle and Pamlico Sounds, so you'll find more crab processors in Manteo and Wanchese, Oriental and New Bern. Most Outer Banks seafood markets will have freshly cooked, picked crabmeat for sale in 1-pound plastic containers.

Crabmeat is sold in three grades. Jumbo and lump both come from the prime lumps of meat found under the shell, and are best served pure and unadulterated. Backfin, a lower grade, includes some lumps but mostly claw meat, and has a more intense flavor that does well for chowder, dips, and pasta. Also look for containers of fresh claw meat still attached to the last claw joint, marketed as "crab cocktail claws," which are great appetizers for dipping into cocktail sauce.

Soft-shells, lined up back-to-belly at the Whalebone Seafood Market in Nags Head, are kept live until they are cleaned. E F Wiegand

Crabmeat must be placed on ice. Place the plastic tub in a deep bowl surrounded with ice in the refrigerator, for up to a week.

Catching crabs is a great pastime for kids and vacationing adults. We collect chicken necks to bait the crab pot we throw off the boat dock on the soundside. When young, our kids entertained themselves for hours holding onto a line loaded with chicken skin or fish bait, trying to pull up a lone, angry crab. And what surf fisherman hasn't had to contend with an ornery, claws-flailing specimen? That's when you understand where the description "crabby" comes from!

Blue crabs have this thing about their outer shell. For starters, they shed their shells in order to grow. Those almost naked soft-shells are themselves a divine gourmet treat. If by chance a crab should lose a claw, it can grow a new one. It can even voluntarily throw off a claw. So beware if you have a crab by its arm—it may just lose it on purpose to escape and then seek revenge!

Soft-shell peeling tanks at Endurance Seafood on Colington Island, which is known as the Soft Shell Capital. E F Wiegand

Crab Boil

Boiling up a big pot of live crabs is an evening's worth of entertainment. Getting enough cleaned crabmeat to make a meal will take hours and several crabs, so make sure you have some cold beer, coleslaw, and good conversations.

Picking crabs yourself will earn newfound respect for the art and hard labor required for providing cleaned, cracked crabmeat in 1-pound containers. Just decades ago, the older women in outlying communities Down East, like Smyrna and Atlantic, as well as in Wanchese, spent hours each day, sitting and chatting while cracking baskets and baskets of crab for commercial distributors. Now, laborers from Mexico stand for hours at huge metal tables, cracking, extracting, and packing crabmeat.

When you serve up a crab boil, have on the table lots of small knives, forks, pliers, lobster crackers, or small hammers, and a roll of paper towels. Let the guests have at it, let conversations roll, and hope no screaming babies demand attention, for you'll have to wash up first.

3 tablespoons Old Bay seasoning

1 tablespoon crushed red pepper

12 live crabs

Melted butter

Cocktail sauce

1. Bring a big pot half-full of water to a boil. Add Old Bay and crushed red pepper. Stir.

2. Add crabs, and reduce heat to medium. Crabs will immediately turn red. Cover and boil for 10 minutes.

3. Drain crabs into sink or pluck from water, and place in a heap on a table covered with several thicknesses of newspapers, directly on the newspaper, with small bowls of melted butter and cocktail sauce placed within easy reach of each person.

YIELD: *3–4 servings*

Stewed Hard Crabs

Live hard crabs made a wonderful one-pot meal when stewed with onions and potatoes, especially when pie bread, or dumplings, were added. The pot could be started early in the day and left simmering or just sitting while other chores were done, says Dennis Williams, who grew up in Kinnakeet.

"There were two things you could do when you got out of school," he says. "Go fishing, or join the Coast Guard." So he left, but returned after thirty years of duty, and now lives in Buxton with his wife, Mary, a romance novel writer born in Hatteras. He shared this recipe he learned growing up.

1. Place salt pork in a large kettle on medium-high heat. Sauté until browned, then remove the pieces.

2. In the hot oil, add onions, stirring for a minute. Add potatoes, then enough water to cover by 3 inches.

3. When potatoes are getting soft, about half done, turn up heat. Add a layer of crabs, then a layer of pie bread. Alternate layers until all are used.

4. Boil until crabs turn color, a bright red, then turn the heat down to allow a bare simmer for an additional 30 to 40 minutes.

YIELD: *6–8 servings*

¼ cup salt pork, diced

2 large onions, sliced

5–6 potatoes, peeled and cut in large dice

Water to cover

2–3 dozen live crabs

Pie bread (see page 224)

Salt and pepper to taste

Writers' Enclave Among the Dunes

Best-selling novelist Nora Roberts has a home on Hatteras Island, and shares friendships with other writers who congregate in Buxton. Perhaps clear thinking and inspiration are gained from walks along the beach, or maybe shared over a steaming bowl of clam chowder.

Crabmeat Sautéed in Butter

There's nothing finer than a pound of jumbo lump crabmeat, for which you'll spend a pretty penny, but my, is it worth it. My philosophy is to not mess with the divine. Do as little as possible with this finest offering from the sea.

4 tablespoons butter

1 pound jumbo lump crabmeat

1 teaspoon Old Bay seasoning, or to taste

1 tablespoon finely chopped chives

Freshly ground pepper

Juice of ½ lemon

1. In large sauté pan, melt the butter. Add the crabmeat, and stir gently to warm. Sprinkle with the Old Bay, chives, pepper, and the lemon juice.

2. When crabmeat is heated through, about 3 to 5 minutes, serve immediately.

YIELD: *3–4 servings*

Two Worthwhile Books from North Carolina authors:

Blue Crabs: Catch 'Em, Cook 'Em, Eat 'Em, by Peter Meyer, Avian-Cetacean Press, P.O. Box 15643, Wilmington, NC 28408. Meyer is an emergency room doctor and nature lover. As the title implies, he tells you how to get them, clean them, and cook them in a variety of ways, with helpful diagrams and photographs.

Crazy for Crab, by Fred Thompson, The Harvard Common Press, Boston, Massachusetts. Thompson is a food writer and stylist who divides his time between Raleigh and New York City. This cookbook offers a variety of recipes for crab cakes, soft-shells, salads, soups, and other ways to prepare crab.

Traditional Outer Banks Crab Cakes

At the Pony Island Restaurant on Ocracoke, Vince O'Neal makes these crab cakes daily. It's a recipe passed down through several generations of his family. His ancestor was the first pilot who established himself in the tiny port, back when it was the only navigable inlet around before Hatteras Inlet opened during two storms. Because Ocracoke's inlet would shift and shoal much as it still does today, it was treacherous to bring in cargo ships. So local men, pilots, would guide the larger vessels in from the ocean to the port. Vince's great-great-aunt was another local legend, the only midwife on the island for years, who delivered babies well into her eighties.

Full of crabmeat, with very little breading, these crab cakes are seasoned in traditional Outer Banks style with dry mustard and Worcestershire sauce. They're usually served with crispy coleslaw and hushpuppies at the Pony Island Restaurant.

I find that crab cakes hold together better if you refrigerate the formed cakes before frying.

1 pound claw crabmeat

1 pound backfin crabmeat

1/3 cup fine bread crumbs

2 teaspoons dry mustard

2 tablespoons mayonnaise

1½ tablespoons Worcestershire sauce

2 eggs

1 teaspoon dried parsley flakes

½ teaspoon Old Bay seasoning

Vegetable oil for frying

1. Place crabmeat in a large bowl, picking through it and carefully removing any remaining shell or cartilage without breaking up any lumps of crabmeat.

2. Sprinkle the bread crumbs over the crabmeat.

3. In a small bowl, whisk together the mustard, mayonnaise, Worcestershire sauce, eggs, parsley flakes, and Old Bay.

4. Gently fold the mayonnaise mixture into the crabmeat. Shape by hand into patties about 3 inches wide. Refrigerate for at least 30 minutes, up to 4 hours.

5. Heat about ¼ inch oil in an electric frying pan to 350 degrees (or on medium-high heat on stovetop). Fry crab cakes until golden brown on both sides. Serve immediately.

YIELD: *about 12 crab cakes, 6 servings*

Beth's Crab Cakes

The less breading, the tastier the crab cake. Cornflakes provide a crispy coating, similar to the potato chips used at Breakwater Restaurant in Hatteras Village, which makes a nice variation from the traditional crab cake.

Refrigerating the cakes before sautéing helps them to keep their form.

To turn this into an appetizer, make the cakes smaller, about the size of a silver dollar. Set on a baking sheet, refrigerate for about 30 minutes to a couple of hours, then bake at 425 degrees for about 10 to 12 minutes, or until coating is golden and crisp and cake is warmed through.

1 ½ cups cornflakes, crushed and divided

1 pound lump or backfin crabmeat

1 egg, beaten slightly

2 tablespoons lemon juice

1 tablespoon Old Bay seasoning

2 tablespoons chopped chives

2 tablespoons chopped parsley

Salt and pepper to taste

2 tablespoons olive oil

4 tablespoons butter

1 lemon, sliced thinly

4 sprigs parsley

1. In a medium bowl, place ½ cup cornflakes, crabmeat, egg, lemon juice, Old Bay, chives, parsley, salt, and pepper. Mix gently, with hands, until mixture is moist and fairly blended.

2. Shape mixture into about 8 cakes about 3 inches wide and 1 inch thick. (It will not want to hold its shape. Just do your best.) Refrigerate for at least 30 minutes, up to 4 hours.

3. When ready to cook, place the rest of the cornflakes in a shallow bowl. Coat each crab cake, pressing the cornflakes to bind with the crabmeat.

4. Add olive oil and butter to a large sauté pan. Cook over low to medium heat, and when butter is melted, add crab cakes. Do not allow sides to touch. Sauté until golden on one side, about 5 minutes, then flip and repeat for the other side.

5. Garnish with lemon slices and fresh parsley, and serve.

YIELD: *4–6 appetizers, or 4 entree servings*

Crab-Stuffed Portabellos with Wine Sauce

Mack Daddy's Seafood Grill & Raw Bar in Avon, on Hatteras Island, goes beyond the expected steamed, fried, or grilled local seafood with nightly specials, including these customer favorites developed by culinary-schooled Chef Anna Mitchell, who runs an all-female kitchen staff. Owner Jomi Price says the catchy name of Mack Daddy's was the result of a brainstorming session. Enjoy a nice selection of fine wines as well.

1. Preheat oven to 350 degrees. Spray a baking sheet with nonstick spray.

2. Pat mushrooms with a damp cloth or paper towel to clean. Place on prepared baking sheet.

3. In a mixing bowl combine crabmeat, bread crumbs, green onion, eggs, mustard, salt, and pepper. Add as much heavy cream as needed to keep mixture moist, a tablespoon at the time. Do not overwork the crabmeat.

4. Fill each mushroom with stuffing mixture. Bake for approximately 10 minutes or until stuffing is raised and lightly browned on top. Remove from the oven and place a slice of Swiss cheese on each mushroom. Return to the oven until cheese is melted, about 5 to 7 minutes.

5. Meanwhile, place all ingredients for the wine sauce into a medium saucepan and bring to a boil. Continue to cook until mixture is reduced by half.

6. Strain wine sauce, then ladle over cooked stuffed mushrooms. Serve immediately.

YIELD: *6 appetizers, or about 4 entrees*

FOR THE MUSHROOMS:

6 portabello mushrooms

8 ounces (1 cup) crabmeat (Anna uses one can pasteurized crabmeat during off-season)

½ cup seasoned bread crumbs

¼ cup thinly sliced green onion

2 slightly beaten eggs

3 tablespoons ground mustard

Salt and pepper to taste

Heavy cream as needed, up to about ¼ cup

6 slices Swiss cheese

FOR THE RED WINE SAUCE:

1 chopped shallot

4 cups dry red wine

1 cup beef stock

Salt and pepper to taste

Crab and Asparagus Pasta

Crabmeat and asparagus complement each other and make for a tasty topping to pasta. This is a good way to use the less expensive backfin crabmeat and stretch it to feed more hungry folks.

1 pound asparagus, preferably thin stalks

4–6 tablespoons butter

1 medium onion, finely chopped

1 large clove garlic, minced

2 tablespoons fresh lemon juice

1 teaspoon salt

½ teaspoon freshly ground pepper

1 teaspoon Old Bay seasoning, if desired

1 pound backfin crabmeat, picked over to remove cartilage

1 pound dried linguine, cooked and drained

2 tablespoons chopped fresh parsley

1. Rinse and snap stems off asparagus. Dry with towels, then cut stalks into 2-inch pieces. Set aside.

2. In a large sauté pan, melt butter over medium heat. Add onion and cook until beginning to be tender, about 3 to 5 minutes.

3. Add garlic and stir for about 1 minute, then add asparagus pieces and continue to cook and stir until asparagus is tender (how long will depend on thickness of asparagus).

4. When asparagus is tender, add lemon juice, salt, pepper, Old Bay, and crabmeat. Gently stir to combine and continue to cook until heated through. If desired, add an additional 2 tablespoons butter.

5. Serve over warm linguine in pasta bowls. Sprinkle top with more Old Bay or perhaps parsley, if desired.

YIELD: *4–6 servings*

Backfin Imperial Crab

This recipe, from the now defunct but renowned Seafare Restaurant, came from Phoebe G. Hayman, one of the four Gould sisters who grew up cooking in the kitchens of the family hotels, The Tranquil House Inn in Manteo, opened in 1898, and also The Arlington Hotel on Nags Head, which was elegantly run from the 1930s through the 1960s. The recipe was copied down by her sister, Natalie, who returned to Manteo at the age of eighty.

4 cleaned crab shells or molds

1 pound backfin lump crabmeat

2 tablespoons mayonnaise

2 tablespoons Durkees dressing

1 tablespoon Worcestershire sauce

1 cup coarsely rolled cracker crumbs
    (Natalie uses Panko instead)

1 tablespoon paprika

2 tablespoons butter, melted

1. Preheat oven to 350 degreees. Lightly spray crab shells or molds with nonstick cooking spray. In a shallow baking pan just large enough to hold the shells, fill with water to 1/4 inch depth.

2. In a bowl, combine crabmeat, mayonnaise, dressing, and Worcestershire sauce, blending lightly so as not to break the crab lumps.

3. Mound the mixture onto four crab shells.

4. Combine the cracker crumbs (or Panko) with the paprika; pat onto filled crab shells.

5. Pour melted butter over crabmeat just before baking.

6. Place crab shells into prepared baking pan, and bake for 12 to 15 minutes, or until tops are golden brown.

YIELD: *4 servings*

Lunch with FDR

To mark the celebration of Virginia Dare's 350th birthday on August 18, 1937, then-President Franklin D. Roosevelt attended the evening performance of *The Lost Colony*, an outdoor play performed every summer since that tells the story of the English colonists and their mysterious disappearance, written by Pulitzer Prize–winner Paul Green, a North Carolina native.

President Roosevelt arrived that morning at the docks of Manteo on a Coast Guard cutter, greeted by a flotilla of boats in Roanoke Sound and hundreds of spectators lining the shore. He gave a brief speech at Fort Raleigh, then left in his open Packard convertible to go to Nags Head, where he had invited himself to lunch with the Buchanan family of Durham at their new beachfront cottage.

No other locals were invited, but they certainly strained to get a look from nearby porches. Roosevelt requested a drink before his meal, which had to be snuck from an upstairs source, as Mrs. Buchanan never served alcohol in her home. The Buchanan's five servants served fifty politicians and thirty security people crab casserole, ham, summer vegetables, rolls, and a blueberry cobbler with hard sauce. Afterward, he sat on the front porch, rocking and watching the ocean while his aides swam in swimsuits borrowed from the servants.

Affordable Crab Salad

What makes this salad affordable is pairing crabmeat with rice and black-eyed peas, a lovely combination worth any cost. Frank White, a Manteo native and retired college professor, shared this favorite lunchtime recipe. He recommends putting any leftover salad in a buttered casserole, dusting the top with saltine cracker "dust" (crumbled), sprinkling with paprika, and then drenching the mixture with as much melted butter as it will take. Heat under a hot broiler.

1. Pick over crabmeat carefully to remove any cartilage that has been missed by the pickers.
2. In a large bowl, using hands, gently mix crabmeat with rice and peas so as not to break up crabmeat any more than necessary.
3. Place the mayonnaise in a small bowl. Blend in the salt and curry.
4. Gently add the mayonnaise mixture to the crabmeat.
5. Scoop the salad onto a bed of lettuce, surrounded by the boiled eggs and tomato quarters.

YIELD: *4 servings*

1 pound picked crabmeat (lump or backfin)

1 cup cooked white rice, cold and fluffed with a fork

1 cup black-eyed peas, cold, rinsed well and drained dry

½ cup good mayonnaise (Frank prefers Hellman's)

Salt to taste

½ teaspoon curry powder (more or less to taste, but do not overdo)

Serve with lettuce, quartered boiled eggs, and summer tomatoes

Crabmeat Omelet

During the warmer weather when my husband and I have a couple of days at the beach, we inevitably seek out fresh lump crabmeat, sold in 1-pound plastic tubs. I always try to save enough from our dinner so that I can make an omelet the next morning. What a decadent way to start a day.

4 tablespoons butter, divided

⅓ pound crabmeat (about 1 cup)

Sprinkle of Old Bay seasoning

1 tablespoon chopped chives

4 eggs

Salt and pepper to taste

1. In a sauté pan, melt 2 tablespoons butter. Add crabmeat and sprinkle with Old Bay and chives. Gently stir crabmeat until heated through, then place crabmeat in a small bowl.

2. In another small bowl, beat eggs together with a fork until creamy and frothy. Melt remaining butter in the same sauté pan over medium high heat, and swirl to coat the bottom and sides of pan. Add eggs, and season with salt and pepper to taste. When mixture has become slightly cooked on the bottom, tilt pan and allow the moist eggs to run beneath the cooked eggs, or if you are skilled, flip the omelet over. Add crabmeat to the center, and fold over the two edges. Remove immediately.

3. Divide omelet in half, and slide onto warmed plates. Sprinkle with more Old Bay if desired.

YIELD: *2 servings*

Old Bay Seasoning

A favorite seasoning for crabs, shrimp, and other seafood that's used up and down the East Coast, Old Bay seasoning is a blend of celery salt, mustard, red pepper, bay leaves, cloves, allspice, ginger, mace, cardamom, cinnamon, and paprika.

However, this spice is not used by most old-timers or traditionalists on the Outer Banks who object to its domineering flavors. Instead you'll find dry mustard, paprika, and native bay leaves.

Crab Eggs Benedict

The Pelican Restaurant and Bar sat among the live oak trees along the shore of Silver Lake, in Ocracoke, for many years. Syd Mulder, originally from Holland, happily found himself marooned there as cook since 1972. Whenever we sailed over to the island, after a needed night's rest, our reward was the Pelican's lovely breakfast. This eggs benedict, served with crabmeat, was a favorite.

1. Fill a 12-inch skillet with water to depth of 2 inches. Add vinegar. Place on medium-high heat, and bring to a simmer. Add salt.

2. Toast the muffin halves in a toaster or oven until slightly crisp.

3. Meanwhile, melt butter in a sauté pan, and add crabmeat. Sprinkle with Old Bay, parsley, scallions, garlic, and sherry. Shake the pan and gently stir just until crabmeat is heated through.

4. Break 1 egg onto a shallow saucer, then slide the egg from the saucer into the simmering water. Add other eggs in the same manner. Cover the pan, and turn off the heat. Let eggs remain in the water for about 5 minutes, or until the whites are cooked through and the yolks are set but still runny.

5. When ready to serve, place the toasted muffins on the plate. Spoon crabmeat over the muffins. Gently lift each egg with a slotted spoon and set on one muffin half. Pour warm Hollandaise Sauce over each egg muffin. Serve immediately.

YIELD: *2 servings*

2 teaspoons vinegar

½ teaspoon salt

2 English muffins, split

2 tablespoons butter

4 to 5 ounces crabmeat

Dash of Old Bay seasoning

1 teaspoon fresh, chopped parsley

1 tablespoon thinly sliced scallions

¼ teaspoon minced garlic

Dash of sherry

4 eggs

1 cup Hollandaise Sauce
(recipe follows)

Hollandaise Sauce

3 egg yolks

1 tablespoon lemon juice

4 tablespoons butter, melted

2 tablespoons hot water

Pinch of cayenne

Pinch of garlic salt

Pinch of salt

1. Use a double boiler or metal bowl that will fit over a pot of gently boiling water. Put the egg yolks in the boiler top and, using a wire whisk, beat until creamy and smooth.

2. Stir in the lemon juice. Pouring in a thin stream, gradually whisk in the melted butter.

3. Gently stir in the hot water, cayenne, garlic salt, and salt.

4. Continue to stir for about 1 minute, until the sauce is thickened. Serve immediately, or you can keep it over warm water for up to 2 hours.

5. If preferred, you may use a blender instead of the above method. Blend the egg yolks first, then on low speed, add the boiling water, then the butter in a slow stream, then the lemon juice and spices.

YIELD: *1/2 cup*

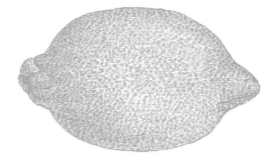

SOFT-SHELLS

In the peaceful backwaters of North Carolina's shallow sounds, the Atlantic blue crab sleeps through the winter in the muck of Neptune's spawning ground. When the water warms, so do the crabs, and come late spring, crabbers get to work pulling the "busters" just before they're ready to shed their outgrown shells.

"The female peelers, the souks, they come in on the first new moon in May, and shed on the full moon," says Mike Cox, who works at Jughead Etheridge's shedder on Manteo's Shallowbag Bay. "The jimmies are earlier, in April."

Those busters that are ready to shed are kept in raised pools, where the temperature of water pumped from creeks or the sound can be monitored. They're watched 24/7 so that the naked crustacean can be plucked from the water as soon as it slips from its old coat, for it forms a paper-like skin within two hours. "When they first come out, they feel just like silk," said a strapping young man helping at another shedder in Wanchese. "We don't sleep if there's a full moon."

Crabs live in tune with the moon, peeling off their skins and mating according to lunar phases. Before they mature, they pass through twenty or more molts. Once mature, females do not ordinarily shed again, and male crabs slow down as they become larger. Market-sized crabs, those about 3 inches across, shed about every twenty days in May and June and continue more slowly during the summer.

Souks are prized more than the males, for they have what some consider a delicious addition, their roe, although with current regulations, if roe are visible, she must be thrown back in. Trapping females in the crabbers' wire traps is a bit like operating a bordello, with genders reversed. "To catch a female, you put a jimmy in the bait pocket, 'cause she's seeking him out when she's ready to mate," Cox explains. "So when the female comes in, he carries her on upstairs. That's when we call her the 'Chandler's wife,' and she'll shed." Actually, the male instinctually cradles her underneath him, protecting her from predators and cannibalism—after he mates with her, that is. A newly molten crab is hungry, and will even eat other crabs. After June, the souks have had enough with the jimmies, says Cox, so they must bait their traps with menhaden.

Once caught, the ready-to-shed crabs are sold to shedders like Jughead's, where Cox watches them night and day, catching naps in the cab of his pickup truck. He peers at each crab, looking for red lines on the claws of the female peelers, and a little blue and pink color on the V-apron. The jimmy has a plain white apron with a little red in the joint of the claw and a "sun glass" effect on his flipper claw. These

Soft-shell peeling tanks at Wanchese. Watching for the soft-shells to shed (especially during a full moon) means babysitting them twenty-four hours a day. E F Wiegand signal when the busters are just about ready to do just that—bust right out of their shells. Then they are quickly sorted by size and packed live, belly to back, traditionally on eelgrass, and shipped off to Fulton's Fish Market in New York City, as well as to area restaurants.

The Outer Banks is considered a mecca for gastronomes in search of the molting Atlantic blue crab. Off a dirt path on Colington Island, claimed by some to be the "soft-shell capital," thirty-year-old Endurance Seafood still packs them by the truckload. Etheridge Seafood in Wanchese built a two-story maze of shedding pools, so that they can better handle higher volumes. O'Neal's Sea Harvest, at the Wanchese Seafood Industrial Park, houses their shedding facility indoors.

When there's a Blue Moon—two full moons within a month, as often happens in May—busters have to repeat their moonlight sonatas. That's good news for soft-shell lovers.

Soft-shell Crab Tips

How to Buy

You want them alive, so poke if you must, or blow across their eyes, to see if they move or spit bubbles. Take a whiff for a clean and astringent smell. If you must store them enclosed in an ice chest and on ice to get them home, it is best to have the crabs cleaned for you at the market.

Sizes range from the smallest, called "mediums," to hotels, primes, jumbos, and whalers, the largest, which can be a bit tough.

How to Store

Do not store live soft-shells directly on ice; rather, place a newspaper or folded paper towels between them and the ice. Keep them in the coldest part of the refrigerator. Cleaned crabs must be stored on ice.

Some believe you must cook soft-shells within 4 hours of cleaning, and others recommend storing cleaned crabs wrapped in plastic for up to 2 days.

How to Clean

This is not a chore for the squeamish. Kitchen shears work great. First, grab the crab in one hand and cut about ½ inch off behind the eyes and mouth. Gently squeeze to remove the yucky contents of the sack at the edge of the cut. Then, lift the pointed end of the crab's outer shell, and remove the Dead Man (the gray-white gills or lungs) on both sides. Turn the crab over, and cut off the triangular flap, called the apron. Rinse and pat dry, then immediately cook or store on ice in the refrigerator.

Basic Sautéed Soft-shell Crabs

½ cup flour

½ teaspoon salt

½ teaspoon ground pepper

1 teaspoon Old Bay seasoning

1 tablespoon parsley, finely chopped

1 tablespoon fresh thyme, minced

8 soft-shell crabs, cleaned

2 tablespoons or more of canola oil

2 tablespoons or more of butter

Thick lemon slices

While others may balk at eating a whole crab—pinchers, paddle fins, and all—I can't wait to taste the succulent, sweet meat and munch on the tender, crackling limbs of a soft-shell crab, just molted and caught with its pants down, so to speak. Besides, there's ten times more edible meat in a soft-shell.

Because crabs are full of water, they will "pop" at you, so beware of the grease splatter. A splatter guard or lid may be used.

1. In a shallow pan, mix together flour, salt, pepper, Old Bay, parsley, and thyme.

2. Rinse crabs and, while damp, dredge in flour mixture, shaking off excess.

3. Heat oil and butter over medium heat in a large saucepan. When butter is melted and hot, add a few of the crabs. Do not crowd the pan.

4. Cook crabs until golden and somewhat crisp on both sides, about 2 to 3 minutes per side. Remove to a heated platter. Cook remaining crabs, adding more oil and butter if necessary.

5. Garnish with parsley and lemon slices. Serve immediately.

YIELD: *4 servings*

Albermarle Sound Soft-shells from The Left Bank

Chef Rhett Elliott pairs the early summer delicacy of soft-shell crabs with two other seasonal delights, sweet corn and May peas, all ingredients found locally, just across the sound from The Sanderling Resort & Spa. The cooking methods are simple, which allow the flavors to really shine, and the addition of optional truffle oil takes it up just a notch.

TO PREPARE THE PEA PUREE:

1. Blanch the peas in heavily salted water for 1 minute or until tender. Plunge into ice water, then drain. Reserve 1/3 cup peas for the corn sauté.

2. Put remaining peas in a blender and add just enough water to spin. Puree until it is perfectly smooth and a sauce consistency. Season with salt and pepper. You could now drizzle the truffle oil to taste, but the puree is fine without it, Chef Rhett notes.

TO PREPARE THE CORN:

1. Blanch corn kernels in heavily salted boiling water for 1 minute. Plunge into ice water, then drain and dry.

2. Render the bacon in a sauté pan until browned and crispy. Pour out all but 1 teaspoon of the bacon fat, and add corn and reserved peas. Cook 2 minutes. Swirl in butter and season with salt and pepper. Add chives.

TO PREPARE THE SOFT-SHELLS:

1. Add oil to a large sauté pan and bring to medium-high heat. Meanwhile, season the crab with salt and pepper and dredge in flour. Shake off excess flour, and immediately add the crabs to the pan.

2. Cook until golden brown. Turn the crabs over and cook until golden brown on the other side, then remove from pan. Blot on a paper towel.

TO ASSEMBLE THE DISH:

1. Divide the corn sauté onto four plates.

2. Drizzle the plate with the pea puree and top with a crab. Serve immediately.

YIELD: *4 servings*

FOR THE MAY PEA PUREE:

1 cup May peas

¼ cup water

Drizzle of truffle oil (optional)

Salt and pepper to taste

FOR THE CORN:

8 ears sweet white or yellow corn, kernels cut from cob

4 slices thick-cut applewood-smoked bacon

1 teaspoon butter

1 tablespoon chopped chives

Salt and pepper to taste

FOR THE CRABS:

2 tablespoons neutral oil (peanut or vegetable)

4 local, soft-shell crabs, cleaned

¼ cup flour

Salt and pepper to taste

The Blue Point, at the Waterfront Shops in Duck

In the summer of 1989, Duck was still a sleepy little village and Highway 12 barely extended beyond The Sanderling Resort & Spa. But two old high school buddies decided that Duck needed a restaurant and bar, so John Power and Sam McGann, from nearby Norfolk, Virginia, opened an oyster bar. With Sam's culinary training at Johnson & Wales, they quickly moved beyond steaming oysters, instead creating a Southern coastal menu which has brought them accolades from the country's top food publications. They seek out local sweet corn, tomatoes, parsnips, or other seasonal produce, and serve a variety of local seafood, such as a stew made with oysters from Rose Bay, a tartare of tuna caught that morning, or she-crab soup made with crabs from Colington Island. You'll also find duck confit and pan-roasted duck, in homage to their home base.

You'll be greeted year-round by John, who manages the operation and the crowds who covet reservations in this delightful bar and restaurant that overlooks Currituck Sound.

There's more to Duck than playing in the sand, but what a pastime. Photo courtesy of Island Photography

Sautéed Soft-shell Crabs

with Green Onion, Country Ham, and Roasted Peanuts

Sam McGann, chef/owner of the Blue Point in Duck, gets his soft-shells from Murray Bridges, of Endurance Seafood on Colington Island, the so named "soft-shell capital." He recommends that if cleaning live crabs is not your "cup of tea," to ask your seafood supplier to show you the live crabs first, then clean them for you.

1. Preheat oven to 350 degrees.

2. Place the crabs in a baking dish and cover with milk.

3. In a separate pan, mix together flour, cornmeal, salt, pepper, and Old Bay.

4. Heat a nonstick sauté pan over high heat. Add enough oil to coat the bottom of the pan.

5. Drain the crab of excess milk and dredge in the seasoned flour mixture. Pat off excess.

6. Pan-fry crabs two at a time, cooking for 2 to 3 minutes per side. Place crabs in a large baking dish to hold until all the crabs have been cooked.

7. Finish cooking crabs for another 3 to 4 minutes in the oven.

8. Meanwhile, over medium-high heat in a separate sauté pan, warm together the ham, green onions, and peanuts in butter.

9. To serve, remove the soft-shells from the oven. Place two crabs on each of four dinner plates. Garnish with the ham mixture over top of the crabs and serve with lemon wedges.

YIELD: *4 servings*

8 prime soft-shell crabs, cleaned

1 cup milk or buttermilk

1 cup flour

½ cup cornmeal

Salt and pepper to taste

1½ teaspoons Old Bay seasoning

1 cup peanut or corn oil

1 cup country ham, sliced thin and julienned

1 bunch green onions, sliced thin

1 cup unsalted, shelled and roasted peanuts

1 tablespoon butter

4 large lemon wedges

Grilled Soft-shells with Creole Sauce

12 medium soft-shells, cleaned

12 tablespoons butter

2 teaspoons minced garlic

1½ teaspoons hot sauce, such as Tabasco, or to taste

2 tablespoons fresh lemon juice

½ teaspoon salt

½ teaspoon freshly ground black pepper

Hot and crunchy is how these soft-shells come straight off the grill. This is one of the easiest ways to prepare this seasonal treat, and allows the succulent texture and taste of the crabmeat to shine.

Simply serve 2 to 3 soft-shells per person over a bed of lightly dressed greens. We found using a perforated grill pan kept the crab legs from falling through the grates and breaking off. If you prefer to leave out the hot sauce, it will still be delicious.

1. Preheat grill.
2. Pat cleaned soft-shells dry, and lay them in a shallow dish.
3. Over medium heat, melt butter. Add garlic and stir for about 1 minute. Remove from heat and add the hot sauce and lemon juice. Stir to mix.
4. Brush the butter sauce over both sides of each soft-shell, then dribble excess over the legs. Sprinkle with salt and pepper. Allow soft-shells to sit until the grill is ready, or about 10 minutes.
5. When grill is medium hot, place crabs evenly over grill without touching. Close the lid and cook for about 3 to 4 minutes, depending on thickness. Turn the crabs over, and cook for another 3 to 4 minutes, or until crabs have gotten a bit crisp and golden brown.

YIELD: *4–6 servings*

CREOLE SAUCE:

½ cup mayonnaise

2 teaspoons drained capers, chopped

2 teaspoons finely chopped chives

2 teaspoons sweet pickle relish

1 generous tablespoon fresh lemon juice

1 teaspoon Tabasco sauce, or to taste

1 teaspoon Old Bay seasoning

¼ teaspoon salt

Several grinds black pepper

Creole Sauce

With just a bit of a kick, this sauce adds a sassy finishing touch to crabs, shrimp, or grilled fish, and it couldn't be easier to make.

Combine all ingredients in a small serving bowl. Taste for seasonings and adjust.

YIELD: *about ³⁄₄ cup*

Fried Soft-shells by Chef Dirt

"Crabmeat has the shelf life of ice cream," says Chef Dirt, a.k.a. Jerry G. Smith, who has demonstrated seafood cooking on local television shows and developed his own line of dips, chowders, and cookbooks. He recommends you clean soft-shells yourself, then immediately cook them. He likes soft bread crumbs as a coating because they won't dry out, and peanut oil, rather than butter, for its cleaner taste when frying. See more helpful hints in the Primer on Frying Seafood, page 160.

2 eggs

1 cup milk

8 stale hamburger or hot dog rolls

2 tablespoons chopped, fresh parsley

1 teaspoon black pepper

1 teaspoon salt

1 teaspoon Old Bay seasoning

6 large soft-shells

Peanut oil for frying

1. Combine eggs and milk in a bowl and beat well.

2. In a food processor, combine rolls, parsley, black pepper, salt, and Old Bay. Process until you have very fine bread crumbs.

3. Place the crabs in the egg wash and let sit in the refrigerator for about 30 minutes.

4. Heat about 1 inch of peanut oil in a large cast-iron skillet, or electric skillet set on 375 degrees.

5. Remove the crabs from the egg wash and coat with the bread crumbs. Fry until golden brown, about 4 to 5 minutes, remove from oil and drain on paper towels.

YIELD: *6 servings*

Soft-shell BLT

4 thin slices pancetta or thickly sliced bacon

4 jumbo soft-shell crabs

4 round, soft sandwich rolls

¾ cup Lynne Foster's Secret Sauce (see page 256) or Creole Sauce (see page 112)

4–8 romaine lettuce leaves or mesclun

4 large slices very ripe tomato

This is a delightful play on the classic bacon, lettuce, and tomato sandwich. Pancetta is an Italian bacon made from the belly of the pig, salt-cured but not smoked.

You choose whether you grill, fry, or sauté the soft-shells. A gas grill is the easiest and less messy for cleanup. Also choose either a savory mayonnaise or a spicier version.

1. Place the pancetta in a skillet and turn heat medium-high. Fry until almost crispy, then drain on paper towels.

2. Prepare soft-shells by either grilling (see page 191), frying (see page 161), or sautéing (see page 108).

3. Meanwhile, place inner sides of sandwich rolls on the grill or under a broiler to toast lightly. Slather with your choice of sauce.

4. Layer the lettuce, tomato, and warm pancetta on each roll. Top with cooked, hot crab, add another dollop of sauce, and serve immediately.

YIELD: *4 servings*

Pocket Buster

4 jumbo soft-shell crabs

4 pita pockets

¾ cup mayonnaise, Creole Sauce (see page 112), or Lynne Foster's Secret Sauce (see page 256)

4 large slices tomatoes

4 large romaine lettuce leaves

A pita pocket seems the perfect place for a soft-shell "buster" to hide in. You choose the method of cooking the soft-shell. We find the grill the easiest and less messy.

1. Prepare soft-shells by either grilling (see page 191), frying (see page 161), or sautéing (see page 108).

2. Meanwhile, prepare pita pockets by cutting off top quarter of the pita circle. Gently open the pocket, and slather with your choice of mayonnaise or sauce. Add tomato and lettuce to pocket.

3. When crab is cooked, slide into pita pocket and serve immediately.

YIELD: *4 servings*

oysters

OYSTERS

Oyster virginica includes all oysters grown on the Atlantic coast. Oysters have been enjoyed as a tasty treat and sustenance for centuries. Mounds of oyster shells at Thicket Lump in Wanchese, and at the northern end of Roanoke, and also at Hatteras, have provided clues to the Algonquians who settled here long before the first European explorers. And when the Englishmen tried to survive those first winters, it was oysters that provided much needed protein and kept them from starving.

Fried oysters, oyster stew, oyster fritters, and steamed oysters are traditional ways these mollusks continue to be served on the Outer Banks. Our favorite way to see in the New Year is sharing an oyster roast with friends, who steam the oysters in a turkey roaster. (I'll tell you how later. Check out favorite Outer Banks oyster stew recipes in the Soups and Chowders chapter.)

Rose Bay, Swan Quarter, Crab Slough, and Engelhard are where local oysters are harvested. Roanoke Sound is the northernmost range you'll find Eastern oysters because of low salinity. They're harvested with tongs or by hand, or in the Pamlico by dredges, from October to March. You'll find these oysters have a salty and rich flavor.

North Carolina's oyster population faced a serious decline during the last decade, especially, but is making a bit of a comeback. Not only do oysters provide food for us humans, but they also help us out by filtering the water they live in, up to 50 gallons a day, which clears out algae, plankton, and pollution. And their beds or reefs provide a nurturing habitat for other sea life, like clams, crabs, and juvenile fish. These beds also help prevent erosion because they break up waves before they hit the shoreline.

And the oyster's reputation about being an aphrodisiac? Blame it on Casanova, that Renaissance lover, who is said to have eaten fifty oysters a day to keep up his stamina.

Oyster Decline and Farming

During the last century, oyster numbers declined 90 percent. What caused this dramatic drop? Overharvesting, habitat disturbance, water pollution, and recently, parasitic disease.

Yet oysters have persisted along the North Carolina coast, and are on a bit of a rebound. That is thanks to oyster farming in Pamlico and Albermarle Sounds, with watermen seeding and providing underwater artificial reefs, and the state's Oyster Sanctuary Programs, which have at least three sites, in Croatan Sound and near Hatteras and Ocracoke Islands. Reefs are being rebuilt with recycled oyster shells, especially, and riprap and limestone marl, which give the oyster larvae something hard to attach to as they mature.

You can take your used oyster shells to recycling bins located at Jockey's Ridge State Park in Kill Devil Hills; The Nature Conservancy, Nags Head Woods; North Carolina Division of Marine Fisheries at Wanchese Seafood Industrial Park; the Village Grocery in Avon; Burrus Red & White in Hatteras Village; and the Recycling Center in Rodanthe Harbor.

In Buxton, high school students are raising oysters from fertilized eggs given to them by the North Carolina Oyster Hatchery Program. When they become "spat," or juvenile, they'll be placed in the oyster sanctuaries.

Oyster farming is nothing new. The Greeks used artificial methods of growing them, as did the Chinese centuries before Christianity. The Romans carted oysters all the way from Brittany to Rome, building a series of ice houses to keep them fresh.

Tips for Oysters

- Buy oysters the day they are to be served.

- Store live oysters in a cool place, preferably outside (perhaps that's why you eat them in "R" months), covered with a damp cloth.

- Use only those oysters whose shells are tightly closed. Discard any with broken shells.

- See A Primer on Frying Seafood, page 160, for helpful hints on frying oysters.

Crab Slough Oysters

Crab Slough is in Pamlico Sound at the southern end of Roanoke Island near Wanchese. It's a well-known area for harvesting prime oysters because the water is slightly rough, being near Oregon Inlet, so that only single oysters, rather than clumps, are formed. The water is rather brackish, which gives the oysters a delicious salty taste. Frequently, very tiny pea crabs, themselves a gourmet treat when eaten whole, are found residing in the oysters. Crab Slough oyster beds were "claimed" and passed down from generation to generation, says Frank White, a Manteo native.

Imagine White's surprise when on a trip to New York City years ago, he found Crab Slough Oysters on the menu at Joe Allen, a restaurant near the theatre district. He adapted the dish by the chef, Ed Gafney.

3 dozen oysters, preferably from Crab Slough, in their shells

2 tablespoons olive oil

2 cloves garlic, minced

1 pound fresh or frozen spinach, thawed

1 ½ sticks butter

1 tablespoon Worcestershire sauce

½ teaspoon hot pepper sauce

1. Open and remove oysters from the shells. If you should find tiny crabs, be sure to save them to include with the oysters. Reserve each of the larger, flat halves of the oyster shells, and place on a large baking sheet or pan.

2. Heat the olive oil in a large skillet over medium heat, and add the garlic, stirring and cooking for just a minute or until the garlic is almost brown.

3. Add the spinach and sauté until fresh spinach is thoroughly wilted or frozen spinach is warm. Drain the spinach in a colander.

4. Divide spinach among the oyster shells. Place one oyster (and one pea crab, if present) on top of the spinach.

5. In a heavy skillet, melt the butter, and add the Worcestershire sauce and hot pepper sauce. Cook slowly, stirring occasionally, until butter is nut brown.

6. Preheat the oven to broil.

7. Drizzle each prepared oyster with the browned butter mixture. Place under hot broiler for 2 to 5 minutes, or until oysters are thoroughly heated. Serve immediately.

YIELD: *9–12 appetizers, or 4 entree servings*

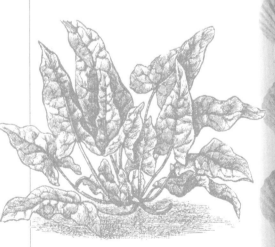

Oyster or Clam Fritters

Mrs. Ivadean Priest, in her seventies, shared the secret to these fritters, and it's this: Rather than mixing the oysters in with the batter, dip the oysters in the batter, then cluster them together to make a fritter, or sprinkle cooking batter with clams. It's like when making blueberry pancakes, you get a better distribution of blueberries if you sprinkle blueberries across a cooking pancake rather than mixing them into the batter.

A cast-iron skillet works best, says Mrs. Priest.

2 eggs, lightly beaten

¼ cup self-rising flour

½ cup oyster or clam juice, water, and/ or milk

Vegetable oil for frying

1 pint oysters (or clams)

Ketchup, mustard, or sour cream

1. Preheat oven to 250 degrees. Line a baking sheet with paper towels.

2. In a mixing bowl, mix eggs and flour together for a thick paste. Add as much of the liquid as is required to make a thin batter that is thick enough to hold together when put into the hot fat.

3. Pour enough vegetable oil into frying pan to reach a depth of ½ to 1 inch. Heat over medium-high heat.

4. When oil is hot, hold the bowl over the pan, and dip oysters into batter individually, then drop 2 to 3 oysters together in a cluster to make one fritter. Or, pour a spoonful of batter into the oil, then quickly add a couple of oysters. If you are doing clam fritters, spoon a dollop of batter into the oil, then quickly add a spoonful of drained clams to the batter. Do not crowd the pan.

5. Cook each fritter until golden, then flip and cook the other side. Remove and drain on paper towels, on the baking sheet kept in the warm oven.

6. Serve stacks of the fritters on a serving platter, along with ketchup, mustard, or sour cream.

YIELD: *1 dozen or more fritters, 4–6 appetizers, or 2–3 entrees*

Indigestion Medicine

Ivadean Priest, who has cooked for most of her seventy-some years in Manteo, pulled out an old cookbook, tattered and stained, without a cover. "I believe it's from Stumpy Point, over on the mainland," she said. "Look here."

Beneath a recipe for fried oyster fritters, the book states: "Now get out this indigestion medicine." And it calls for:

1 gallon boiled rainwater

5 heaping teaspoons soda

2 ounces spirit of ammonia, and

1 ounce of spirits of peppermint.

It doesn't say how much, or how often. Ivadean admits she has never tried it.

How to
Do Your Own Oyster Roast

SUPPLIES NEEDED:

Several pairs of heavy gloves, preferably rubber

Scrub brush

Outside water hose

Bucket

Outside picnic table or plywood set on two sawhorses

Turkey fryer or grill (charcoal or gas)

Oyster knives

Saltine crackers

Bowls of melted butter and cocktail sauce

Small plastic bowls and forks

Iced tea, bourbon, or beer

Newspapers

Garbage can for shells

Bushel or two of raw oysters

An oyster roast is a great way to see in the New Year, shake and greet a politician, or use as an excuse to gather friends and family. Many families on the Outer Banks celebrate Christmas with a family get-together around a table full of steaming oysters they've harvested from nearby waters.

The rule of oysters being safe to eat only in the "R" months—such as November, January, or March—is just a myth. Instead, it was rather a necessity prior to refrigeration. And, during the summer months, oysters are rather milky and lack a bit of flavor because they're in their spawn cycle. Therefore it really is best to eat them in the cooler months, which happen to have an "R."

So when the weather is nice and cold, buy a bushel or two of oysters. Keep them covered with wet burlap, and cool, without putting them directly on or under ice, which will do them in (another reason to do this in the winter).

1. Wear thick rubber or work gloves to prevent being cut by the sharp oyster shells. Oyster cuts tend to get infected or, at the least, be very sore.

2. The oysters need to be rinsed with cold water and may need scrubbing with a brush to remove the mud. An old table, a piece of roofing tin on two sawhorses, or an extra-large bucket is handy for the big and wet job of rinsing. All shells should be closed, or close when you handle them or tap on them. Shells that remain open mean the oyster is dead and should not be eaten.

3. The handiest thing for steaming that we've found is a turkey fryer. Place the cleaned oysters in the steamer basket, then into the fryer that's been filled with water to a depth of about 3 to 4 inches. As the oysters begin to open, their juices will feed the steaming water. Steam for about 8 to 10 minutes, or until oysters open easily. Check the pot after every batch to make sure you have sufficient water.

4. Or, place oysters on a hot grill for about 8 to 10 minutes. You may find a grated tray helpful. Remove oysters when they open easily.

5. Cover an outside picnic table with newspapers. Have oyster knives ready, along with saltines, bowls of melted butter, and cocktail sauce. When the oysters are done, dump them directly onto the table.

6. Enlist the help of several experienced folks, wearing gloves, to open the oysters for you and your guests. Have them toss the opened shells into the garbage can.

7. Oyster shells can be used as a compost or mulch to "fertilize" bushes, fruit trees, and fig trees, especially,

Kinnakeet Oysters

The women at Kinnakeet wanted a church. There wasn't much money to be donated, so they talked their menfolk into getting together and harvesting the large number of oysters that "miraculously" appeared in Pamlico Sound. They took the oysters to market, and with their profit paid for the building supplies. Legend has it the villagers were so excited when the boat arrived, they carried the lumber to the site on their backs. The South Banks Methodist Episcopal Church was consecrated in 1880.

Oyster shells can cut bare feet when wading in the sound, so beware. E F Wiegand

Christmas on the Outer Banks

Christmas comes twice a year on the Outer Banks.

In addition to December 25, Old Christmas is celebrated on the Saturday closest to Epiphany, particularly on Hatteras Island in the village of Rodanthe, near the old Chicamacomico Lifesaving Station.

When the English Crown finally adopted the new, Georgian calendar in 1752, the year was shortened by eleven days. Residents of the Outer Banks were so isolated that they did not receive word of this change for years. Even then, they were known for their eccentricity and refused to adopt the changes, and continue to this day to celebrate "Old Christmas" on what Elizabethans called the "Twelfth Night."

During the 1800s, the men in Rodanthe had shooting contests in the afternoons, while children "pulled" taffy candy. Women worked together to prepare an evening feast of fish, chicken, greens, and cold sweet potato pie. There was a parade with fife and drums and the church choir. Folks dressed in costume, in old clothes with stockings on their faces, and told jokes and made merry, with square dancing added in later years. There are stories of men dancing until the buttons on their drawers popped off, or drinking eggnog, with or without the egg, until daybreak. One of the keepers of the Chicamacomico Lifesaving Station reportedly shot apples off the heads of his crewmen.

Today, Rodanthe residents still gather for a lively celebration beginning with an "oyster shoot," the prize for the best shot being a basket of oysters. A chicken and pastry dinner is offered, along with a huge oyster roast, music by a local band, stockings for all the children in attendance, and a parade led by "Old Buck."

Old Buck is a mythical bull who supposedly ran wild in nearby Trent Woods, with a roar that was said to be louder than a winter nor'easter. He occasionally ran wild through the village as well, terrorizing all. Even after he was "felled" by a hunter, he would always make an appearance at the Old Christmas celebrations. Today's Old Buck appears much as he did a hundred years ago with the help of two men carrying a bleached cow skull attached to blankets, sometimes cow skins, over barrel hoops for the body and ribs, to "terrorize" children and lead revelers through the crowds.

Farther north, the villagers of Duck had their lively parties on December 25, and on Old Christmas, a solemn, religious observance with no drinking, dancing, or carousing. You have to wonder if there were not partygoers who traveled from one village to the other to keep the parties rolling.

Outer Bankers celebrated the holidays with what they could scavenge from nature, but what treats nature provided! Christmas tables were laden with ducks and geese, as well as oysters, drum, bluefish, and mullet. Helen Daniels of Manteo recalls "her daddy hunting down at Pea Island" so that each family member had their very own duck to eat at their Christmas dinner. Or sometimes it was a big goose, baked with apples. Up at Duck, folks referred to swans as their "white turkey" when served at holiday dinners.

Old Buck, a deranged bull, makes an appearance each year at the Old Christmas celebration at Rodanthe. Photo courtesy of the Stick Collection at the Outer Banks History Center

In Nags Heads Woods, sharpshooters would shoot mistletoe from treetops. The mistletoe was packed into barrels and shipped by boat to New York, sold, and with the profits, new clothes were bought and packed in those barrels to be sold back in Manteo. Holly trees were gathered from the woods, set inside homes, and decorated. Oranges, apples, nuts, and candy were brought by supply boats, bought with fishing and hunting income, and became prized stocking stuffers for delighted children.

Even in 1585, Christmas was a significant occasion for a couple of native Outer Bankers. Two Algonquians, Manteo and Wanchese, made the return voyage back to England with the explorers who were attempting the first colonization in the New World. During that winter, they witnessed the holiday merry-making and, on the Twelfth Day of Christmas, Queen Elizabeth proclaiming Sir Walter Raleigh a knight and Governor of Virginia.

scallops

SCALLOPS

A bivalve mollusk with a pretty crinkle-edged shell, a scallop actually swims or propels itself by snapping its shells together, thus "body-building" the muscle we eat. Its bright blue eyes stick out on short stalks among the tentacles of the mantle. Scallops only live for about two years, although most North Carolina bay scallops are harvested at twelve to sixteen months of age.

Bay Scallops

The creamy, sweet, and tiny bay scallops of North Carolina are in trouble. Their numbers have dwindled to almost nothing, and that's due to being low on the environmental food chain.

An increasing number of cownose rays swoop through the sounds on an eating rampage during the summer when scallops are breeding, and eat all the scallop babies. The cownose are more prolific now because of a dwindling population of great sharks. Sharks eat rays, and rays eat scallops. With smaller numbers of sharks, there are more rays, less scallops. Blame it on the demand for sharkfin soup and shark meat in foreign markets.

Sea Scallops

There are two other kinds of scallops found in the deeper waters off North Carolina's coast, the calico and the larger sea scallop. The calicos have been scarce, also, and that leaves the sea scallop. It's about 1 to 2 inches wide, and its flavor is much milder and more briny than the bay scallops.

Cleaning them is a messy job, so appreciate the nicely packed plastic containers you'll find at seafood markets. (Europeans actually prefer the roe and guts along with the adductor muscle we eat.) Keep them in the cooler part of your refrigerator.

Look for packages with little liquid, and make sure you drain the scallops well and pat them dry with a towel before cooking. Scallops are frequently frozen and lose little flavor, but it's best to use them within three or four months.

However they are cooked—sautéed, grilled, broiled, or fried—make sure not to overcook them, as they can get tough real fast. And never overcrowd them in a pan, as they'll steam instead. Check out helpful hints on frying scallops in A Primer on Frying Seafood on page 160. Scallops also toughen the longer they sit after cooking, so serve them immediately.

Scallops in Lime and Rosemary

Rosemary has an intense smell and taste, one that overpowers many other foods. But when paired with lime, it brings out the sweetness of sea scallops, giving it a unique accent.

Warn your guests to remove the rosemary sprigs before eating, because they will be tough and unsavory.

⅓ cup extra-virgin olive oil

4 sprigs fresh rosemary, 4 inches long (¾-ounce package)

3 tablespoons lime juice (2–3 limes), divided

2 teaspoons finely grated lime zest, divided

Pinch of salt

Several grinds black pepper

1 pound sea scallops, drained and patted dry

3 tablespoons butter

1. In a small saucepan, heat olive oil to the point where it is bubbling on the sides of the pan. Remove from heat and add 2 large sprigs of rosemary. Allow to steep for 30 minutes, then discard the rosemary.

2. Pour rosemary oil into a long, shallow baking dish.

3. Add 1½ tablespoons lime juice, 1 teaspoon zest, salt, and pepper, and mix together. Add scallops, and turn to coat the scallops well. Set aside to marinate for at least 20 minutes, turning occasionally.

4. Preheat grill or broiler.

5. Snip remaining 2 sprigs of rosemary into 1-inch pieces. Poke one of these shortened sprigs into the middle of each scallop.

6. Place scallops on a heated, designated grill pan and sear until just cooked, about 3 minutes or less per side. Or, place in broiler pan and broil 6 inches from heat, turning scallops after 3 minutes and cooking for an additional 2 to 3 minutes or until cooked through and slightly browned. After turning scallops, brush lightly with any remaining rosemary oil. Do not overcook, or scallops will be tough.

7. Meanwhile, melt butter, add the remaining lime juice and zest, and season with salt and pepper. Pour over scallops and allow to puddle on serving plates.

8. Serve immediately. Spinach wilted in butter and fresh garlic makes a nice presentation with the scallops.

YIELD: *4 appetizer servings, or 2–3 entrees*

Simply Seared Scallops

Botticelli portrayed the birth of the Roman goddess of love, Venus, by showing her emerging in all her unadorned beauty from a scallop shell. I prefer scallops simply prepared, without too much "adornment," so that the beauty of the flavor shines through.

This dish must be served immediately, so have everything else for dinner done and your guests ready.

1. In a heavy sauté pan, heat butter and olive oil over medium-high heat. When hot, add scallops, a few at a time. Do not crowd, or they will be steamed instead of seared.

2. Cook for about 2 to 3 minutes per side, just until edges begin to brown. Remove from pan, and continue to cook until all scallops are finished.

3. Divide among four plates, and sprinkle with parsley and garnish with lemon wedges. Pour browned butter and oil over, if desired.

YIELD: *4 appetizer servings, or 2–3 entrees*

3 tablespoons butter

3 tablespoons olive oil

1 pound large sea scallops, rinsed and dried

Sea salt and freshly ground pepper to taste

1 tablespoon chopped Italian parsley

1 lemon, quartered

Filet Coquille

Sir John Colleton was given the first British land grant in North Carolina, a spit of sandy hills surrounded by Currituck, Albermarle, and Roanoke Sounds, near Kill Devil Hills. He attempted to grow grapes for wine, corn, and tobacco on his plantation. Cattle were more successful, and indeed, they roamed the swamps and steep hills, even into the 1930s. The island was eventually settled by fishermen, and is known for its soft-shell crabs and other seafood.

With a nod to this historical background, Carlen Pearl of the charming and cozy Colington Café serves this popular entree. Carlen's menu reflects her French heritage as well as her love for the local cuisine of the Outer Banks. Look for the beautiful, 300-year-old live oak with lights, on Colington's winding road, which was once an Indian and cow path.

1 tablespoon olive oil

4 4-ounce fillets of beef tenderloin (filet mignon)

1 pound large sea scallops

1/3 large red pepper, thinly sliced

1/3 large yellow pepper, thinly sliced

1/3 cup chopped yellow onion

1/3 cup sliced mushrooms

1/3 cup diced tomatoes, fresh or canned

1/4 cup red marsala

5–6 tablespoons demi-glace (Knorr's made according to package directions is fine)

1/2 teaspoon prepared pesto

1/2 teaspoon crushed garlic

1 tablespoon A-1 sauce

1 teaspoon Worchestershire sauce

1. Heat the olive oil in a large sauté pan over high heat. Add the fillets and sear for 3 to 4 minutes.

2. Add scallops, peppers, onions, and mushrooms to the pan, and cook for 3 to 4 more minutes. If you desire medium-rare, remove fillets to an ovenproof plate, and place in a warm oven.

3. Continue to cook until the peppers are soft, and scallops are cooked through. Remove scallops to the ovenproof plate with the fillets.

4. Add tomatoes, marsala, and demi-glace to pepper mixture. Add pesto, garlic, A-1, and Worchestershire sauces. Cook down for 1 to 2 minutes.

5. Place the fillets on each plate, top with scallops, then the pepper mixture and sauce.

YIELD: *4 servings*

Beach (Cow) Boys

Free-range cows and pigs foraged up and down the Outer Banks, along with the wild horses, for over two centuries until the 1930s. The islands were ideal for raising livestock—no fencing was needed, there was grass in the marshlands, and it was relatively easy to round them up. Many Bankers were stockmen who managed the herds that roamed the islands.

During the summer in the early 1900s, Outer Banks boys got to be cowboys. They'd flush the long-horned, scraggly cows and their calves from the marshes, woods, and underbrush, running barefooted on the hot sand, to shoo them to the beach. There they'd form a human fence to corral the cows so that the grown men could count and mark them. Then the men, on horseback, would drive the yearlings, especially, to the soundside, where they were loaded onto barges and boats to float to Norfolk. Or, sometimes there were cattle drives that lasted for a couple of days, with one contingent of men riding horseback along the beach and another along the sound, all the way from Oregon Inlet up to the Virginia border.

Helen and Luther Daniels remember when concern for Rocky Mountain spotted fever caused a 1930s federal requirement that wild cattle be dipped into a huge vat that had been dug out of the ground and filled with carbolic acid to keep the ticks off.

In 1933, two hurricanes ravaged the islands and killed many livestock. And, the CCC, the Civilian Conservation Corps, began building over a hundred miles of oceanfront dunes and planting beachgrass to stabilize them. With free-ranging animals, that was a problem, so the state outlawed open grazing and most were rounded up.

But there was one last cowboy at Carova in the late 1980s, before the roadless area beyond Corolla began getting built up with massive beachfront homes. Ernie Bowen raised hybrid Cenipoles from the Virgin Islands, and white Charolais cattle from France, along with horses. He even tried buffalo, and produced the first purebred buffalo calf ever to be born on the Outer Banks. He also succeeded in breeding a cross, a "beefalo." But alas, the open range gave way to open development. Beachgoers don't like sharing their oceanfront with cattle seeking relief from the heat and mosquitoes.

Pecan-Encrusted Scallops with Fresh Peach Salsa

Pecan trees provide much shade to many backyards on Roanoke Island. And on Knotts Island to the north, peaches grow abundantly. Here's a recipe that combines these sweet bounties along with a bounty from the sea, sweet scallops. Add some jalapeño pepper to the peach salsa, and serve with just about any firm, white fish that's grilled or pan-roasted.

FOR THE FRESH PEACH SALSA:

3–4 ripe but firm peaches, peeled and finely diced

⅓ cup finely diced red bell pepper (about ½ pepper)

¼ cup finely diced sweet onion (try North Carolina's Mattamuskeet Sweets)

1 large garlic clove, minced

2 tablespoons chopped fresh flat-leaf parsley

1 tablespoon lime juice

½ teaspoon salt

½ teaspoon freshly ground black pepper

Pinch of sugar

FOR THE SCALLOPS:

1 pound sea scallops, rinsed and patted dry

¼ cup milk

½ cup finely chopped pecans

2 tablespoons butter

1 tablespoon olive oil

1. Prepare the fresh peach salsa: In a small saucepan, mix all ingredients, and allow to marinate together for at least 1 hour at room temperature.

2. For the scallops: Place scallops for just a second into the milk, then press into the pecans, just on one side. When all scallops have been dipped and pressed, heat butter and oil in a large sauté pan.

3. When pan is hot, add scallops, pecan-side down, and cook for just 1 minute. Turn each scallop over and cook for another 2 to 4 minutes, depending on the thickness of the scallop. Do not overcrowd the pan, as the scallops will steam and not sear.

4. Remove each scallop as it is finished to a warm platter.

5. To serve, divide the peach salsa among four plates (those large "scallop" shells or dishes are pretty), then place scallops on top.

YIELD: *4 servings*

Pesto Scallops

Café Atlantic uses sea scallops when preparing this popular menu item from a recipe developed for them by local chef and artist, Debbie Wells, who used to own The Back Porch restaurant, also in Ocracoke. Co-owner Ruth Toth says that it takes some prepping to get all the ingredients ready, but it's really simple.

1. Slice bacon into thin strips and cook until it is crunchy. Drain off fat.

2. In a large sauté pan, melt butter over medium-high heat. Add scallops, in batches if needed so as not to crowd the pan. Cook scallops until browned and not quite cooked through.

3. Add tomatoes, cooked bacon, scallions, and lemon juice. Heat until all ingredients are hot.

4. Serve in a shallow dish to hold all the juices. Top with a generous dollop of Basil Mayonnaise. Garnish with lemon and chopped parsley.

YIELD: *4 servings*

12 slices bacon

4 tablespoons butter

1½ pounds sea scallops

1⅓ cups tomatoes, chopped

1 cup scallions, chopped

4 teaspoons lemon juice

½ cup Basil Mayonnise (recipe follows)

4 lemon wedges

2 tablespoons chopped fresh parsley

Basil Pesto

Ruth makes this pesto during the summer when basil is plentiful, then freezes 1-cup amounts in ziplock bags for year-round use.

2½ cups packed fresh basil leaves

2 teaspoons minced garlic

½ cup walnuts (or pine nuts or almonds, if preferred)

½ cup grated Parmesan cheese

½ teaspoon black pepper

½ cup olive oil

1. Using a food processor, place all ingredients except for the olive oil in the work bowl. Pulse until it makes a paste.
2. With the machine running, add the olive oil in a stream and process for just a few seconds more.

YIELD: *about 1 cup*

Basil Mayonnaise

Ruth also uses this mayonnaise on BLTs and other sandwiches.

1 cup Basil Pesto

1 cup mayonnaise

1 tablespoon fresh lemon juice

Whisk all ingredients together in a bowl.

YIELD: *2 cups*

Prosciutto-Wrapped Scallops and Spinach

This is an adaptation of an occasional special on the menu at The Lone Cedar Café on the Manteo–Nags Head Causeway. It's a pretty presentation, and the flavors are so complementary.

1. Soak 2 to 3 dozen wooden skewers in water for at least 30 minutes. Preheat grill. Line a baking sheet with foil.

2. Rinse scallops and pat dry. Cut each prosciutto slice in half, lengthwise. Wrap each scallop's edge, if possible, with prosciutto, and secure with 2 wooden skewers. Place the wrapped scallops on the baking sheet.

3. Mix together the butter, lemon juice, garlic, and parsley. Using a brush, coat each scallop on both sides with the butter mixture.

4. When ready to cook, place scallops on lightly oiled grill rack. Cook for about 3 minutes, basting with the butter mixture, then turn and baste again, and cook for about 2 to 3 more minutes, or until scallop is white and cooked through. Be careful not to overcook.

5. In a large, deep skillet or pot, melt butter with garlic. Add spinach, and stir to coat. Cook for about 3 to 4 minutes, or until spinach just begins to wilt. Add salt and freshly ground pepper.

6. Arrange spinach on bottom of plates, and lay scallops across. Serve immediately.

YIELD: *4 appetizer servings, or 2–3 entrees*

1 pound large sea scallops

¼ pound thinly sliced prosciutto

4 tablespoons butter, melted

2 tablespoons lemon juice

1 clove garlic, minced

2 tablespoons finely chopped fresh parsley

2 tablespoons butter

2 large cloves garlic, minced

8 ounces baby spinach

½ teaspoon salt

Freshly ground pepper

Coquilles Ocracoke

1 pound sea scallops

½ cup white wine

½ cup water

2 tablespoons finely chopped sweet onions

1 small bay leaf

4 tablespoons butter, cold, cut into small pieces

1 tablespoon finely chopped chives

1 tablespoon finely chopped parsley

Salt and freshly ground pepper to taste

¼ cup coarsely grated Parmesan cheese

Baguette, for sopping up juices

Coquilles St. Jacques, French for "shells Saint James," generally refers to a creamy baked gratin of scallops. Saint James supposedly wore a scallop shell as his emblem. After he died, he was carried to Santiago de Compostela in Spain to be entombed. After the knights carrying his remains crossed an inlet to the sea, they found scallops clinging to their clothing and the horses' blankets, and thought it was a sign. Visitors to his tomb then received a scallop shell to prove where they'd been.

Given the wild horses of Ocracoke, the pretty calico scallop shells you find on the beaches there, and the inlet, it seems appropriate to name a variation of this classic recipe after North Carolina's island.

Place in serving shells or gratins along with a French baguette to sop up the juices, and a green salad.

1. Drain and rinse scallops. If using large sea scallops, quarter them.
2. Place the wine, water, onions, and bay leaf in a medium saucepan with lid. Bring to a boil, then reduce heat and simmer for 5 minutes.
3. Add scallops, cover pan, and simmer for just 1 minute. Remove the pan from heat and allow scallops to sit in the poaching liquid for 10 minutes.
4. Remove scallops with a slotted spoon and place in a bowl. Preheat broiler.
5. Return the pan to the stove, and boil the liquid over high heat until syrupy, about 3 to 5 minutes. Add butter, one piece at a time, whisking until each piece is melted before adding the next one. Whisk in the chives and parsley, then salt and pepper. Add scallops, and stir to coat.
6. Arrange 4 serving shells (or gratins) in a broiler pan. Divide scallops equally among the shells. Sprinkle with Parmesan cheese.
7. Place under broiler just until cheese is melted and slightly golden, about 3 minutes. Serve immediately.

YIELD: *4 servings*

Scallops and Scallions on Polenta Medallions

Cheat a little with purchased rolls of polenta. Smother them with this tomato-butter sauce, then surround the discs with golden scallops. This is a pretty, quick, and easy dish.

1. In a large skillet, heat the olive oil. Sauté the scallions for about 2 minutes, then add garlic and stir.

2. Add the tomato, and continue to stir for another minute, then add the wine or chicken stock and bring to a boil. Reduce to about half, stirring occasionally. Add salt and pepper to taste.

3. Meanwhile, preheat oven to 400 degrees. Cut polenta into 3/4-inch circles. Place circles on greased baking sheet, and place in oven until heated through, about 5 minutes.

4. Rinse scallops and pat dry. In another large skillet, heat olive oil with butter until melted. Add scallops, working in batches if necessary, so as not to crowd the pan. Cook until the first side is golden brown, for about 4 minutes, then turn and cook an additional minute. Place on a warmed plate while the other scallops are being cooked.

5. To serve, place the warmed baked polenta circles in the center of the plate. Place the scallops around them, then ladle the tomato and scallion mixture over all. Garnish with basil. Serve immediately.

YIELD: *4 servings*

2 tablespoons olive oil

1 bunch scallions

1 garlic clove, minced

1 tomato, peeled and diced

½ cup white wine or chicken stock

Salt and pepper to taste

1 roll store-bought polenta

1 pound large sea scallops

2 tablespoons olive oil

1 tablespoon butter

6 large basil leaves

Scallops Gremolata

Gremolata is a traditional Italian preparation that usually includes garlic, parsley, and grated lemon peel. It's a great complement to scallops that can sometimes be rather bland tasting. Do not overcook the scallops, as they can quickly turn to rubber.

1 pound sea scallops

1 lemon or lime, zested and juiced

3 tablespoons finely chopped parsley

1 tablespoon minced garlic

1 teaspoon salt

Freshly ground pepper

2 tablespoons olive oil

½ cup white wine

2 tablespoons butter

1. Drain and rinse the scallops, then pat dry with paper towels.

2. Grate the lemon or lime zest and set aside. Finely chop parsley and garlic on a cutting board. Add the zest, salt, and a grind or two of pepper to the parsley, and mix with your knife blade.

3. Pat both sides of each scallop into the mix.

4. In a large sauté pan, heat the olive oil on medium-high heat. When oil is hot, add scallops, a few at a time so that they do not touch, and sear for 1 to 2 minutes, until just brown, then flip and sear for another 1 to 2 minutes, depending on thickness.

5. Place scallops as they are cooked on individual serving plates or serving shells.

6. When all scallops are cooked, add wine and lemon or lime juice to the pan and stir to scrape up any bits left. When it has thickened slightly, add the butter, 1 tablespoon at a time, and stir until butter is melted. Pour evenly over the cooked scallops.

YIELD: *4 servings*

Broiled Scallops

Broiling is a very easy way to prepare delicious sea scallops. But keep a watchful eye while cooking, for scallops are like rubber disks when overcooked.

1. Grease a shallow baking pan. Preheat broiler.

2. Drain and rinse scallops, and pat dry with paper towels. If using large, thick sea scallops, cut in half horizontally.

3. Place scallops in pan, and brush with half of melted butter. Sprinkle with paprika, then sprinkle half of parsley and lemon juice evenly over scallops. Season with salt and pepper.

4. Broil for 2 to 3 minutes, then remove pan from oven and turn scallops over. Brush that side with melted butter, then again sprinkle with remaining parsley and lemon juice. Broil again for another 1 to 2 minutes, or just until scallops are done. Serve immediately.

YIELD: *4 servings*

1 pound scallops

4 tablespoons butter, melted

¼ teaspoon paprika

2 tablespoons finely chopped parsley

3 tablespoons lemon juice

Salt and freshly ground pepper to taste

shrimp

SHRIMP

During the warmer months of the year, you'll see large shrimp boats, their wing-like arms extended to support their large nets, trawling just offshore out of Oregon and Hatteras Inlets or inside the more shallow Pamlico Sound. Wanchese serves as a home port for a large fleet of shrimpers who bring in the second most valuable catch in North Carolina.

Today's favorite seafood used to be considered pests, or "bugs," that fouled nets. Old-timers talk about "going bugging."

Shrimp are spawned in the ocean and, from there, are carried by tides and wind-driven currents into the sounds and estuaries where they overwinter. They're fast growers, doubling in size every two weeks, and when almost fully grown, leave their nesting waters for the ocean.

Brown shrimp are the most plentiful and sweetest of the species caught along North Carolinas's coast, especially during the summer when they reach their maximum life span of eighteen months. Spring and fall find more pink or spotted shrimp, which can grow up to 11 inches. Fewer white shrimp, locally called green tails (white- or green-tailed) are harvested, mostly in the fall. These are the ones most prized by chefs in the Outer Banks.

E F Wiegand

The success of the shrimping season is weather-related. A cold winter means a small shrimp population during the spring. And lots of rain pushes the shrimp out of the estuaries into the ocean before they're fully grown.

Shrimp Tips

- Two pounds of shrimp in their shells yields about 1¼ pounds when peeled.
- Allow ¾ pound headless unpeeled shrimp per person, or ⅓ to ½ pound peeled per person.
- When sold by count per pound, the smaller the size, the higher the counts. Jumbo means 8 to 10 shrimp per pound, large is 10 to 25, medium 26 to 40, small 41 to 60.
- Most people prefer to devein shrimp, but it is not necessary.
- When peeling shrimp before cooking, save shells in freezer until you have enough to make a shrimp-based stock to enrich soups, chowders, and pasta dishes. Better yet, buy shrimp with heads on and use them in your stock.
- For tips on frying shrimp, see A Primer on Frying Seafood on page 160.

Shrimp 'n' Beer

Serve with ice cold beer and perhaps a potato salad—and lots of napkins for sticky fingers.

2 pounds shrimp, unpeeled

1 12-ounce beer (not lite)

1 cup water

1 medium onion, sliced

1 lemon or lime, sliced

4 garlic cloves, slivered

1 bunch parsley, coarsely chopped

1 tablespoon salt

2 tablespoons Old Bay seasoning

1 teaspoon red pepper flakes

1 teaspoon whole black or mixed
   peppercorns

1 cup prepared cocktail sauce

1. Rinse shrimp and set aside to drain.

2. In a large pot, add beer and all other ingredients. Over medium-high heat, bring to a boil, and allow to bubble for 2 minutes, reducing heat if necessary to keep from boiling over.

3. Make sure beer mixture is at a raucous boil, then add the shrimp. Stir often, and cook just until the mixture returns to the boil and the shrimp turn pink. Drain.

4. Serve in a large bowl, with an extra bowl for discarded shrimp shells, and a small bowl of cocktail sauce.

YIELD: *6–8 appetizers, or 4 entree servings*

Pork and Shrimp Tarragon

Carlen Pearl has a passion for food, and for knowing her customers, honed by years in the restaurant industry. But it was from her mother, who was raised in Provence, France, that she learned the art of making everything from scratch, the art of seasoning with herbs and spices, and using fresh ingredients available locally.

The Colington Café, which the Pearls have run for over eighteen years, now sits in a beautiful and homey cottage under the shade of a three-hundred-year-old live oak tree, the oldest on the island.

1 12-ounce pork tenderloin, cleaned

Flour for dredging

Salt and pepper to taste

1 tablespoon each unsalted butter and oil, mixed

¼ sweet onion, chopped

18 large shrimp, peeled and deveined

¼ cup white wine, preferably a chardonnay

¼ cup heavy cream

1–2 tablespoons coarse French mustard (or smooth, if you prefer)

1 teaspoon chopped fresh tarragon

1. Cut pork tenderloin diagonally into 1-inch slices. Lightly dredge in flour that has been seasoned with salt and pepper. Preheat oven to 250 degrees.

2. Heat the butter/oil mix in a large sauté pan over medium-high heat. (Unsalted butter is best because it won't burn.) Add the pork medallions and chopped onions and cook until pork is brown, 3 minutes on each side. Transfer pork to an ovenproof platter.

3. Add shrimp to the pan, and cook for 1 minute each side. Add white wine and cook down to half, about 2 to 3 minutes. Remove shrimp with a slotted spoon and fan on top of the pork medallions on platter. Place platter in oven.

4. Add cream, mustard, and tarragon to the reduced wine. Cook for an additional 3 to 4 minutes, or until thick. Add salt to taste.

5. Pour sauce on top of pork and shrimp, or arrange on individual plates and top with sauce.

YIELD: *6 large servings*

Colington Café sits on a rise along the curvy island road that follows an old meandering cow path. Admire the 300-year-old live oak tree. E F Wiegand

Shrimp and Grits

Chef Bud Gruninger of Basnight's Lone Cedar prefers the taste of green tails, the white shrimp that are only caught in Pamlico Sound during a few weeks of late summer and early fall. He carefully freezes hundreds of pounds to use for the restaurant. And he also prefers the taste of grits that are stone-ground. Here's his take on shrimp and grits, which is a traditional Low Country dish, whether you are in the coastal waters of North or South Carolina. Prepare the shrimp while grits are cooking.

FOR THE GRITS:

2 cups chicken stock

4 tablespoons butter

1 teaspoon sea salt, or to taste

¼ teaspoon cracked pepper, or to taste

½ cup yellow grits, preferably stone-ground

½ pound sharp white cheddar cheese, grated

FOR THE SHRIMP:

2 tablespoons canola oil

½ pound andouille sausage, sliced

2 pounds shrimp, preferably green-tails, peeled and deveined

1 small onion, diced small

1 small red pepper, diced small

½ green pepper, diced small

1 large clove garlic, minced

3 to 4 scallions, thinly sliced

1 tablespoon butter

1 tablespoon Texas Pete sauce, or more to taste

1. To start the grits: In a medium saucepan, bring chicken stock, butter, salt, and pepper to boil over medium-high heat.

2. Slowly add grits, stirring constantly. Lower heat and simmer for 15 to 20 minutes, stirring occasionally. When most of the liquid has been absorbed, turn off heat. Add cheese and mix until incorporated. Cover and keep grits warm by wrapping in a kitchen towel or placing pot over steaming water.

3. For the shrimp, heat oil in large skillet. Add andouille sausage and brown over medium-high heat.

4. Add shrimp, onions, peppers, and garlic and cook for 3 minutes. Add scallions, butter, Texas Pete, salt, and pepper and cook for an additional 3 minutes.

5. Divide grits evenly among four bowls. Spoon shrimp mixture over grits and serve immediately.

YIELD: *4 servings*

Pancetta-Wrapped Shrimp over Cheese Grits

Here's a variation of shrimp and grits with pancetta providing an Italian twist to the classic country ham flavor.

"Corncob" shrimp is the nickname given to those extra-large shrimp caught as a by-product in nets intended for mullet, croakers, or other fish found in Pamlico Sound.

If you prefer, the pancetta-wrapped shrimp are also good served over wilted spinach and garlic.

1. Place shrimp in a small bowl, and drizzle with 1 tablespoon olive oil, 1 tablespoon lemon juice, and the zest. Toss and allow to sit for 5 minutes.

2. Cut pancetta into 16 equal long, thin strips. Wrap each strip around the fleshy part of the shrimp.

3. Start the grits. In a large saucepan, bring water and milk to a boil. Toss in the salt. While stirring constantly, add grits slowly, in a steady stream. Lower heat to a simmer and stir occasionally.

4. Meanwhile, in a small bowl, beat eggs, then add cheese and cayenne pepper. After about 10 minutes, the grits should be pulling away from the pan. When most of the water is absorbed, add a dollop of the grits to the eggs and cheese mixture, stir, then stir the egg mixture into the remaining grits (that's called "tempering" the eggs so that they do not cook from the heat of all the grits). Continue to cook over low heat, stirring constantly, until cheese is melted and the mixture is thick. Set aside.

5. Heat the remaining 2 tablespoons olive oil in a sauté pan over medium heat until oil is hot, then add shrimp. Sauté until pancetta is golden brown and crisp and shrimp are pink, about 5 minutes. Remove the shrimp from the pan, then deglaze the pan with Worcestershire sauce and 1 tablespoon lemon juice.

6. To assemble the dish, spoon cheese grits in a mound onto center of plate. Add shrimp around the mound, then drizzle sauce around shrimp. Sprinkle with parsley and chives, then serve immediately.

YIELD: *4–6 appetizers, or 3–4 dinner entrees*

FOR THE SHRIMP:

1 pound extra-large shrimp (about 16), peeled with tails intact

3 tablespoons olive oil, divided

2 tablespoons lemon juice, divided

1 teaspoon lime zest

½ teaspoon red pepper flakes

About 4 ounces thinly sliced pancetta

2 tablespoons Worcestershire sauce

Salt and freshly ground pepper to taste

2 tablespoons chopped fresh parsley

1 tablespoon chopped fresh chives

FOR THE CHEESE GRITS:

2 cups water

1 cup milk

1 teaspoon salt

¾ cup stone-ground grits

3 eggs

1 cup grated cheese (Parmesan or Asiago)

¼ teaspoon cayenne pepper

Shrimp and Baked Grits

This variation of a favorite Low Country dish served with baked cheese grits makes a beautiful appetizer or a lovely entree. Buttered Green Corn provides a tasty topping, a pair of corn flavors, from the grits to the "green" kernels.

1 batch Baked Cheese Grits Cakes (see page 235)

1½ tablespoons butter

1½ tablespoons olive oil

2 pounds large shrimp, peeled and deveined, with tails intact

3 thick slices bacon, cooked, fat removed, and meat diced

1 large clove garlic, minced

2 tablespoons fresh lemon juice

2 tablespoons chopped fresh parsley

1 teaspoon Old Bay seasoning

Salt and freshly ground pepper to taste

3 tablespoons butter, room temperature

1 batch Buttered Green Corn (see page 230)

2 tablespoons grated Parmesan or Asiago cheese (same as used in baking grits)

1. Preheat oven to 400 degrees. Using a small bowl as a template, cut cheese grits into four 4-inch circles, or do squares or triangles if desired. Place on foil-lined baking sheet, and heat in oven for about 7 to 10 minutes, or until warm.

2. Heat butter and olive oil in a large sauté pan. When hot, add shrimp, and cook quickly, stirring, until they just start to turn pink.

3. Add bacon, garlic, remaining lemon juice, parsley, and Old Bay, and season with salt and pepper.

4. When shrimp are totally pink and done, add butter in several pats, stirring until melted and then quickly remove from heat.

5. Place one round of cheese grits on plates. Spoon the shrimp and butter sauce over baked cheese grits.

6. Spoon Buttered Green Corn over the shrimp and onto the plate. Sprinkle the whole mixture with Parmesan or Asiago cheese. Serve immediately.

YIELD: *6 appetizers, or 4–6 entrees*

Margarita Grilled Shrimp

A Happy Hour on skewers, these shrimp are delicious served over a bed of greens and chopped red tomatoes, or simply pulled from the skewers as an appetizer. You'll need about a dozen 8-inch or about 6 to 8 12-inch skewers.

1. Place ingredients for marinating the shrimp in a bowl or plastic resealable bag. Add shrimp, and stir or shake to coat. Refrigerate while marinating, for about 30 minutes.

2. Preheat grill or broiler. If using wooden skewers, soak in water until needed.

3. Thread shrimp on skewers, not packing them too tightly together so they will cook evenly.

4. Place shrimp on grill (or under broiler), and cook for a total of 5 to 6 minutes or until pink and firm, turning at least once. Remove from heat.

5. Prepare bed of greens and tomatoes on each plate. Whisk together the olive oil, tequila, and lime juice, then season. Pour over greens and tomatoes. Divide skewers evenly and cross over plates, then serve.

YIELD: *4–6 servings, or about 25 appetizers (shrimp alone)*

FOR THE SHRIMP:

¼ cup tequila

2 tablespoons lime juice

Zest of 1 lime

¼ cup thinly sliced green onion

¼ cup finely chopped cilantro

1 small jalapeño, minced

1 teaspoon salt

2 tablespoons canola oil

2 pounds shrimp, peeled and deveined

FOR THE VEGETABLES:

6–8 cups mixed lettuce

2 tomatoes, chopped

4 tablespoons olive oil

1 tablespoon tequila

1 tablespoon lime juice

Salt and freshly ground pepper to taste

Ginger-Beer Shrimp Kabobs

Our daughter Kate tells us she devised this recipe as her teenager's excuse to get into her parents' stash of beer when we were away. It's a good recipe, with no excuses needed!

You'll need about 10 short, 8-inch skewers or about 6 12-inch ones. Serve these kabobs with seasoned rice and a salad.

1 12-ounce beer (not lite)

2 teaspoons minced fresh ginger

2 large cloves garlic, minced

1 teaspoon celery salt

1 tablespoon soy sauce

½ teaspoon freshly ground pepper

1½ cups mushroom caps, or large caps quartered

1 whole green pepper, cut into chunks

1–2 zucchinis, sliced into thick chunks

1–2 Vidalia onions, cut into 6 chunks

1½ pounds shrimp

4 cups cooked white rice

2 tablespoons chopped fresh parsley

1. In a large bowl, mix beer, ginger, garlic, celery salt, soy sauce, and freshly ground pepper together.

2. Add mushrooms, pepper, zucchini, and onion, and stir to coat. Allow to marinate for about 30 minutes.

3. If using wooden skewers, soak for at least 20 minutes to prevent burning. Preheat grill.

4. Place shrimp in a bowl, and drain marinade from vegetables over the shrimp. Stir to coat, and allow to sit for about 10 minutes.

5. When ready to cook, alternately thread veggies and shrimp onto skewers. Meanwhile, bring any marinade left to boil in a small pan.

6. Place on grill, and cook on medium to low heat for about 10 to 15 minutes, or until shrimp turn pink and are cooked all the way through. Brush with hot marinade to prevent drying.

7. Place skewers across individual plates filled with rice. Sprinkle with parsley and serve immediately. Heat the marinade to boiling again if a sauce is desired.

YIELD: *4–5 servings*

Grilled Shrimp Salad

This version of grilled shrimp topping a salad has a bit of a kick to it. Use one of those lovely perforated grill pans or use skewers.

1. In a small bowl, place shrimp and stir in ½ cup vinaigrette. Allow to marinate for at least 30 minutes, up to 1 hour.

2. Preheat grill.

3. In a large bowl, combine salad greens, peppers, onion, and olives. Just before placing shrimp on grill, toss salad with enough of the remaining vinaigrette for the leaves and vegetables to have a "gloss."

4. When ready to serve, place shrimp on grill (best to use a grill pan). Grill for about 5 minutes, turning at least once, until shrimp are pink and translucent. Or, you may thread on skewers if desired.

5. Divide salad among four plates.

6. Top with grilled shrimp. Sprinkle with minced cilantro. Serve immediately.

YIELD: *4 servings, as lunch or appetizer*

1 ½ pounds large shrimp, peeled and deveined

1 cup Chile-Lime Vinaigrette (see page 255)

1 package (8 to 10 ounces) of mixed baby greens, spinach, or arugula

½ red bell pepper, medium dice

½ yellow bell pepper, medium dice

½ small, sweet onion (try North Carolina's Mattamuskeet Sweet)

½ cup kalamata olives, pitted

1 tablespoon minced fresh cilantro

Shrimp and Honeydew Salad

During the heat of the summer, this salad is cool and refreshing. You can make it early in the day, then enjoy the sun and surf!

About 3 cups 1-inch-cubed honeydew melon

1 pound shrimp, cooked, cooled, and peeled

1 large cucumber

2–3 tablespoons minced fresh dill

2 tablespoons lime juice

½ teaspoon salt

Freshly ground pepper

⅓ cup olive oil

1. Place melon and shrimp in a large serving bowl.

2. Peel cucumber. Cut in half lengthwise. Scoop out seeds, then cut into ½-inch slices. Add to the honeydew and shrimp.

3. Sprinkle the dill over the mixture.

4. Place lime juice, salt, and pepper in a small bowl. Whisk in olive oil. Pour over shrimp mix.

5. Stir gently.

6. Salad may be served immediately or refrigerated for several hours.

YIELD: *4 servings*

South of the Border Shrimp Salad

Chill out with this colorful shrimp salad that can be made ahead.
    Always save lemon and lime halves that have already been squeezed for their juice, because they can still impart a good citrus flavor to the water when boiling shrimp.

1. Fill a large saucepan with water to a depth of 2 inches. Add lemon or lime slices, onion slices, peppercorns, and Old Bay. Bring to a boil over high heat, then add shrimp. Stir, and when water returns to the boil, the shrimp should be done within 1 minute. Drain, and cool shrimp in refrigerator.

2. In a large serving bowl, place black beans, cooked corn, red pepper, jalapeño, cilantro, garlic, and minced onion. Stir gently. Add shrimp, and gently stir in.

3. In a small bowl or cup, whisk together the lime juice, olive oil, Tabasco sauce, salt, and pepper. Pour over shrimp mixture, and again, stir gently.

4. Salad may be served immediately or chilled in the refrigerator for up to 4 hours.

YIELD: *4–6 luncheon servings*

1 lemon or lime, sliced

1 medium yellow onion, sliced

½ teaspoon whole peppercorns

1 tablespoon Old Bay seasoning

1 pound shrimp, peeled and deveined

1 14-ounce can black beans, drained and rinsed

2 cups cooked corn, drained

½ cup chopped sweet red pepper

1 tablespoon chopped fresh jalapeño pepper

¼ cup chopped fresh cilantro

1 tablespoon minced garlic

¼ cup minced red or yellow onion

2 tablespoons lime juice

⅓ cup olive oil

1 teaspoon Tabasco sauce

1 teaspoon salt

½ teaspoon freshly ground pepper

Warm Shrimp Pasta Salad with Goat Cheese

⅔ pound dried pasta shells or bowties

1 lemon, juiced, then quartered

1 tablespoon Old Bay seasoning

1 pound shrimp, shelled and deveined

½ cup goat cheese, or to taste

¾ cup chopped cherry tomatoes

2 tablespoons finely chopped chives

2 tablespoons finely chopped basil

1 tablespoon finely chopped dill

½ teaspoon salt

Several grinds black pepper

This tastes as delicious as it looks, and makes for a quick supper or lunch.

1. Bring a large pot of water to boil. Add 2 teaspoons salt and pasta, and cook until al dente, or according to package directions. Drain, and place pasta in large serving bowl.

2. Fill a large saucepan with water to depth of 3 inches. Add juiced lemon quarters and Old Bay, and bring to a boil. Add shrimp, and after water has returned to a boil, cook for about 2 minutes longer or until shrimp are done. Drain shrimp and add to pasta.

3. Crumble or cut goat cheese into small pieces, and add to warm pasta and shrimp. Stir to combine.

4. Add cherry tomatoes, chives, basil, dill, and lemon juice. Season with salt and pepper. Mix thoroughly, then serve immediately.

YIELD: *4–6 servings*

Pickled Shrimp

Serve these spiced, "pickled" shrimp in a large glass bowl for a beautiful presentation. This is a very old, very Southern way of serving shrimp. The nice thing about this dish is that it can be done ahead and served chilled.

Some feel they get more flavor when shrimp is boiled with the shells on than peeled. However, it's easier to remove the vein with that special shrimp-peeler tool if done while raw. Then you can also freeze the shells to use to make shrimp broth. You decide.

1. Fill a large pot with water to a depth of 3 inches and bring to a boil. Add shrimp and bring to a boil again, then cook for about 2 more minutes or until shrimp are pink. Drain, then peel under running water, leaving the shrimp tails attached.

2. In a large serving bowl, layer shrimp, onions, lemon slices, capers, and bay leaves.

3. In a small mixing bowl, blend the remaining ingredients, whisking well. Pour over the shrimp layers. Cover tightly, and refrigerate for at least 8 hours, up to 3 days. Be sure to stir the mixture occasionally.

4. Serve as an hors d'oeuvre with toothpicks, or over a bed of chopped iceberg or romaine lettuce.

YIELD: *serves 12 or more as appetizer, or 8 or more as entree*

3 pounds shrimp, unpeeled

3 sweet onions (try North Carolina's Mattamuskeet Sweets)

1 large lemon, very thinly sliced

2 tablespoons capers

4 bay leaves

1 teaspoon dry mustard

1 teaspoon celery seed

1 teaspoon salt

2 teaspoons sugar

1½ teaspoons freshly ground pepper

1 teaspoon Worcestershire sauce

1 teaspoon Tabasco sauce

½ cup tarragon or white wine vinegar

2 tablespoons fresh lemon juice

1 cup olive oil

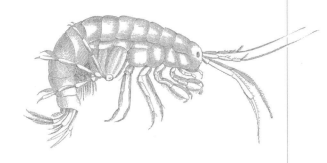

Grilled Mozzarella and Shrimp Sandwich

Save a handful of shrimp from dinner to make a fabulous sandwich for lunch the next day.

⅓ cup mayonnaise

1 tablespoon prepared horseradish

1 teaspoon minced garlic

½ teaspoon salt

Freshly ground pepper

8 slices rye or whole-wheat bread, toasted lightly

½ pound shrimp, peeled, deveined, and cooked

½ cup thinly sliced mushrooms

4 sandwich-size slices mozzarella cheese

2–4 tablespoons butter

4 large lettuce leaves or 4 handfuls green sprouts

1. In a small bowl, mix together the mayonnaise, horseradish, garlic, salt, and pepper. Spread mixture on one side of all slices of the toasted bread.

2. Place shrimp evenly over four slices. Place mushrooms in a layer over shrimp. Cover with cheese.

3. Melt butter in a large skillet or griddle over medium-high heat. Place the four slices topped with shrimp et al in the melted butter and cook until browned and mozzarella begins to melt.

4. Top each sandwich half with lettuce or sprouts, then add the top toast slice. Flip the sandwich, and warm the other side briefly, for about 1 to 2 minutes. Serve immediately.

YIELD: *4 servings*

Guacamole Shrimp Wrap

Wraps are a fun treat to eat on the beach since they hold everything together so well. This is a quick and easy recipe.

1. Place avocado and lime juice in a mixing bowl, and mash with a fork or potato masher until still somewhat chunky. Add onion, jalapeño, tomato, cilantro, salt, and pepper. Gently mix. (Mixture may be covered with plastic wrap and refrigerated for up to 2 hours.)

2. Lay 1 tortilla wrap on each plate, and spread two-thirds of tortilla with a layer of guacamole. Top with shrimp, laid two-by-two in a column down the length of the tortilla. Spoon a tablespoon or more of salsa over shrimp, then a layer of lettuce. Fold and wrap tortilla. Serve immediately.

YIELD: *4 servings*

2 large very ripe avocados, halved, pitted, and peeled

2 tablespoons fresh lime juice

¼ cup minced onion

1 tablespoon minced fresh jalapeño pepper

½ cup chopped fresh, ripe tomato (about 1 medium)

2 tablespoons chopped fresh cilantro

½ teaspoon salt

Freshly ground pepper

4 flour tortilla wraps

1 pound shrimp, peeled, deveined and cooked

½ cup prepared tomato-based salsa

1 cup thinly sliced lettuce

A Primer on Frying Seafood

It's a tradition in most Outer Banks restaurants and households to fry seafood that's been battered in hot oil. In spite of health concerns, sometimes it's the best—and most delicious—method. Nothing can beat a perfectly fried, succulent oyster from Rose Bay.

What you aim for when frying is crisp on the outside, moist on the inside. Quick cooking seals the juices in. Here are the secrets for crisp fried seafood:

- Hot oil, cold batter.

- An electric deep-fat fryer or deep electric skillet that can keep the temperature maintained at 350 or 375 degrees. Or, use a deep cast-iron skillet.

- Peanut or vegetable oil that can tolerate high heat. Butter can be added to oil when pan-frying. Discard oil after each use.

- Local cooks and chefs tend to use a local seafood breader mix made by Abbitt's out of Williamston, North Carolina.

- Coat the seafood in batter just when you're ready to drop it into the oil to prevent the coating from being too heavy.

- Fry scallops, shrimp, and oysters at 350 degrees, fish at 375 degrees.

The following recipes will make about 4 servings each:

Fried Oysters

2 eggs
½ cup flour
2 tablespoons cornmeal
¼ teaspoon salt
¼ teaspoon pepper
1 pint raw, shucked oysters, drained, juice reserved

1. Combine eggs, flour, cornmeal, salt, and pepper. Add just enough of the oyster liquid to make the batter moist but not runny.

2. Dip drained oysters into batter and drop into hot oil. Cook until golden brown, about 4 to 5 minutes. Drain on paper towels.

Fried Shrimp

2 eggs, beaten
1 teaspoon salt
¼ teaspoon black pepper
½ teaspoon Tabasco sauce, if desired
½ cup flour
½ cup cornmeal or dry bread crumbs, plain or seasoned
2 pounds shrimp, any size, cleaned, with or without tails

1. Combine eggs, salt, pepper, and Tabasco sauce. In another bowl, combine flour and cornmeal, or if you prefer, bread crumbs.

2. Dip peeled shrimp into egg mixture, then into flour mixture. Immediately drop shrimp into hot oil, and fry until golden brown, about 6 minutes. Drain on paper towels.

Fried Scallops

2 eggs

1 teaspoon salt

Black pepper

¼ teaspoon cayenne pepper (optional)

1 cup flour

1 pound sea scallops, rinsed and patted dry

1. Combine eggs, salt, pepper, and cayenne pepper, if desired. Place flour in a shallow dish.

2. Dip scallops into flour, and shake off excess. Dip into egg mixture, then drop into hot oil, and fry until golden brown, about 3 to 4 minutes. Drain on paper towels.

Fried Flounder, Spot, Croaker, Mullet, or Other Fish

If using a deep-fat fryer, cut fish into small chunks. If pan-frying, fillets or whole fish can be used.

1 egg

1 tablespoon milk or water

1 teaspoon salt

⅛ teaspoon pepper

½ cup cornmeal

½ cup flour

1 pound skinless fish fillets, whole or cut into chunks

1. In a bowl, combine egg and milk (or water), salt, and pepper. Mix cornmeal and flour in another bowl.

2. Dip the fish in the egg mixture, then roll in the flour mixture.

3. Fry in deep fat at 375 degrees until golden brown, about 8 minutes. Or fry in pan in oil about ½ inch deep, turning when golden brown. Drain on paper towels.

Canadian Hole Breakfast

Technically, on the map, it's known as Haulover Bay, where a boat's cargo was transferred from sound to ocean at this thin point on Hatteras Island, which circumvented the need to go through the dangerous inlet.

But most folks know it as The Canadian Hole, a wide, shallow bay on Pamlico Sound with a white, sandy beach, where favorable winds allow windsurfers and kite boarders to zip along at crazy speeds. Some days there are literally hundreds of kites and sails on the water, and the license tags from 95 percent of the vehicles parked there are from Canada. Hatteras Island has quite the reputation in Québec and Toronto, especially in late spring when our warmer weather is a bit of Southern heaven to them.

Here is a hearty and tasty breakfast to start the day's activities, whether it's out on the water or watching from the beach. Leftover cooked shrimp always comes in handy.

PER SERVING:

1 slice Canadian bacon

3–4 medium cooked shrimp

½ English muffin

1 slice Muenster, mozzarella, or cheese of your choice

1 teaspoon butter

1 egg

Salt and pepper to taste

1. In a small, nonstick sauté pan, place Canadian bacon and cooked shrimp over medium-high heat.

2. Meanwhile, toast the English muffin.

3. When Canadian bacon and shrimp are heated through, place on toasted muffin half. Place cheese on top.

4. Meanwhile, melt butter in the sauté pan over medium heat, and add the egg. Cook until white is set, pushing it up to make a nice rounded egg. When the yolk is just beginning to cook, flip the egg over and turn off heat. Allow egg to remain in pan to "set" the yolk for just a minute, then flip egg pretty-side up over the cheese/Canadian bacon.

5. Season with salt and pepper, and serve immediately.

Shrimp boats head out for days, with their nets extended like wings while they drag the nets. E F Wiegand

fish

FISH

Until the development of the fishing charter industry in the late 1930s, most Outer Bankers seldom went out to the Gulf Stream to fish. That's why traditional recipes call for drum, trout, bluefish, or mackerel that are caught in the sounds or just off the beach. Bankers traded their catch for corn or bought supplies with their proceeds. Captain Irv Stowe owned the *Ethel,* a supply boat that ran from Hatteras to Elizabeth City from the late 1920s to early 1930s. It would take iced-down fish, and return with store goods, lumber, and hardware.

Today the seafood markets in the Outer Banks contain a wonderful selection of fish, both from the Gulf Stream, less than an hour offshore, and fish that make Pamlico and Currituck Sounds their feeding grounds. Tuna, wahoo, grouper, flounder, dolphinfish, snappers . . . there's such a wide variety. If you're lucky, you can catch them yourself!

Grill, bake, or broil your catch, then add a salsa, or just enjoy the fish by itself. Or try pan-searing, which seals in the moisture and allows you to add all kinds of wonderful sauces.

Tips for Fish

- Keep fish on ice in your refrigerator.
- Always rinse, to make sure there are no scales left hovering around.
- Use tweezers to remove bones.
- The skin is usually removed from dolphinfish and tuna, as well as grouper, and larger fillets of flounder, rockfish, and trout when they are cleaned. However, you can easily remove the skin from raw fish fillets yourself. Peel the skin back slightly from one corner with a sharp knife, then, with the skin side down on the cutting board and holding onto it with one hand, insert the knife blade and pull it down, pressing it between the flesh and skin.
- Remember the saying, Fish and Guests Begin to Stink After Three Days.

The Demise of the Fish Houses

Fish houses are that vital link between commercial fishermen and the markets. They're where fishermen go to unload and sell their catch, and where those fish are cleaned, sorted, iced down, packed up, and shipped out. But fish houses are gradually disappearing from the North Carolina coast.

They are victims of declining harvests, pollution, governmental regulations, and perhaps even more importantly, of rising demand, and cost, of waterfront property. By necessity, they sit on the water, most on prime real estate that could be used for pricey condos or a restaurant. A third of the fish houses in the state closed over the last six years.

Which means it's harder for fish to find their way to the market.

In 2006, Ocracoke's last remaining fish house, located in a prime spot on Silver Lake, threatened to close for good. To understand why, look at the numbers—just thirty years ago, there used to be fifty fishermen who set out crab pots, but now there are five. Only a few pound netters still set their nets. So a group of those fishermen and charter boat operators formed the communal Ocracoke Working Watermen's Association, to operate the Ocracoke Seafood Company. Fish fries, bake sales, and oyster roasts were held to help them raise the needed capital. They continue to struggle to keep afloat.

That gives us, as consumers, even more reasons to buy local.

Graybeard's Seafood in Wanchese still brings in catches from the day boats to sell at market. E F Wiegand

Flaked Fish Cakes

Outer Bankers have never wasted anything, much less good food. When your fisherman brings in a large catch, especially those fish with white, flaky meat such as flounder, drum, grouper, or mahimahi, go ahead and cook extra fish with that first dinner. With the leftovers, you can make fantastic fish cakes for future meals.

1. In a large skillet, heat oil over medium heat. Add onions, and sauté for about 5 minutes or until tender. Add garlic, and stir for about 1 minute. Place onions and garlic in a large bowl.

2. Add fish, egg, bread crumbs, lemon juice, thyme, chives, and parsley. Add salt and pepper to taste. Mix gently, then form into 8 small patties.

3. Refrigerate for at least 30 minutes and up to 4 hours.

4. When ready to cook, heat olive oil and butter together, using the same large skillet used to fry the onions, if you prefer. When butter is melted, add fish cakes, making sure not to crowd them. Sauté until golden brown on one side, about 4 to 5 minutes, then turn and cook until golden brown on the other. Garnish with lemon slices.

YIELD: *4 servings*

2 tablespoons olive oil

½ cup finely chopped onions

1 clove garlic, finely minced

About 2 cups cooked, flaky white fish, deboned and skinned

1 egg, slightly beaten

½ cup bread crumbs (I like Old Bay's)

2 tablespoons lemon juice

1 teaspoon fresh thyme, de-sprigged and chopped

1 teaspoon finely chopped fresh chives

2 tablespoons finely chopped parsley

Salt and pepper to taste

2 tablespoons olive oil

2 tablespoons butter

4 lemon slices

Drum, Outer Banks Style

A boiled drum dinner is quite a tradition on Hatteras and just about every other island of the Outer Banks. But what is interesting is the variation that each village or family has for serving this dinner. Some have raw onions, some no onions, and some with onions slightly cooked. Some serve all the ingredients in one large bowl, and others keep them separate. Boiled eggs are added sometimes, whereas other Bankers would be aghast at the very idea.

Basically, a very large drum, about a foot and a half long with the head and tail removed, is boiled in water with salt and pepper. Potatoes are also boiled, separately, until soft. What is constant among all the village variations is the dice of salt pork that's fried crisp, "cracklins," along with the grease available for pouring over the fish at the table. Onions are diced, usually into a separate bowl.

The drum is usually brought to the table on a big platter, along with the potatoes, served separately. Diners place a large hunk of the fish on their plate, and usually mash the potatoes, sometimes mixing the fish in with the potatoes. Onto that, sprinkle onions, if you desire, the salt pork, and the grease, if you want to be really traditional. Mix what's on your plate together as you desire.

Drum, or channel bass as it is also known, used to be quite prolific in the waters of the Outer Banks, but its numbers are dwindling now. They spawn in the fall in the waters of Pamlico Sound, when the males produce a drum-like noise by vibrating a muscle in their swim bladder. Juveniles, who spend the first years of their life in quiet, shallow waters, are called puppy drum. Like many Bankers, when they mature, they seek the more thrilling waters of the ocean, returning to the sounds only to feed and spawn.

Trophy-size fish have been caught near Oregon Inlet and also Hatteras Island, one weighing 94 pounds and believed to be sixty years old. They are prized catches in the surf as well as on charter boats just offshore.

In the old days, folks would salt and dry the fish, then stack it in a dry spot for storage. When ready to cook, it then had to be "soaked out." Pressure cookers allowed later cooks to preserve the fish.

Now, it's only served fresh, in season. Darrell's Restaurant in Manteo serves a boiled drum special every Monday while the fish is in season during the colder winter months.

Crab-Stuffed Flounder

Flounder is a sweet white fish, one-sided though it may be, that camouflages itself into the sandy bottom with only its eyes and faint outline to be seen by the observant.

Flounder pairs well with crabmeat, which also wanders the bottom of the sounds and surf surrounding the Outer Banks. We've tried stuffing whole flounders, or layering crabmeat between two matching fillets, and decided that fillets are more appealing to us because the fish cooks more quickly and evenly. For this preparation, the fish stays moister when the skin is left on.

1. Preheat oven to 350 degrees. Butter a baking dish large enough to hold two fillets side by side, or line baking sheet with foil.

2. Rinse flounder fillets and pat dry. Place two thickest fillets, skin-side down, in the dish. Brush with about 2 tablespoons of melted butter.

3. In a small bowl, gently mix together the rest of the ingredients with the remaining 2 tablespoons butter. Divide into mounds on each of the fillets, then spread it outward, keeping it on top of the fillet.

4. Brush the flesh side of the other two fillets with melted butter and season with salt and pepper. Place the fillets over the mound of crabmeat so that the skin side is facing up.

5. Place in oven and bake, checking after 20 minutes to make sure top fillet is not burning; if so, cover loosely with foil. Continue to bake until the bottom fillets flake when fork is inserted, about 30 to 40 minutes total.

6. Cut each stuffed fillet halves in two, and serve immediately.

YIELD: *4 servings*

4 tablespoons butter, melted and halved

4 large flounder fillets (about 1½–2 pounds)

½ pound backfin crabmeat

2 scallions, finely chopped

2 tablespoons lemon juice

1 teaspoon Old Bay seasoning

1 egg, beaten

Salt and freshly ground pepper to taste

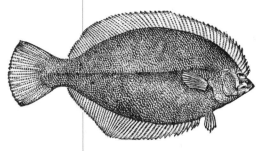

Flounder French Market Style

Summer flounder, basil, fresh tomatoes, freshly grated cheese—you really could imagine yourself walking through a market in Marseilles, or better still, gathering ingredients from around Currituck Sound, as does chef/owner Wes Stepp of Red Sky Café in Duck.

Prep work is 90 percent of cooking, says Chef Stepp. That includes cutting, chopping, grating, measuring, and having pans easily accessible. Be sure to have all the rest of your dinner and recipe ingredients ready to go, for this recipe goes fast.

Flounder has a very mild taste, so this dish has a very delicate flavor. Chef Stepp serves this with Cilantro-Lime Slaw (see page 238) and Rice Salad (see page 239).

¼ cup olive oil

½ cup flour

1 tablespoon finely chopped fresh basil

½ teaspoon kosher salt

½ teaspoon freshly ground black pepper

About 2 pounds flounder fillets, at least 4 portions, skinned

2 eggs, beaten with 2 tablespoons water

Thin slices of tomato, 1 per fillet

¼ cup freshly grated Romano or Asiago cheese

¼ cup dry white wine

½ lemon, juiced

1 tablespoon chopped fresh parsley

4 sprigs fresh rosemary

4 scallion flowers (see note)

4 lemon slices

1. Preheat oven to 400 degrees. Heat olive oil in a large sauté pan over medium-high heat.

2. In a bowl, mix together flour, basil, salt, and pepper. Lightly dredge each fillet in the flour mixture, then dip into the eggs.

3. Place fleshy side of fish down first, and cook for about 2 to 3 minutes per side, just enough to begin browning. Be sure to keep your pan hot so that the egg wash doesn't become like an omelet, Chef Stepp warns.

4. Remove pan from heat, and place a tomato slice on top of each fillet. Season with salt and pepper, then sprinkle with cheese. Add wine to pan, squeeze lemon juice over the fish, and sprinkle parsley.

5. Place pan in oven for 6 minutes, or until fish is white and flaky and still tender. Do not overcook.

6. Garnish with fresh rosemary, a scallion flower, and lemon slices, and serve immediately.

YIELD: *4 servings*

NOTE: Scallion flowers can be made ahead of time by removing the root fibers of each scallion, then cutting the green top so that each scallion is about 5 inches long. Gather the top shoots of each scallion together on a cutting board, then carefully make thin slices down to the top of the white root bulb, but not all the way through. Place these in a bowl of iced water, and place in the refrigerator until ready to use. The top part of the scallions will make nice curls, or flowers.

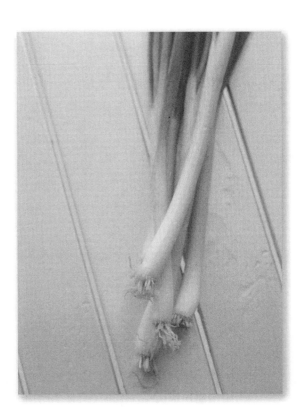

Fish Camps

Fish camps used to dot the sounds and beaches of the Outer Banks. They varied from having just enough construction to call them a shack to being a fairly substantial cottage. Those on the soundside were perched on pilings just feet away from water level. Along the beach, they were rude shelters made by weaving rushes, grasses gathered from the marsh, with wooden lathes, with tiers of bunk beds inside, lined with more grass. Most were owned by fishermen from the mainland, used for sleep and a respite against the weather. A very few that have survived have lately become retreats and playhouses as well.

You can rent The Fish Camp that's within sight of the Manteo–Nags Head Causeway by the week from The Roanoke Island Inn. The only access is by boat, but you'll find gracious accommodations and a fully functioning kitchen where you can cook up the crabs or fish you catch off the dock, or jump in your boat to go to dinner. Climb the three-story tower to watch the sun, moon, and stars over the water.

The Ice Plant

Ice is an important commodity for fishermen as well as for home food storage. Until ice was readily available at the turn of the twentieth century, fish had to be salted or smoked for storage.

An ice plant was dug into the small island just off the Manteo docks, where Roanoke Festival Park is now located. It provided ice for fishermen to load with their catches on sailboats and steamers bound for Elizabeth City, Norfolk, and other towns along the water. It burned in the early 1920s, and was rebuilt across Dough Creek along the Manteo waterfront.

The *Trenton,* a steamer, was loaded with ice each morning before leaving for Nags Head and other points along the Outer Banks.

Tom Skinner, a retired attorney, remembers as an older kid spending his summers in Nags Head helping to deliver ice from Jethro Midgette's cart, then later a truck, to iceboxes in the Cottage Row beach houses.

Gremolata Flounder

Gremolata is a wonderful combination of lemon zest, garlic, and parsley, and is a great way to add flavor to a mild fish such as flounder. And, a food processor can make it quick work!

1. Preheat oven to 425 degrees.

2. In a food processor, place parsley, garlic, zest, salt, and pepper and process until parsley is minced and all is blended. Add mayonnaise and lemon juice, and pulse until blended.

3. Cover a baking sheet with foil, then place fish on top. Spread mayonnaise mixture over each fillet.

4. Bake for 15 minutes, or until fish flakes with a fork.

YIELD: *4 servings*

½ cup packed Italian flat-leaf parsley

2 cloves garlic

1 teaspoon lemon zest

1 teaspoon salt

¼ teaspoon black pepper

¼ cup mayonnaise

1 tablespoon lemon juice

4 6-ounce flounder fillets (or other firm, white fish) skinned

Fish en Papillote

As the name implies, this is a French rendition. Fish fillets enclosed in a paper heart, seasoned with herbs, turn out marvelously moist. It is such an easy entree, as you can prepare them beforehand, then enjoy your company while they bake in the oven. The papillotes, which look like butterfly wings (papillons), will impress your guests. Or, just make packets from aluminum foil.

The secret here is to cut all vegetables into like sizes and thicknesses, so that they will evenly cook.

4 boneless, skinless fillets (4–6 ounces each) of flounder, grouper, tilapia, or other mild white fish, rinsed and patted dry

1 bunch of green vegetables in season: asparagus, thin green beans, sugar snap peas cut in half lengthwise; or zucchini sliced lengthwise into thin "logs"

1 small bunch of carrots, cut to match the thickness of the green vegetable

1 bunch green onions, cleaned and chopped

3–4 tablespoons fresh herbs—chives, thyme, parsley, or combination

Salt and freshly ground pepper to taste

4 tablespoons butter, cut into thin slices

1. Preheat oven to 350 degrees. Coat a baking sheet with nonstick spray.

2. Cut 4 pieces of parchment, 12 to 16 inches square depending on size of fillets (or use aluminum foil). Fold parchment squares in half, then cut half of a heart, like you did in grade school for Valentine's Day, from the end of one fold to the bottom, so that when the paper is opened, it looks like a whole heart.

3. Place folded hearts on baking sheets. Open the heart, and place a fillet in the center next to the fold.

4. Evenly divide the vegetables among the four hearts, arranging them on top of the fish fillet. Sprinkle the herbs over, and season with salt and pepper. Place slices of butter on top of fish and veggies.

5. Fold the paper back down, and roll the edges of the heart together to seal the seams so that they stay together on their own. (May be refrigerated for up to 4 hours at this point.)

6. Bake in preheated oven for 10 to 15 minutes, depending on the thickness of the fish. Fish should be flaky and vegetables tender. In order to check for doneness, you'll have to sacrifice the presentation of one papillote, but you can claim that one.

7. To serve, place one papillote on each serving plate. Allow guests to open their butterfly wings at the table.

YIELD: *4 servings*

Black Sea Bass Baked with Herbs

Black sea bass is literally a beautiful fish, with its long, graceful fins that look like angel wings. A very sweet-tasting, white and tender fish, it's best to treat it very simply to allow its flavor to shine through. Fresh herbs are a real asset, too.

There's something organic about serving a whole fish to each diner that makes you feel that connection from the water to the table. Serve with a spinach salad and perhaps some herbed orzo.

1. Preheat oven to 375 degrees.

2. Place one sheet of aluminum foil over a baking pan large enough for both fish. Place fish, opened, on pan.

3. Sprinkle butter, then lemon juice over the fish. Place lemon slices over flesh of the "down" side, then add sprigs of thyme and chopped chives, and sprinkle with salt and pepper.

4. Close fish together, then cover pan with foil and seal all edges.

5. Place in oven, and bake until fish is firm and white, about 20 to 30 minutes, depending on thickness.

6. The whole fish can be placed on each dinner plate. The backbone can be removed whole, along with the thyme sprigs, which will make eating the fish a bit more pleasant.

VARIATION: Add ¼ cup lump crabmeat to the inside cavity of each fish, in addition to the herbs and butter.

YIELD: *2 servings*

2 whole black sea bass (about 1 pound each), headed, scaled, cleaned, and butterflied

2 tablespoons melted butter

1 lemon, juiced

1 lemon, very thinly sliced

4 large stems fresh thyme

1 tablespoon chopped fresh chives

Salt and freshly ground pepper, to taste

Baked Catch of the Day

2 large onions, sliced very thin

4 large white potatoes, peeled and sliced very thin

2 pounds whole, dressed fish (Della prefers fresh bluefish)

½ pound sliced bacon

Salt and pepper to taste

The Basnights are a prominent family that has been in the Manteo area for generations. My friend Della Basnight returned to the street where she grew up after doing a few films and some television in Los Angeles, then working in Raleigh for decades. Her brother Marc owns Basnight's Lone Cedar Café on the Manteo–Nags Head Causeway, and has served as the North Carolina Senate Pro Tempore for years. Brother Saint is in construction, and her four sisters all live in town. Their mother, Cora Mae, played Agona, the Indian queen, in the annual summer production of *The Lost Colony* for twenty-five years; Della played several roles growing up. Della now sells fine wines to area restaurants, and entertains friends with stories of growing up on the Banks and having Andy Griffith, another *Lost Colony* co-star, as her godfather.

This is her favorite way to prepare fresh fish.

1. Preheat oven to 400 degrees.

2. In an ovenproof pan large enough to hold the fish, place a layer of thinly sliced onions.

3. Top onions with sliced potatoes.

4. Rinse fish and pat dry. Cut three to four ¼–½-inch scores diagonally across fish. Place fish on top of onions and potatoes in pan.

5. On top of each score, place a slice of bacon, and wrap around the fish, tucking bacon ends under the sides of the fish. Salt and pepper to taste. Add water until it covers the layers of potatoes.

6. Bake for 35 to 50 minutes, depending on the thickness and size of the fish.

YIELD: *4 servings*

Alice's Famous Fish

Alice Skinner summered at Nags Head with her husband Tom for six decades, and finally, in their eighties, they have retired there. Tom is very fond of her Famous Fish fillets. When asked what kind of fish she prefers, she answered, "Whatever anyone gives me!" Fortunately, they have quite a few fishing buddies.

4 tablespoons butter, divided

½ cup finely chopped onion

½ cup chopped mushrooms

½ cup finely chopped green pepper

1 cup commercial breading

4 large fish fillets, preferably rockfish, trout, or flounder, skinned and washed

Salt and pepper to taste

4 slices Swiss cheese

1. In a medium sauté pan, melt 2 tablespoons butter. Add onion and cook over medium-low heat for 2 minutes. Add mushrooms and green pepper, and sauté for another 5 minutes or just until vegetables are tender. Set aside.

2. Preheat oven to 350 degrees. Spread breading in a shallow pan. Place fish fillets in pan, turning fillets over into breading until covered on both sides. Season with salt and pepper to taste.

3. Melt remaining 2 tablespoons butter in a large frying pan that can be put into the oven. When butter is melted, add breaded fillets. Cook for 3 to 5 minutes per side, depending on thickness, until almost done.

4. Add sautéed vegetables to the top of the fish, and slide the frying pan into the oven. Bake for just a few minutes, until fish is done or flakes when forked.

5. Add Swiss cheese slices to each fillet, and return to oven. Turn the oven off, shut the door, and leave fish until cheese is melted. Serve immediately.

YIELD: *4 servings*

Baked Fish
with Parmesan Crust

2 cups freshly grated or shredded
   Parmesan cheese

¼ cup melted butter

¾ cup mayonnaise

¾ cup chopped green onions

4 teaspoons minced garlic

1 teaspoon hot sauce

4 large (4–6 ounces) fish fillets, preferably puppy drum, or flounder, trout,
or rockfish, skinned

At Café Atlantic on Ocracoke, Ruth Toth likes to use local puppy drum for this most popular item on her menu. But that's a seasonal fish, so if Farris O'Neal, the fisherman who supplies the restaurant, finds flounder, trout, rockfish, or possibly bluefish or Spanish mackerel in his nets that morning, that's what is used.

1. Preheat oven to 425 degrees. Place aluminum foil over baking sheet or pan.

2. Mix all ingredients, except fish, together in a mixing bowl.

3. Spread cheese mixture evenly over fillets, and place in oven. Baking time will depend on the thickness of the fillets, but will take about 12 minutes for fillets ³/₄ inch thick.

YIELD: *4 servings*

Baked Flounder

Jeanie Williams, a Kinnakeeter who raised her children in Manteo, dedicated this recipe to the memory of her daughter, Sandra W. Merritt, who really loved this dish. A very traditional Outer Banks preparation, note its similarity to Della's Baked Catch of the Day and Baked Rockfish. Whereas Della likes bluefish, this variation calls for flounder and the addition of tomatoes. Della and Sandra were best friends.

1. Preheat oven to 350 degrees. Grease the bottom of a large, rectangular baking dish.

2. Clean flounder and leave whole. Place in baking dish.

3. Cut three slashes across fish and place a strip of salt pork or bacon over each slash.

4. Surround fish with potatoes and onions. Add the can of tomatoes, juice and all. Sprinkle with salt and pepper.

5. Bake uncovered for 1 hour, basting occasionally. Serve straight from the oven.

YIELD: *4–6 servings*

1 3-pound flounder

3 strips salt pork or bacon

4 medium potatoes, quartered

1 onion, sliced

1 14-ounce can diced tomatoes

1 teaspoon salt

½ teaspoon pepper

Pecan-Encrusted Trout

2 cups chopped pecans

1 cup House of Autry Seafood breader
or other commercial breading

6 fillets of trout (speckled, gray, or
rainbow), skinned

Salt and pepper to taste

⅓ cup buttermilk

3 tablespoons oil for frying

WINE SAUCE

1½ cups dry red wine

2 cups commercial Sauce Espagnole
(Mother brown sauce) or
2 tablespoons (1½ ounces) Glace
de Viande Gold, a concentrate
available at specialty foods stores
mixed with 2 cups hot water

½ cup brown sugar

Salt and pepper to taste

Chef Anna Merrill of Mack Daddy's in Avon takes this deliciously prepared trout to the next level with the complex flavors of her brown sugar wine sauce, made with a classic "Mother" sauce, the Sauce Espagnole, a brown roux enhanced by a mixture of onion, carrot, celery, and ham. Chef Anna learned these international culinary lessons well at the Winner Institute of Arts and Sciences in Pennsylvania before migrating to the Outer Banks. The Sauce Espagnole can be purchased at gourmet specialty stores, or you can substitute other prepared brown sauces.

Without the sauce, the trout is still lovely. Sea trout is lean, and has a delicate and sweet meat. Speckled or gray trout, called a weakfish because the flesh around its mouth tears easily when hooked, can be found in waters off the Outer Banks almost all year long.

1. Preheat oven to 350 degrees. Coat a baking sheet with nonstick spray.

2. In a flat dish, combine pecans and breader. Season fish with salt and pepper. Dredge fish in buttermilk, then pecan breader.

3. In a large sauté pan, heat oil over medium-high heat. When oil is hot, add fish, and pan-fry until lightly browned but not quite cooked, about 3 minutes per side. Do not burn the pecans.

4. Place fillets on prepared baking sheet, and place in oven for 4 to 6 minutes, depending on thickness of fillets. When fillets are cooked, remove from heat, and place on plates. Top with wine sauce.

YIELD: *6 servings*

Brown Sugar Wine Sauce

1. Combine red wine and brown sauce in a medium saucepan. Bring to a boil, and reduce by half.

2. Add brown sugar, and cook for 1 minute longer. Season with salt and pepper.

YIELD: *about 1½ cups*

Pan-Roasted Fish

Thick and firm-fleshed fish, such as grouper, mahimahi, or rockfish (or salmon, definitely not a local fish!), do best with this quick and easy preparation.

Choose a salsa, pesto, or herbed butter (see below) to add further flavor to the fish. If I'm in a hurry, a store-bought red pepper pesto adds just the right touch, both in flavor and in presentation.

1. Preheat the oven to 450 degrees.

2. Salt and pepper the fish. Sprinkle with lemon juice. If using a salsa, pesto, or herbed butter, you may spread a thin coating on each fillet.

3. In an ovenproof large skillet, heat the olive oil over medium-high heat.

4. Place the fish in the oil, skinned-side down. Sear the fish for 1 minute, then transfer the pan to the oven.

5. Roast fish for 6 to 10 minutes, depending on thickness and desired doneness. (Check with a fork to see if fish flakes or is no longer pink.)

6. Remove fish to plates, and if desired, top with optional salsa, pesto, or butter.

YIELD: *4 servings*

4 6-ounce fish fillets, skin removed

Salt

Freshly ground pepper

½ lemon, juiced

Tomato or fresh fruit salsa, prepared pesto, or herbed butter (optional)

2 tablespoons olive oil

Herbed Butter for Fish

1. In a small bowl, mash the butter with the salt and pepper. Add the herb(s) and combine well.

2. May be stored in the refrigerator for up to a week.

YIELD: *About ⅓ cup*

HERBED BUTTER

4 tablespoons butter, softened

¼ teaspoon salt

Freshly ground pepper

1 tablespoon finely chopped thyme or dill, chives, and/or parsley

Grouper Floating on Succotash

Mild, firm, and flaky, grouper is an excellent fish to pan-roast, starting on the stovetop and finishing off in the oven. It's so easy. The succotash complements the sweetness of the grouper, while taking advantage of two prime vegetables grown on nearby Currituck farms—sweet corn and tiny baby butterbeans. You can find both at farm stands and farmers' markets, or use frozen. Small lima beans would be a good substitute for butterbeans.

FOR THE SUCCOTASH:

1 pint (2 cups) baby butterbeans, shelled, washed, and picked over

2 cups chicken broth (if using canned, dilute by half with water)

4 ears sweet corn, shucked and silked

1 large tomato, peeled, seeded and finely chopped

1 tablespoon finely chopped chives

1 tablespoon finely chopped parsley

3 tablespoons butter

Salt and freshly ground pepper to taste

FOR THE GROUPER:

3 tablespoons butter, divided

1 tablespoon olive oil

4 6-to 8-ounce grouper fillets, skin removed

Salt and pepper to taste

1 lemon, juiced

4 sprigs parsley

4 sprigs chives, cut into 2-inch pieces

TO PREPARE THE SUCCOTASH:

1. Place butterbeans in chicken broth in a large saucepan, and bring to a boil. Immediately reduce heat and simmer until butterbeans are almost tender, about 15 minutes. Make sure there is enough liquid to cover the butterbeans, and add water if needed.

2. With a sharp paring knife, with corncobs held vertically inside a large bowl, cut off kernels. Run the dull side of the knife down the cob to extract the "milk" or juice. Add both to the cooking butterbeans.

3. Simmer for an additional 5 minutes. Taste for tenderness, cooking more if necessary. When tender, add tomato, chives, parsley, butter, salt, and pepper to taste. Stir to mix in.

TO PREPARE THE GROUPER:

1. Preheat oven to 300 degrees.

2. In a large ovenproof sauté pan (or use two medium-size pans), heat 2 tablespoons butter with oil. When hot, add fillets, skinned-side up. Season with salt and pepper. Cook for about 2 minutes. Turn fish over, and add the remaining tablespoon of butter. Place pan in oven.

3. Cook until fish is firm and just beginning to lose that translucent color, about 10 minutes or more, depending on thickness.

TO ASSEMBLE THE DISH:

1. Reheat the succotash if necessary. Place in shallow pasta bowls.

2. Place fish on top of succotash. Squeeze lemon over fish, and add a sprig of parsley and chives on top of the grouper for a garnish.

YIELD: *4 servings*

Dolphinfish with Crabmeat Fromage

FOR THE FROMAGE:

4 egg yolks

½ cup mayonnaise

½ cup Parmesan cheese

¼ cup each sweet red and yellow pepper, finely diced

½ pound backfin crabmeat

FOR THE FISH:

¼ cup olive oil

4 4–6-ounce fillets, preferably dolphinfish, skinned

¼ cup flour

1 lemon, juiced

1 tablespoon finely chopped fresh parsley

Salt and freshly ground pepper to taste

Mahimahi is the Hawaiian name for the common dolphinfish and also the preferred name on menus and at markets to keep anyone from thinking they're being asked to eat Flipper or Hatteras Jack. To confuse matters even more, sometimes fishermen call it dorado.

Locals just call this beautiful species "dolphin." Its colors are brilliant blue and green in the water, but change to an intense yellow and almost purple when they are brought up. With very short snouts, they look as though they ran real hard into a wall.

Dolphinfish hang out in the Gulf Stream just a few miles out from Oregon and Hatteras Inlets. Sport fishermen usually allow their boat to drift while they cast to schools that congregate under the sargasso grass, their reward being a 5- to 25-pound catch.

Dolphinfish has a firm, flaky flesh that's mild and sweet and good for a variety of preparations. It is usually skinned when cleaned and cut into fillets or chunks.

Other white, firm and flaky fish, such as wahoo, flounder, trout, or red snapper could be substituted in this recipe, says Chef Wes Stepp of the Red Sky Café, who shared this creative preparation. He slices thick fillets in half lengthwise, on the diagonal, so they are thin and cook more evenly and fast, searing in the juice and flavor. He also likes to use the flavorful crabmeat from nearby Lake Mattamuskeet.

1. Prepare the fromage: Beat egg yolks till creamy, then stir in mayonnaise and Parmesan cheese. Mix in sweet peppers, then stir in crabmeat. Mix well. Set aside.

2. Preheat oven to broil. Pour olive oil into an ovenproof sauté pan, and heat over medium-high heat.

3. Dust fillets with flour, shake off excess, then place into hot oil. Brown quickly on both sides, about 2 to 3 minutes per side. Remove pan from heat.

4. Squeeze lemon juice over each fillet, sprinkle each with parsley, and season with salt and pepper. Spread a dollop of the crabmeat fromage across each fillet.

5. Place under broiler until tops are brown, about 2 to 3 minutes.

6. To serve, spread tomato slices across the middle of each plate. Sprinkle with fresh basil, salt, and pepper, and drizzle with olive oil.

7. Place fish on top of tomatoes. (Chef Stepp goes one step further by angling a Parmesan crisp on top.)

YIELD: *4 servings*

FOR THE GARNISH:

8 or more thin slices red tomatoes

2 tablespoons fresh basil, rolled and thinly sliced

Salt and freshly ground black pepper

2 tablespoons olive oil

Sweet Ginger-and-Soy-Glazed Dolphinfish

1/4 cup soy sauce

Juice and zest from 2 limes (at least 3 tablespoons)

2 tablespoons honey

1/4 teaspoon cayenne powder

1 tablespoon canola oil

1 tablespoon dark sesame oil

1-inch cube of fresh gingerroot, minced (about 2 tablespoons)

1 tablespoon minced garlic

4 4–6-ounce dolphinfish fillets, skinned (or grouper, wahoo, or tilapia)

Dolphinfish has such a sweet flavor, and is perfect for this recipe, yielding moist, bronzed fillets glazed with a wonderful tropical flavor. Serve over seasoned rice or orzo, garnished with fresh pineapple chunks.

1. In a small bowl, mix together the soy sauce, lime juice and zest, honey, and cayenne.

2. In a large sauté pan, heat both the oils. When hot, add ginger and garlic, stirring constantly so garlic doesn't burn. Stir in soy sauce mixture and bring to a boil.

3. Carefully add fish fillets, skinned-side down, and cover the pan. Cook for about 4 minutes.

4. Turn the fillets over, and cook for an additional 2 to 5 minutes, depending on the thickness of the fish.

5. To serve, place fish on plate over rice or orzo. Drizzle with the sauce, and serve immediately.

YIELD: *4 servings*

Spanish-Style Dolphinfish

Lynne Foster is spoiled, she says. If the fish isn't just off the boat that day, it really isn't fresh to her. Given that she is married to a charter fishing boat captain, she is allowed to be that picky. Fresh fish is simply grilled with a little butter and herbs. Day-old fish is given more elaborate, flavor-enhancing cooking techniques.

Lynne was in the marketing world of fashion and cosmetics in London and traveling around the world before meeting Ernie Foster on a fishing trip to Hatteras. He was the captain, head of the Albatross Fleet, the original charter-boat business in Hatteras Village. Now she helps him run the business while attending to many civic duties and writing and editing, including *A Hatteras Anthology: The Voices of Hatteras Island Women*.

This recipe reminds Lynne of many beautiful evenings spent along the Spanish coast. She uses a huge cazuela, a terracotta dish seasoned to handle temperatures on the stovetop and in the oven that looks attractive enough to go right to the table. The Spanish-style sweet peppers and paprika impart a smoky flavor to the fish. Shrimp and clams work as well as dolphinfish, she says.

Make sure you serve lots of crusty bread to dip into the fish broth. A green salad dressed with a simple sherry vinaigrette, and figs with Manchego cheese, would complement the Spanish flavors.

½ cup olive oil

2 medium onions, thinly sliced

1 8-ounce jar smoked pepper strips, preferably fire-roasted piquillo peppers

2–4 slices Serrano ham (a special cured Spanish ham), sliced into thin strips

1 teaspoon sweet smoked paprika

1 14-ounce can good-quality tomatoes, preferably San Marzano, juice only

1 8-ounce bottle clam juice

1½–2 pounds dolphinfish fillets or chunks, skin removed

4–6 large sprigs fresh thyme

Salt and pepper to taste

1. In a heavy-bottomed pot (e.g., Le Creuset), heat olive oil over medium-low heat. Add onions and cook until softened.

2. Add smoked pepper strips and Serrano ham, and sprinkle with paprika. Stir for 2 minutes.

3. Drain the juice from the tomatoes into the pot, and set tomatoes aside for another use. Add enough clam juice to make the mixture a bit soup-like. Cook for about 5 minutes to allow flavors to meld.

4. Add the dolphinfish, and cover with the thyme sprigs. Turn the heat to low, and continue to cook until fish is cooked through, flaky yet firm, for about 5 to 10 minutes, depending on the thickness of the fish. Do not overcook. Season to taste with salt and pepper.

YIELD: *4 servings*

Captain Ernie's
Beer-Batter Dolphinfish

1 bottle or can of beer, warm and flat

1 egg, beaten

1 teaspoon salt

About 2 cups flour

1½–2 pounds dolphinfish, skin removed, cut into thumb-size chunks

Peanut oil for frying

Captain Ernie Foster, of the famed Albatross Fleet in Hatteras, catches dolphinfish all summer long. He learned the art of fishing from his father, the late Ernal Foster, who was the first to start running commercial charter fishing parties from Hatteras in 1937, and helped put Hatteras on the map, or chart, rather. It's now known around the world for its spectacular sport fishing. The Gulf Stream is less than an hour's boat ride from the inlet, and that's where the dolphinfish hang out, along with striped bass, king mackerel, and wahoo. The Giants—the huge bluefin tunas and blue marlins—are also caught right offshore.

The Albatross Fleet, located at Foster's Quay at the Hatteras Harbor, features boats made locally in a unique style, from the flare of the bow to the rounded stern, which allows fish to be reeled in without catching on the corners. They also sport distinctive red-and-white, candy-caned outriggers. Captain Ernie is one of the very few native guides left, continuing a second-generation family tradition, and frequently employs female crew.

Here is how Captain Ernie, who has also been a high school guidance counselor, cooks the dolphinfish he brings home. He uses an electric fryer so that the temperature can be consistently maintained.

1. In a large bowl, mix and beat the beer, egg, and salt together. Add enough flour to make the mixture the consistency of pancake batter.

2. Heat oil in the electric fryer to 375 degrees.

3. Add chunks of dolphinfish, a few at a time, to the batter, turning to evenly coat.

4. Drop the battered chunks into the hot oil, a few at a time, and cook until browned and crunchy, about 6 to 10 minutes. Captain Ernie warns not to cook too many at a time, since that will lower the temp of the oil and result in soggy fish.

5. Drain the cooked fish on paper towels, and eat immediately. Serve with Lynne Foster's Secret Sauce (see page 256).

YIELD: *4 servings*

Beautiful dolphinfish, whose brilliant blue and green colors in the water change to a brilliant yellow when brought up. E F Wiegand

Grilled Mahimahi Sandwich

Mahimahi, the Hawaiian name for the common dolphinfish, seems to have more of a ring to it when grilling for a sandwich. Add a more spicy sauce or aioli, if you prefer, such as those found in the Sauces chapter.

4 6-ounce mahimahi (dolphinfish) fillets, skin removed

1 lime or lemon, juiced

2 tablespoons finely chopped fresh dill or 1 teaspoon dried dill

Salt and pepper to taste

2/3 cup mayonnaise

4 large sandwich rolls, sliced

1 large ripe tomato, cut into 4 slices

4 lettuce leaves

1. Preheat grill.

2. Wash fillets, pat dry, and place in a large, flat dish. Reserve 1 tablespoon of lime or lemon juice, then sprinkle the rest over the fish. Evenly distribute 1 tablespoon of the fresh dill over the fish, then salt and pepper to taste.

3. In a small bowl, mix rest of dill with mayonnaise, 1 tablespoon lime or lemon juice, and salt and pepper to taste.

4. Place fish on hot grill, and grill just until flaky, about 5 to 6 minutes total, turning fillets once.

5. Meanwhile, place cut side of sandwich rolls down on grill, and heat through, about 2 to 3 minutes.

6. Spread mayonnaise over each of the roll halves. Add grilled fish, then top with slice of tomato and lettuce.

YIELD: *4 servings*

Hatteras Jack

Hatteras Inlet has always been a shifting, shoaling channel that was especially treacherous for sailors before the days of navigational aids and dredging. But legend has it that there was help—in the form of an albino bottle-nosed dolphin, who approached each boat as they entered the inlet, and with his jumps and glides, guided them to water deep enough to pass through. When they were safely through the inlet, he would perform jumps, barrel rolls, and tail walks to celebrate. Known as Hatteras Jack, the white dolphin never lost a ship in the inlet. After the federal government placed a bell, buoy, and horn system to guide ships in, he disappeared, his services no longer needed.

A Primer on Grilling Fish

Dolphinfish (mahimahi), grouper, red snapper, and mackerel fillets, as well as tuna steaks, are great for grilling—so simple and quick. Here are a few secrets for a successful fish grill:

- Dolphinfish and grouper are usually skinned at the dock when they are cleaned, and cut into fillets or chunks. Mackerel is often cut into steaks, "in the round," which includes the backbone and skin. Most of the time, the skin is left on red snapper and mackerel fillets, which will help protect the flesh from falling through the grill or getting too dried out. However, it is best to remove the skin as soon as you pull it off the grill, before serving. Usually the fleshy side is placed facing down on the grill first, then it is turned over to brown the skin or skinned side.

- Fish that has been skinned, especially, should be "wet" with a marinade or just rubbed with olive oil to prevent it from drying out. Coat with oil or marinate fillets in lemon or lime juice, salt and pepper, or seasoned salt, or blackening or Cajun spices for at least 30 minutes and up to 2 hours before grilling.

- Always preheat the grill to at least medium heat. After the grill is hot, carefully spray the grates with nonstick cooking spray, or wipe them with a towel soaked with vegetable oil.

- Most fillets will not need to be flipped or turned over, especially if they still have the skin on. However, they look better with a nicely browned top, so try putting the good side down first, then flipping after 2 minutes.

- Monitor the fish closely, for it only takes about 5 to 10 minutes total to cook, depending on the thickness of the fillets or steaks. Remove from heat when fillets are no longer translucent and flake easily with a fork.

- A rectangular tray with punctured holes specifically designed to keep vegetables, fish, or other food items from falling through the grill works wonders. It can be sprayed or greased to make flipping and removal easier.

Salsas for Grilled Fish

Serve one of these salsas (or one of the choices in the Gulf Stream Fish Grille recipe, page 194, or the Tomato and Black Olive Salsa on page 257) over or with the fish:

Avocado and Tomato. Finely chop 1 clove garlic, 1 jalapeño pepper, and $\frac{1}{4}$ cup onion together, either on a chopping board or in a small food processor. Chop a small fistful of cilantro (if using food processor, pulse till chopped coarsely). Add 1 firm but ripe avocado and 1 fist-size ripe tomato, and coarsely chop. Add to the rest of the mixture. Squeeze in the juice of 1 lime, salt, and pepper to taste.

Mango Salsa. As above, except use 1 large, ripe mango with its juice instead of the avocado and tomato.

Tomato and Cukes. Coarsely chop 1 ripe tomato, with its juice, and a matching amount of peeled cucumber. Add about 2 tablespoons of chopped chives or scallions or onions. Sprinkle with just a bit of balsamic vinegar and an equal amount of olive oil. Add salt and pepper to taste.

Fish or Shrimp Tacos from The Bad Bean Taqueria

FOR THE FISH:

About 2½ pounds fresh dolphinfish (mahimahi), or tilapia or tuna may be used instead, cut into 2-ounce portions, or 2 pounds medium shrimp, shelled and deveined

1 lime, zest and juice

1 tablespoon ground cumin

3 tablespoons canola oil

FOR THE SLAW:

1 large jicama

1 head green cabbage

2 teaspoons granulated sugar

Salt (preferably sea or kosher salt) to taste

1 lime, zest and juice

1 cup homemade or store-bought mayonnaise

1 tablespoon cumin

1 teaspoon ground cayenne pepper

1 bunch cilantro, washed and chopped

When Chef Rob Robinson found free time while working at The French Laundry, Aqua, and other esteemed California restaurants, he'd visit taquerías along the West Coast that sold fish tacos and other authentic Mexican food. He returned to the Outer Banks, where after a stint as executive chef at The Left Bank at The Sanderling Inn, Robinson found himself wanting to reach a broader audience. So he and partner John Lenhart opened an Outer Banks version of a taquería. The Bad Bean in Timbuck II in Corolla features locally caught fish, homemade salsas, classic mole, burritos, and heavenly sopaipillas. And none of their beans are bad, for they are made with authentic Mexican oregano and fresh epazote.

TO PREPARE THE FISH:

1. The day before serving, place fish (or shrimp) in a medium bowl or resealable plastic bag.
2. Zest and juice lime, and sprinkle both over the fish.
3. Sprinkle cumin and canola oil over the fish, then toss to blend flavors.
4. Refrigerate overnight.

TO PREPARE THE SLAW:

1. Remove the outer skin of the jicama and then cut into thin strips.
2. Clean the cabbage, removing some of the outer leaves. Cut into quarters and remove core from each. Slice each quarter as thinly as possible.
3. In a large bowl, toss together the jicama and cabbage with the sugar and salt to taste. Let sit for 30 minutes.
4. Zest and juice the remaining lime.
5. In a small bowl, mix together the mayonnaise, cumin, cayenne pepper, lime zest and juice. Add salt to taste.
6. Add the mayonnaise mixture to the jicama and cabbage. Add the chopped cilantro, and toss all together. Taste and add salt, if necessary.

TO ASSEMBLE THE TACOS:

1. Heat a large, heavy cast-iron pan over medium-high heat until a drop of water sizzles. Add fish, and sear on both sides until just cooked through, making sure not to overcook and allow the fish to dry out. If using shrimp, sauté until they just turn pink.

2. Preheat grill or heat a nonstick pan over high heat. Place tortillas on hot grill or pan and toast lightly.

3. Assemble the tacos by placing fish, then slaw in toasted tortilla. Top with salsa or guacamole or hot sauce.

YIELD: *10–12 tacos (4–6 servings)*

FOR ASSEMBLY:

10–12 flour tortillas

Fire-Roasted Tomatillo and Poblano Pepper Salsa (optional; recipe follows)

Guacamole or hot sauce

Fire-Roasted Tomatillo and Poblano Pepper Salsa

1. Preheat grill or broiler. If using broiler, line a cookie sheet with aluminum foil.

2. Place the tomatillos and peppers in a large bowl, and toss with 2 tablespoons canola oil to coat lightly. Sprinkle with 1 teaspoon salt.

3. Toast the tomatillos and peppers on all sides until well darkened all over. If using broiler, reserve the liquid released from the tomatillos and peppers. When cool, puree in a blender, leaving the mixture somewhat chunky.

4. Add 2 tablespoons canola oil to a large, heavy-bottomed pot and heat over medium heat. Add onions and garlic, and sauté until onions are translucent and begin to turn slightly brown and caramelize. Add the coriander and cook for only 10 to 20 seconds.

5. Immediately add the tomatillo and pepper puree and the 2 cups water. Bring mixture to a boil, reduce to a simmer and cook for about 10 minutes to incorporate the flavors.

6. To finish, fold in the cilantro and season with salt as needed. Cool the salsa immediately. It will thicken as it sits in the refrigerator.

YIELD: *about 2 cups*

20–25 fresh tomatillos

4 poblano peppers

1–2 jalapeño peppers, to taste.

3–4 tablespoons canola oil

Salt

1 white onion, chopped

4 cloves fresh garlic, minced

1 teaspoon ground coriander

2 cups water

2 bunches fresh cilantro, washed and coarsely chopped

Gulf Stream Fish Grille with Three Salsas

4 5-ounce pieces of fresh fish, about 1½ inches thick, skinned (Chef Gruninger suggests tuna, wahoo, grouper, dolphinfish, rockfish, or cobia)

2 tablespoons olive oil

Sea salt and cracked pepper to taste

Choice of salsas (recipes follow)

It takes only about 45 minutes from Oregon Inlet, via a fast motorboat, for anglers to reach the Gulf Stream, nicknamed "The Yellow Brick Road" for the line of amber sargassum seaweed where fish, especially dolphin-fish (mahimahi), grouper, and wahoo like to hang out to feed.

At Basnight's Lone Cedar Café, Chef Bud Gruninger takes whatever fresh catch the boats bring in, seasons the dressed fish, and tosses it on the grill. He then tops it off with one of the following salsas.

1. Preheat grill.
2. Season the fish by rubbing with olive oil, then sprinkling with salt and pepper.
3. Place on grill and cook 4 to 5 minutes per side until fish flakes or is no longer pink in the middle

YIELD: *4 servings*

Pineapple Salsa

1 medium pineapple, peeled and cut into ½-inch dice
1 jalapeño pepper, chopped fine
3 scallions, thinly sliced
1 small red pepper, chopped fine
2 limes, juiced
1 bunch cilantro, chopped fine
Sea salt to taste

1. In a medium bowl, combine all ingredients.
2. Cover and refrigerate for 2 to 4 hours.

YIELD: *About 3 cups*

VARIATION: *For a Melon Salsa, substitute cantaloupe or honeydew melon, or a combination, for the pineapple, then continue as above.*

Pico de Gallo

8 Roma or plum tomatoes, chopped into ¼-inch dice
2 limes, juiced
1 onion, chopped fine
3 scallions, thinly sliced
2 jalapeño peppers, chopped fine
1 bunch cilantro, chopped fine
Sea salt to taste

1. In a medium bowl, combine all ingredients.
2. Cover and refrigerate for 2 to 4 hours.

YIELD: *4 servings*

Basnight's Lone Cedar Café

If it's not local or seasonal, it will not be served at Basnight's Lone Cedar Café. No oysters unless they're plucked from Hyde or Dare county waters, shucked that day. If there's a storm, there's no fresh fish until the boats can get back out. If the rockfish are running, the staff member whose only job is to obtain the best, local seafood will make sure he gets them on the menu. One soft-shell crabber dedicates his catch to the restaurant. Ninety percent of the produce is also local, like the Mattamuskeet Sweets, the local variety of sweet onions, or tomatoes from Edenton and asparagus from Currituck. Farms in North Carolina provide the pork and poultry, too.

Opened in 1995 by Sandy and Marc Basnight, North Carolina Senate President Pro Tempore for many years, the cafe and its standards are now overseen by their daughter Vickie. But Marc is often there, greeting customers, cleaning tables, and tending the fresh herbs in the gardens out back, while head chef Bud Gruninger supervises the grill and kitchen. You'll also find a unique selection of wines.

In May 2007, the restaurant burned to the ground one night after closing. Other restaurants quickly hired some of the staff on a part-time basis until the Lone Cedar could be rebuilt, and the community held fish fries to raise money for other waitstaff and kitchen crew. Re-opened a short four months later, the new, two-story design now affords better views of the water.

In June that same year, Sandy Basnight died, leaving the restaurant in the good hands of daughter Vickie.

Basnight's Lone Cedar Café is located on the Manteo–Nags Head Causeway, 252-441-5405.

Grilled Dolphinfish
(Mahimahi)

Also known as mahimahi, dolphinfish is one of those fish that takes to the grill so readily. With firm, white, and thick flesh, it simply needs to be rubbed with olive oil and seasoned with salt and pepper. Then serve with any number of flavorful salsas, butters, or aiolis you'll find in the chapter on Sauces and Dressings or in the preceding Gulf Stream Fish Grille.

4 6-ounce mahimahi fillets, skinned

¼ cup olive oil

½ teaspoon salt

Freshly ground pepper

1. Preheat grill.
2. Lightly rub the fish fillets with the olive oil, then season with salt and pepper.
3. Grill over medium-high heat, turning once, until lightly browned and cooked through, about 8 minutes.
4. Serve immediately with your choice of salsa, butter sauce, or aioli.

YIELD: *4 servings*

Fish Throats

Fish throats seem to be a coastal secret, something that anglers and those who clean fish for the market may keep for themselves. With more rounded fish like red snappers, groupers, and mahimahi, the upper part of the fish's breast, cut out in the shape of a V, contains more fatty tissue, and is quite a delicacy.

Treat a fish throat much like you would a fillet, brushing it with butter or oil, seasonings, and lemon juice before broiling or grilling.

Fresh Grilled Grouper and Peaches

Knotts Island, just across Currituck Sound near the Virginia border, is known for its peach orchards. During the summer, you'll also find peach stands along the roads leading to the Outer Banks. Chef Bud Gruninger combines two of summer's treasures: succulent, local peaches, and grouper freshly caught from the Gulf Stream which runs just offshore.

1. Split peaches in half.

2. Mix together Key lime juice, 2 tablespoons olive oil, brown sugar, honey, and cinnamon in a small bowl. Coat peach halves with mixture, then refrigerate for 1 to 2 hours.

3. Wash grouper fillets and pat dry. Coat with olive oil, then season with sea salt and Caribbean jerk seasoning.

4. Preheat grill. When hot, place fillets on grill and cook for about 8 minutes each side.

5. Place peach halves cut-side down and grill 4 to 5 minutes, then turn over and grill for 3 to 4 minutes more.

6. Serve 2 peach halves with each grouper fillet.

YIELD: *4 servings*

4 large ripe peaches

4 tablespoons (2 ounces) Key lime juice

2 tablespoons olive oil

1 tablespoon brown sugar

2 tablespoons honey

½ teaspoon cinnamon

4 12-ounce boneless, skinless grouper fillets

3–4 tablespoons olive oil

Sea salt to taste

Caribbean jerk seasoning, to taste

Grilled Wahoo

Wahoo are one of the fastest fish in the ocean, and most caught near Hatteras are in the 25–50-pound range. Peak times are late summer and early fall, although they can be caught during April, May, and June. In Hawaii, it's known as ono.

Wahoo is a firm, white fish with lots of flavor, and can be simply basted, then grilled. Because of its size, it's usually cut into thick steaks.

4 tablespoons butter, melted

¼ cup olive oil

2 teaspoons minced garlic

2 tablespoons lemon juice

¼ cup finely chopped parsley

2 teaspoons Old Bay seasoning.

¼ teaspoon salt

Freshly ground pepper to taste

4 wahoo steaks, about 4–6 ounces, 1-inch thick

4 thick lemon slices

1. Preheat grill.

2. In a small bowl, whisk together butter, oil, garlic, lemon juice, parsley, Old Bay, salt, and pepper.

3. Brush both sides of each steak with butter sauce. Place steaks on medium-high heat on the grill, and cook, basting occasionally. Turn and baste again. Cook until fish is lightly browned and flakes, about 7 to 10 minutes total.

4. Garnish with lemon slices and serve immediately.

YIELD: *4 servings*

Wasabi Sesame Tuna

Tuna is caught in the Gulf Stream just offshore from the Outer Banks. Chef Wes Stepp of Red Sky Café in Duck says to look for dark red meat, which indicates freshness, when shopping for tuna. He likes to cut portions from a whole loin just over an inch thick, thick enough that the tuna won't overcook, especially in the middle, which you want to remain pink.

Serve this tasty tuna with Cucumber Vinaigrette (see page 258) and perhaps a seasoned rice.

1. Mix together the wasabi and soy sauce in a non-metallic bowl.

2. Place tuna in a shallow baking casserole, and pour wasabi-soy marinade over. Allow to marinate for 5 to 6 minutes.

3. Place sesame seeds in a small, shallow dish, and place each tuna steak on top, pressing to coat each with seeds just on one side.

4. Heat olive oil over medium-high heat. When hot, add tuna, seed-side down, and sear until seeds are browned, about 2 to 3 minutes. Turn tuna over and cook for just another minute, until tuna is still soft and red in center, for it will continue to cook when off the heat.

5. Serve immediately with Cucumber Vinaigrette and additional wasabi mixture.

YIELD: *4 servings*

1 tablespoon wasabi paste (mix equal parts wasabi powder and water) or to taste

⅓ cup soy sauce

4 tuna steaks, 1¼ inch thick

½ cup black and white sesame seeds

¼ cup olive oil

An additional mixture of 1 tablespoon wasabi paste (equal parts wasabi powder and water) as a condiment

Red Sky at Night, Diners' Delight

The Red Sky Café faces the sunset over Currituck Sound, and just as the sky can explode into a profusion of color, so do the range of flavors and talent at this delightfully cozy café in Duck.

Chef and owner Wes Stepp has cooked for years in Outer Banks kitchens, and was head chef at Kelly's before opening his own café in Duck. He draws inspiration from around the world to prepare local seafood, like crabmeat from Lake Mattamuskeet, and vegetables gathered from gardens just over the sound in Currituck. He also offers Chefs On Call which delivers the chef, food, dishes, and anything else needed to create a party, as well as more typical catering services.

Tuna Udon

Beautiful loins of dark, red tuna are available fresh from the day boats at O'Neal's Sea Harvest in Wanchese or at any of the seafood markets along the Outer Banks. For a fascinating diversion, catch the charter boats when they return to Oregon Inlet Fishing Center or to the docks in Hatteras Village late in the afternoon, to watch them unload, or rather heave onto the boardwalk the big, torpedo-like yellowfin tunas caught offshore. At Hatteras Village, the local watermen at the fish cleaning stations make quick work of peeling the skin, then quartering the tuna to extract the loin. Loins are then cut crosswise into steaks.

This dish makes a beautiful presentation, with the contrast of the bright colors of the veggies in the udon noodles. The tuna is very tender, almost like butter, when marinated in oil.

FOR THE TUNA:

4 tuna steaks, at least 1 inch thick

½ cup extra-virgin olive oil

2 teaspoons chili oil

3 strips lemon peel, ½ inch wide

3 sprigs fresh thyme

2 large garlic cloves, slivered

Salt and freshly ground pepper

FOR THE UDON:

3 tablespoons white sesame seeds

1 tablespoon minced garlic

1 tablespoon minced fresh gingerroot

¼ cup soy sauce

¼ cup canola or vegetable oil, plus 1 tablespoon

½ teaspoon Tabasco or other hot sauce

½ cup chopped red pepper

3 green onions, chopped

½ pound fresh asparagus and/or 2 cups sugar snap peas

1 package (8 ounces) dried udon pasta

1. At least an hour before cooking, marinate tuna steaks. In a plastic, resealable bag, place the olive oil, chili oil, lemon peel, thyme, and garlic. Squish it around to blend, then add the tuna steaks. Place bag in refrigerator until time to cook.

2. Start to prepare the udon noodles. In a small skillet, over medium heat, place the sesame seeds, and shake the pan to stir them around as they toast. When lightly browned, after about 3 to 5 minutes, remove from heat.

3. In a small mixing bowl or jar with a tight lid, combine the garlic, gingerroot, soy sauce, oil, hot sauce, red pepper, and onions. Whisk, or shake the jar, to combine. Let sit so that the flavors will meld.

4. If you are using asparagus, snap the tough ends off, rinse, then cut into 2-inch pieces on the diagonal to make it attractive. Place in a skillet, barely cover with water, and set on stove. Turn heat to medium-high, and as soon as the water begins to boil, drain the asparagus, then immediately run cold water over the pieces to stop the cooking process and give it a bolder green color.

5. When you are ready to serve within 30 minutes or less, put a large

pot of water on high. When it begins to boil, add the udon noodles, and time for about 9 to 10 minutes, or until pasta is al dente. Drain, and place in a large serving bowl.

6. In a small skillet, place 1 tablespoon oil, red pepper and green onions, and (if using) the sugar snap peas over medium-high heat. Cook and stir for just about 2 minutes, just enough to warm the vegetables but still keep them crisp. Remove from heat and add to the udon noodles.

   Add asparagus, if using.

7. Whisk or shake the soy sauce combination, then pour over the noodles and vegetables. Stir to combine. Sprinkle with toasted sesame seeds.

8. Remove tuna from the bag and make sure none of the garlic or herbs have stuck to its sides. Strain the oil into a large sauté pan, and place over medium-high heat. When oil is hot, add tuna and season with salt and pepper. Sear quickly, 2 to 3 minutes for the first side, turn and sear for an additional minute but no more than 3, depending on how rare you desire. We prefer tuna that is still red in the center, about 4 minutes total. Remove from pan immediately.

9. Place dressed noodles and vegetables in the center of each plate, and make a well in the center. Place tuna in center. Serve immediately.

YIELD: *4 servings*

Skilled watermen clean the catch, making quick work of skinning, then cutting the loin from large yellowfin tuna at Hatteras Harbor. E F Wiegand

Tuna Carpaccio with Shaved Fennel and Arugula

1½ pounds fresh, grade 1+, center-cut tuna

¼ cup currants

¼ cup port wine

2 fennel bulbs

4 tablespoons extra-virgin olive oil, divided

2 teaspoons red wine vinegar

Kosher salt and ground black pepper, to taste

1 tablespoon fresh lime juice

¼ cup toasted pine nuts

6 basil leaves

2 cups arugula, washed well and dried

The Kill Devil Grill may look like an old-fashioned diner, and it is listed in the National Registry for Historic Buildings, but the food is anything but old-fashioned. Chef Bill Tucker prepares new-style cuisine, like this recipe, using fresh local ingredients, simply prepared from scratch.

Yellowfin tunas swim close to the shore of the Outer Banks to feed during most of the year.

Chef Tucker says to make sure the tuna is very fresh and kept well chilled.

1. Cut tuna into thin slices.

2. Place slices between plastic wrap, and pound gently until paper-thin. Refrigerate.

3. Place six appetizer plates in the refrigerator.

4. Plump the currants in the port wine and chill.

5. Trim the fennel bulbs. Remove the outside layer and core. Using a mandoline or Japanese slicer, shave fennel.

6. Mix 2 tablespoons of olive oil and red wine vinegar with kosher salt and freshly cracked black pepper to taste.

7. Mix remaining olive oil with the lime juice, and season with salt and pepper to taste.

8. When ready to serve, divide tuna evenly on the well-chilled plates. Splash with the lime and olive oil. Strain the currants, and sprinkle them, along with the pine nuts, on top of the tuna. Stack the basil leaves, roll, and thinly slice. Sprinkle the basil on top of the tuna.

9. In a separate bowl, toss the arugula and fennel in the red wine vinaigrette. Arrange them on top of the tuna, without covering the tuna completely.

YIELD: *6 appetizer or lunch servings*

The front section of the Kill Devil Grill Diner is from another era. E F Wiegand

Fresh Tuna Salad from The Great Gut Deli

5 pounds fresh tuna loins

Olive oil

Salt and pepper to taste

1½ cups finely chopped celery

¾ cup finely chopped onion

2 cups heavy mayonnaise

Tuna Belly

Bluefin tuna sometimes make a detour run off the Outer Banks during the colder months from the Labrador current while seeking their gourmet delight, bluefish. Bluefins are usually not brought to local market; rather, they are sold for a very fetching price to the Japanese who prize bluefin for sushi.

That said, you might find toro or otoro, Japanese for tuna belly, on the most upscale or experimental Outer Banks menus. It may come from the more available yellowfin rather than bluefin tuna, but it's still considered the most prized sushi in the world. Taken from the tuna's belly loin, it has a higher fat content than other pieces of the fish, which gives it a rich and butter-like taste. But order it only in season, during the winter, when it is caught fresh and locally.

There's no sign for The Great Gut Deli, but workmen in Wanchese boatyards and office workers in Manteo head there at lunchtime for delicious soups, salads, wraps, and sandwiches made fresh daily. It's located at Thicket Lump Marina in Wanchese, where owner and chef Annie Davis takes seafood straight off the boats to work her magic. And she also makes hand-rolled meatballs, from her Italian heritage, featured in a terrific sub.

During the summer, her husband, Wade, a boatbuilder like his father, and their two kids net shrimp right out in front of the "gut" or cut in the sound. Or the kids might dig for arrowheads and shards of pottery in the ancient oyster mounds left by the Algonquians.

Annie does not offer this tuna salad unless she has a fresh catch. She recommends small tuna loins.

1. Place tuna in a sealable container and cover in salted water (about 1 tablespoon salt per quart of water). Soak for at least 12 hours.

2. Preheat oven to 400 degrees. Take tuna out of water and pat dry, and place in foil-lined pan.

3. Drizzle with olive oil, sprinkle with salt and pepper, and bake for 30 to 45 minutes, until it starts to brown.

4. Let tuna cool, then flake with a fork or with your hands.

5. In a large mixing bowl, place the flaked tuna, and add celery, onion, and mayonnaise. Season with salt and pepper to taste.

YIELD: *About 2 quarts*

Grilled Tuna Burger

Fresh tuna is such a treat. Sometimes you can purchase long loins, which will yield quite a few triangular-shaped steaks, enough to indulge in a splurge for lunch. A lemon or lime-flavored mayonnaise or aioli complements the tuna flavor, whereas the Wasabi Aioli will give it a bite. Your choice.

1. Preheat grill to medium-high heat.
2. Cut the top off the red pepper and remove the core and seeds. Cut horizontally into rings. Coat red pepper and onion slices with olive oil.
3. Brush olive oil on both sides of tuna steaks, then season with salt and pepper.
4. Place tuna, onions, and red pepper on grill. Cook all about 3 minutes, then turn. Cook tuna for an additional 2 minutes, then remove. Cook pepper and onions for another 3 minutes or more after turning.
5. Meanwhile, heat rolls on the sides or upper grate of grill.
6. To assemble, spread aioli on both halves of the warmed buns. Place tuna, then onion and red pepper on bun. Top with shredded lettuce. Serve immediately.

YIELD: *4 servings*

1 large red pepper

4 thick slices sweet onion (Vidalia, or try North Carolina's Mattamuskeet Sweets)

¼ cup olive oil, divided

4 4–6 ounce tuna steaks, about 1 inch thick

Salt and freshly ground pepper to taste

4 sandwich buns

¼ iceberg lettuce head, shredded

1 cup Lime-Mustard Aioli (see page 259) or Wasabi Aioli (page 259)

Streaking Stripers

We were walking down the beach at Nags Head one winter afternoon, when we came upon a convention of fishermen, about fifty of them lined up, frantically casting over and over into the surf. Fish 2 feet long or more flopped about in the sand, littering our path. As soon as the lines were cast, the tips of the rods bent almost double. The men would reel their catch in, run it up, and drop it into a cooler, or frantically shake it off into the sand.

One man came over the dune, literally at a gallop, clutching his rod and reel in one hand, his tie tucked between the buttons of his white shirt, his dress pants' legs stuffed into wading boots. "What are they taking?" he shouted to a buddy. "Anything," was the reply.

What we had walked onto was a school of stripers, also known as striped bass or rockfish, making their way down the coastline at Nags Head. They had created a fishing frenzy. One fellow said he was working on a new house when his cell phone rang. It was a buddy working a few miles north, who from his vantage point on the roof of a house under construction had seen the large school of fish "working" or feeding in the surf.

"This looks exciting," I said to another guy dropping his catch into a large cooler.

"Ma'am, I haven't had this much excitement ever in my life," he said, a big grin on his face. "Nothing could be better than this."

"Not even sex?" I asked.

"Ma'am, that lasts for only a minute. This has been going on for hours."

That night, rockfish was on the menu, grilled and topped with a lemon-butter wine sauce.

Stripers migrate from the north back south during their annual late-winter, early-spring migration, and then head up freshwater rivers. where they came to life themselves, to spawn. That creates yet another fishing frenzy. Fishermen are limited by dates and location in order to give the fish a fighting chance to stay viable.

A prized catch, striped bass, also known as rockfish, caught during the late winter and brought into the Oregon Inlet Fishing Center. E F Wiegand

Baked Rockfish or Striped Bass

This is one of the most traditional recipes for fish caught in North Carolina, whether near the Outer Banks when they run along the beaches, or inland, where the fish are caught while making their way up the Roanoke River to spawn. Folks look forward to the annual run of rockfish, and other than grilling, would prepare the fish no other way. This preparation is similar to the traditional recipes for bluefish, and also flounder (see recipes on pages 176 and 179).

1. Preheat oven to 350 degrees.

2. Place fish in large covered casserole or ovenproof pot. Make 3 to 4 diagonal slices through the skin but not quite to the backbone. Wrap bacon around the fish, covering the slashes.

3. Place potatoes and onions to the side of the fish, and sprinkle salt and pepper over all. Add enough water to come up two-thirds of the side of the fish.

4. Cover and bake until fish is flaking and almost done, about 45 minutes. Uncover, turn oven up to 375 degrees, and bake for about 15 minutes to brown the bacon.

5. To serve, quarter the fish and place each serving on a plate. Divide potatoes and onions among the plates, and pour the pan juices over the fish and vegetables.

YIELD: *4 servings*

1 whole rockfish (striped bass), cleaned and gutted, about 2 pounds

4 slices bacon

6 medium white potatoes, peeled and cubed

4 medium onions, peeled and quartered

1 teaspoon salt

1 teaspoon freshly ground pepper

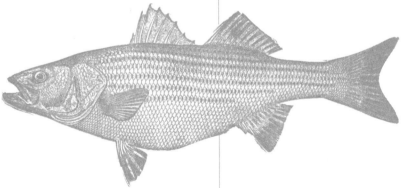

Grilled Striped Bass

Grilled "in the round" or whole, or with a couple of large fillets, this is a simple and easy way to showcase the delicate flavors of the striped bass, whether caught in the wild or farm-raised. Striped bass are also known as rockfish or stripers.

Hybrid striped bass are a cross between striped bass and white bass, and are a tasty alternative when their wild cousins are unavailable. There are several of these environmentally sound fish farms near the coastline in eastern North Carolina that began less than a decade ago but now produce over a million pounds of fish. You'll find them at your local inland fish market and upscale grocery stores.

1 whole striped bass, about 2 pounds or 4 skinless fillets, about 7 ounces each

4 tablespoons butter, melted

2 tablespoons finely chopped fresh parsley

2 tablespoons finely chopped scallions

½ teaspoon salt

Freshly ground pepper

2 tablespoons lemon juice

1 lemon, thinly sliced

1. Prepare or preheat grill. Coat either a fish basket or a perforated grill pan with nonstick spray.

2. Mix together butter, parsley, scallions, salt, pepper, and lemon juice. Brush butter mixture on fish or fillets, and if using whole fish, in the center cavity. Place lemon slices over fish.

3. Place fish on grill, cover, but baste occasionally with butter mixture until fish flakes easily, about 20 minutes and turning once for the whole fish, or about 8 to 10 minutes total for fillets, depending on thickness. Garnish with lemon slices.

YIELD: *4 servings*

Bluefish

"The blues are running . . . " is the song and title of a Broadway show written by the Chapel Hill–based Red Clay Ramblers, and aptly describes what happens on the North Carolina coast during the annual migration of bluefish.

During our honeymoon many years ago, my husband raced up the beach casting his line over and over, each time reeling in one big bluefish after another. I gathered his catch up in a big bucket until it just couldn't hold any more. Any more than one per person is a waste, anyway, because they are so perishable. Bluefish need to be cooked the day they are caught. That night we passed up an intimate romantic dinner in favor of feeding our neighbors.

Bluefish (*Pomatomus saltatrix*), known as the "bulldog of the ocean," are exciting to catch because they get into such a feeding frenzy. And with an incredible amount of teeth, you don't need to get your fingers or toes in their way. These fish migrate south, seasonally, to spawn, and show up on our coast during the late summer and early fall, although you might find them earlier during the summer.

An oily fish, bluefish are chock full of omega-3 fatty acids, so they're really good for you. However, some object to the strong fishy flavor of that dark, oily strip that runs down the center and discard it before eating.

Bluefish is best broiled or grilled and very good for smoking. To offset its high oil content, you need to prepare it with lemon or lime juice, and/or fresh tomatoes.

Broiled Bluefish

If you've spent a couple hours chasing the blues from the beach, you don't want to mess with much in the kitchen, especially after you have to clean your catch. This is such a simple recipe to prepare, and enhances the bluefish flavor.

4 8-ounce (more or less) bluefish fillets

2 tablespoons fresh lemon or lime juice

½ teaspoon chili powder

1 teaspoon salt

Freshly ground pepper

3 tablespoons (or more) freshly grated Parmesan cheese

1 tablespoon finely chopped parsley or cilantro

1. Preheat broiler. Line a shallow baking pan with foil, or coat with a nonstick cooking spray.

2. Rinse fillets and pat dry. Lay them in the pan, skin-side down. Sprinkle with lemon or lime juice, the chili powder, salt and pepper. Then lightly coat each fillet with the cheese.

3. Place fish under broiler, and cook, without turning, for about 7 to 8 minutes, or until fish are lightly browned.

4. Slide a spatula between the flesh of the fish and its skin, to remove the skin, when transferring the fish to individual plates, Sprinkle with the parsley or cilantro.

YIELD: *4 servings*

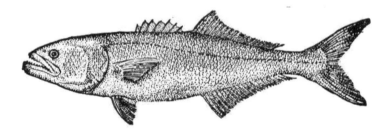

Bluefish Cakes

Jeanie Williams, ninety-four, grew up as a Kinnakeeter, although she lived in Manteo for most of her life. She serves these delicious fish cakes with tartar sauce.

1 3–4-pound bluefish, dressed

2 potatoes, peeled and diced

1 onion, diced

½ teaspoon salt

½ teaspoon black pepper

½ cup plain flour

2 tablespoons vegetable oil

1. Place bluefish in a large saucepan, and add just enough water to cover. Bring to a boil over high heat. Cover and simmer until the fish flakes. Drain.

2. Remove the fish from the skin and bones, and flake.

3. Meanwhile, boil potatoes until tender.

4. Mix together flaked bluefish, potatoes, and raw onion. Season with salt and pepper. Shape into patties. Roll in flour.

5. Heat oil over medium-high heat, then add fish cakes. Cook until browned on both sides and heated through.

YIELD: *12–14 cakes, 4–6 servings*

Mullet in the Round

"In the round" is a Carolina coastal expression that means dressed but not filleted, or rather, the whole, cleaned fish. Fishing buddies taught us how to make this dish.

4 small mullets, cleaned and dressed

1 cup water

1 small bunch spring onions, cut into ½-inch pieces

Salt and pepper to taste

FOR THE SAUCE:

½ cup white vinegar

½ teaspoon crushed red pepper

¼ teaspoon black pepper

1 teaspoon minced fresh garlic

½ teaspoon salt

Ground black pepper to taste

2 tablespoons butter

1. Place the fish in a sauté pan, and add water. Add onion, salt, and pepper. Cover and cook about 20 minutes, or until tender.

2. While fish is cooking, combine sauce ingredients in small saucepan, and heat until butter is melted.

3. When fish is done, pour sauce over, cover and continue to cook for 1 minute.

YIELD: *4 servings*

Mullet

Best known for their jumping ability, mullets (*Mugil cephalus*) don't get much more respect in North Carolina than the haircut so named does. Often seen as trash fish caught in backyard fishnets, they are sooner tossed than cooked in some households. However, the mullet's firm flesh is good enough to smoke, or to be used in a stew or deep-fat fried.

Mullet has lots of omega-3s and, because it's an oily fish, doesn't keep for long. But that makes it good for smoking. After cooking, remove the strong-tasting, oily dark flesh from the middle.

Old-timers along the North Carolina coast like the "pluck," or gizzard, from the mullet, which is dredged in flour and fried beside the fish, or sometimes fried in salt pork, then covered with water along with the mullet liver and cooked until tender. A more contemporary recipe calls for sautéing in butter, then seasoning with chopped parsley and lemon.

And why do mullets jump? They have a special air pocket that fills up during their leaps, which allows them more time on the bottom to feed.

Ocracoke Caviar: Roe Mullet

The plump, golden yellow roe of the gray mullet, caught during the fall off Ocracoke, in Albermarle Sound and along Bogue Banks, is considered quite a delicacy, perhaps more so in Taiwan than in North Carolina. There, eating it on New Year's Eve is a tradition that promises to bring you lots of good fortune during the year. Most of the commercial catch of roe mullet is sold to companies from the Far East, where even the rich and tender meat is used in rice noodle soup.

But a "mullet blow" during a cold front and a nor'easter is a tradition along the shores of the Outer Banks. Mullet come down south to spawn in inshore waters between October and December, then migrate back. One old Wanchese fisherman claimed roe mullet have their right eye to the shore when moving southward. Most roe mullet are caught in a four-mile stretch between Manns Harbor and Manteo, and then along the ocean shore at Ocracoke, using a seine net hauled from the beach in a dory and drawn back in using a tractor or truck. *Trick Oar Treat,* a dory owned by Ocracoke fishermen, hauled in 25,000 pounds on a recent Halloween.

"Ocracoke caviar" is traditionally deep-fat fried, like shad roe, or added to hush puppy batter.

chicken and duck

CHICKEN AND DUCK

Duck hunting has always been a successful endeavor in the sounds of the Outer Banks. Waterfowl migrate to the marshlands full of grasses and delicious bites of fish, and hunters migrate here in the cold winter months to bag their share.

Hunting was a huge industry here at the turn of the twentieth century, especially before stringent restrictions were made in the 1920s and '30s. More tourists came during the winter than the summer, with locals serving as their hunting guides. Hotels and their dining rooms took care of the comfort needs of those who did not belong to the exclusive "hunting clubs" lodged on many of the smaller islets in Pamlico and Currituck Sounds.

In *The Roanoke Island Womens Club Cookbook,* published during the 1960s, Mrs. Woodie Fearing shared this recipe:

> Parboil duck for five minutes with small piece celery and small sliced onion. Drain; rub inside and out with salt and pepper and pinch of ground ginger. Place inside duck a half of small onion, piece of apple studded with cloves and a small white potato. Bake 20 minutes at 450 degrees uncovered; reduce heat to 350 degrees and bake covered 15 to 20 minutes per pound. Baste with equal parts melted butter, hot water and red wine or orange juice.

An outdoorsman I spoke with told me this was how he prepared his wild duck:

Place duck in large baking pan. Salt and pepper inside and out. Add onions, carrots and potatoes. Pour one bottle of red wine over the duck. Bake at 350 degrees for about one hour. While duck is baking, open another bottle of red wine and drink. After the hour is up, remove duck from oven, and if inedible, throw duck away with empty bottles and open another bottle of wine.

On Roanoke Island, backyards in Wanchese and Manteo were "manicured" by each household's free roaming chickens. Chicken was not served any day, rather it was considered a special Sunday or company treat. And early Bankers did not have the luxury of boneless chicken breasts to cook in a hurry. They had to deal with the whole chicken, from its killing, plucking and cleaning to cutting it into pieces and then cooking. Few could master fried chicken as tender and succulent as well as Lola Browser, the servant who cooked for Della Basnight's grandmother. "There's nothing real good that black pepper don't make better," she is remembered as saying.

Pan-Roasted Duck Breasts

You can't "do" the Outer Banks without doing duck, given its history with hunting wild fowl, as well as the village of Duck on the northern Banks.

Mass-produced duck breasts are now available in most grocery stores, and the more robust, gourmet-style ones are available at specialty food stores or through the Internet. The less expensive, smaller breasts render a lovely dinner entree or salad that's easy, yet delicious.

This method of cooking is quick and simple. We have experimented with leaving the skin intact, removing the skin entirely, and this compromise, which seems to work the best both in the pan and on the grill.

4 small duck breast halves (about 8 ounces each)

2 teaspoons quatre epice, a French blend of ground pepper, cloves, nutmeg, and ginger, found in gourmet food stores

1 cup pinot noir wine

4 tablespoons cold butter

Salt and pepper to taste

1. Trim the skin on the duck breast by snipping and lifting the layer of skin from the edges of the breast. Cut away all but a 2-inch-wide strip of skin running down the middle of the breast. Score the skin in three places (cut through the top layer of skin but not meat). Reserve removed skin.

2. Rub the quatre epice into each breast, and let it sit for about 30 minutes.

3. When ready to cook, preheat oven to 400 degrees. Place reserved pieces of skin into a large skillet over medium heat. Render the skin to get enough fat to cover the bottom of the skillet. Remove pieces of skin.

4. Turn heat to medium-low, and add duck breasts, skin-side down. Cook until the skin is crisp and brown, about 8 to 10 minutes. Turn and cook for another 2 minutes. Remove duck breasts to an ovenproof platter, and place in heated oven, then turn oven off.

5. Turn heat for the skillet to medium-high, and when pan is hot, add wine, stirring to clean any duck residue from the pan. Continue to cook until wine is reduced to about 1/3 cup, about 5 minutes. Add butter, a tablespoon at a time, and stir until incorporated. Add salt and pepper to taste.

6. Place duck breasts on plates, and spoon wine sauce over.

YIELD: *4 servings*

The Whalehead Club was built as a private residence. It sat empty for decades until it was restored by Currituck County, and is now open for tours. Photo courtesy of Island Photography

Pan-Seared Duck Breast with Barley Risotto and Orange Confit

FOR THE ORANGE CONFIT:

10 oranges

¾ cup sugar

FOR THE BARLEY:

2 tablespoons butter

1 Vidalia onion, diced small

1 pound barley

½ cup white wine

4–5 cups vegetable stock

2 tablespoons chopped tarragon

Salt to taste

FOR THE DUCK:

4 duck breast halves

Salt and pepper to taste

2 tablespoons neutral oil (peanut or vegetable)

2 tablespoons butter

Rhett Elliott, one of the chefs at the acclaimed The Left Bank, the upscale restaurant of The Sanderling Resort & Spa, shared this recipe for duck breasts. Given the history of the waterfowl in the upper reaches of the Outer Banks, The Left Bank always includes duck on the menu.

TO PREPARE THE ORANGE CONFIT:

1. Cut 6 of the oranges into segments, and put in a heatproof container.

2. Juice the rest of the oranges until you get 1³/₄ cups.

3. Combine the juice and sugar, and simmer until the mixture coats the back of a spoon. Add the juice to the segments and let cool to room temperature.

TO PREPARE THE BARLEY:

1. In a medium saucepan, melt the butter over medium heat. When the foam subsides, add the Vidalia onion. Sweat for 3 minutes (there will be no color).

2. Add the barley and toss until well coated in butter. Add wine and reduce until there is no longer any smell of alcohol.

3. Add vegetable stock to cover by 1 inch, and lightly simmer. Begin to check after 30 minutes, and simmer until barley is cooked through, adding more stock as needed.

4. Add tarragon, season with salt, and reserve.

TO PREPARE THE DUCK:

1. Season duck with salt and pepper. Heat the oil in a medium sauté pan on medium-high heat. Add the duck, skin-side down, and cook until the skin is golden brown.

2. Reduce the heat to medium-low and flip the duck. Add the butter and baste for approximately 1 minute or until duck is cooked to medium. Let rest for 5 minutes.

TO ASSEMBLE THE DISH:

1. Divide the barley between four plates.

2. Thinly slice the duck breasts, and fan them onto the barley.

3. Spoon the confit on the duck. Serve immediately.

YIELD: *4 servings*

The Sanderling Resort & Spa

The Sanderling Resort & Spa is the premier resort of the Outer Banks, located five miles north of Duck, and touches both Currituck Sound and the Atlantic and neighboring Pine Island Audubon Sanctuary. Built in 1988, its cedar-shingled buildings reflect traditional architectural details found along North Carolina's coast.

Menus in both award-winning restaurants, The Left Bank and The Lifesaving Station, strive to highlight the bounty available from the waters they overlook.

The Lifesaving Station Restaurant is sited in exactly what its name implies—a restored building from 1899, filled with nautical artifacts. You can enjoy a range of appetizers, soups and salads, and lovely entrees and seafood, as well as special wine dinners. Executive chef Christine Zambito shared several lovely recipes here.

The Left Bank, as its name implies, takes some influence from the French while playing homage to contemporary American cuisine, while also playfully referring to its soundside location. It has earned the coveted AAA Four-Diamond Award, as well as a host of others. Expect a superb dining experience.

Grilled Duck Breasts on a Bed of Greens

4 duck breast halves (about 8 ounces each)

Salt and pepper to taste

4 large handfuls mixed greens, washed and dried

4 beets, roasted, skins removed, and quartered

½ cup toasted pecans

½ cup goat cheese, crumbled

FOR THE VINAIGRETTE:

2 tablespoons balsamic vinegar

6 tablespoons olive oil

1 teaspoon minced garlic

1 tablespoon chopped chives

½ teaspoon salt

Freshly ground pepper

Duck breasts can present quite a challenge when trying to grill or cook over high heat, as the large amount of fat under the skin can cause grease flare-ups and quickly char your delightful entree. So we've hit on this happy compromise, leaving a strip of skin on the breast, because removing the skin entirely makes it too dry.

Instead of the green salad, you may serve this with the Fresh Peach Salsa (page 134) and fresh steamed green beans.

1. Preheat grill. Trim the skin on the duck breast by snipping and lifting the layer of skin from the edges of the breast. Cut all but a 2-inch-wide strip of skin running down the middle of the breast. Score the skin in three places (cut through the top layer of skin but not meat). Reserve removed skin.

2. Salt and pepper each breast and, when grill is ready, place skin-side down. Do not cover with lid. Cook until skin is browned, about 8 minutes. Turn breasts over and cook for an additional 3 minutes, or until the internal temperature reads 140 degrees. Take breasts off grill, and allow them to rest for 5 minutes.

3. Meanwhile, place greens in a large bowl, and toss with vinaigrette. Divide evenly among four plates. Place beets to one side, then sprinkle the salad with the pecans and goat cheese. Season with salt and pepper as needed.

4. Cut each breast into thin slices, and fan onto individual plates by the salad. Dribble any collected juices over the duck meat. Serve immediately.

YIELD: *4 servings*

Bourbon Pecan Chicken

On the Back Road of the village of Ocracoke, The Back Porch Restaurant sits nestled among twisted live oaks. Owner Daphne Bennink recently expanded the restaurant's bar, since Ocracoke finally voted to allow mixed drinks.

North Carolina shrimp and crabmeat from the Cedar Island area are featured on the menu, along with fresh catches from local fisherman Hardy Plyler. But one of the more popular dishes, developed by former owner Debbie Wells, is this Bourbon Pecan Chicken, using two favorites on the Outer Banks—pecans and bourbon.

1. Whisk together mustard, sugar, bourbon, soy, and Worcestershire. Set aside.

2. Mix together pecans and bread crumbs. Press chicken breasts firmly into crumbs, coating well.

3. Heat 2 tablespoons butter in large skillet until bubbly hot. Add chicken breasts and cook until nicely browned on both sides and cooked through. If necessary, cook chicken in batches, wiping pan clean, and replenishing butter between batches.

4. In a small saucepan, bring the bourbon mixture to a low simmer, watching carefully. Remove from heat and, whisking constantly, add the 6 ounces of butter, one piece at a time. Allow each piece of butter to melt before adding another. Do not reheat sauce.

5. Arrange chicken on plates, allowing two pieces per serving. Pour sauce over chicken and sprinkle with sliced scallions.

YIELD: *4 servings*

½ cup Dijon mustard

¼ cup dark brown sugar

2 tablespoons plus 2 teaspoons bourbon

1 tablespoon soy sauce

1 teaspoon Worcestershire sauce

½ cup finely ground pecans

½ cup dry bread crumbs

4 double breasts of chicken, boned, trimmed and split into 8 pieces

4–6 tablespoons clarified butter

6 ounces chilled, unsalted butter, cut into 12 pieces

½ cup scallion tops, sliced into small rounds

Mrs. Tark's Sunday Stewed Chicken

2 whole chickens, about 3–4 pounds each, cleaned and plucked, head and feet removed

4 teaspoons salt, divided

3/4 teaspoon pepper, divided

4 cups plain flour

Boiling hot chicken broth

Ice water

At the Tarkington house in Manteo, the whole family looked forward to Sunday Dinner because they were certain to have chicken, which was not an everyday occurrence. This recipe was started on Saturday night; the pie bread, what Outer Bankers call pastry for dumplings, was made early Sunday morning; and the dish was completed after church.

Frank White, grandson of "Mrs. Tark," remembers having to chase down the chosen chicken, then watching the cook prepare it. For this recipe, cooks used old hens that had quit laying, because they could cook them until they became tender. Frank also remembers that if you mistakenly killed a chicken that had egg yolks in its egg bags, the cooks added those to the boiling broth to enrich the stew.

1. Cut up chickens and wash thoroughly. Put chicken pieces, with skin, in a very large pot and cover with water. Add 2 teaspoons salt and 1/2 teaspoon pepper, and bring to a boil. Simmer until chicken is tender, about 30 to 45 minutes.

2. While chicken is cooking, mix flour with remaining salt and pepper in a large bowl.

3. When chicken is tender, remove from broth and place in a large baking pan, while allowing the broth to continue to boil.

4. To make the pastry, make a "well" in the middle of the flour mixture, and stir in about 1 cup of the hot broth. Continue to add more broth, 1/4 cup at a time, until the flour is almost moistened enough to create a ball. Add 2 to 5 tablespoons of ice water until the dough forms a loose ball.

5. Lightly flour a work surface and your hands. Turn out dough and knead about 10 times until somewhat smooth. With a rolling pin, roll the dough to a 1/2-inch thickness.

6. Cut the dough into 2½-inch-wide strips, and hang them over the rim of the work bowl to dry. (At this point, Frank says "go to church," leaving the chicken broth, drying pastry, and chicken pieces.)

7. After several hours, or "after church," return the broth to a boil and place the pan of chicken in a 350-degree oven to heat and dry out slightly. When broth is boiling, drop the pieces of pastry carefully into the pot. Cover and cook for 20 minutes.

8. Remove chicken to a deep bowl or serving dish. Add pastry and ladle some broth over it to keep it moist. If desired, you may thicken the broth with a flour slurry (a bit of broth mixed with 2 or more tablespoons of flour, mixed, then added back to the broth).

9. To serve, pour more broth or thickened gravy over the chicken and pastry.

YIELD: *8 or more servings*

Chicken aux Pêches

8 3–4-ounce boneless, skinless
chicken breasts

Flour for dredging

4 tablespoons unsalted butter

2 tablespoons chopped onion

2 tablespoons chopped country ham

2 tablespoons sweet marsala

2 tablespoons chicken stock

1½ cups sliced fresh or canned
peaches

1 teaspoon cracked black pepper

At the Colington Café, Carlen Pearl strives to give local ingredients
a starring role on her menu. As her mother learned growing up in
Provence, France, Carlen gathers and preserves fresh, seasonal fruit, like
peaches from nearby Knotts Island, Currituck corn and strawberries,
and blackberries she picks from the thickets down near Salvo. Shrimp
comes from the surrounding sounds, and fishermen call on their cell
phones about the catch they're bringing in, like tuna or grouper.

With this recipe, Carlen likes this combination of sweet and salty,
with the country ham, marsala, and peaches. Serve it with rice pilaf.

1. Lightly dredge chicken breasts in lightly salted flour (reserve that
   flour). Heat butter in large sauté pan.

2. Add chicken breasts and onion. Saute for about 3 minutes each side.

3. Add ham. Sprinkle ½ teaspoon of reserved flour into pan. Slowly add
   marsala and chicken stock. Stir with a fork. With chicken still in pan,
   reduce liquid by half.

4. Add sliced peaches and cracked pepper. Cook for 1 minute.

5. Remove breasts to plates, and pour sauce on top.

VARIATION: If you want to prepare this recipe ahead of time, cook the
chicken breasts for 2 minutes on each side. After the liquid has cooked
down, turn the heat off and let the chicken sit. Refrigerate if it will be
more than 30 minutes before you plan to serve the meal. Before serving,
reheat the chicken, adding peaches at this time, and cook for another
minute.

YIELD: *4–8 servings*

vegetables and salad

VEGETABLES AND SALAD

Sometimes it's the side dishes—the vegetables and salads—that really make a meal or that hold a special place in some food lover's memory bank. Traditionally, Southerners serve two to four or more seasonal and fresh vegetables, along with at least one salad, to accompany a meal's meat or fish.

Most Outer Bankers grew what they could, especially tomatoes, cucumbers, and potatoes, in their backyard gardens. But sometimes they did not have easy access to fresh vegetables, and so they'd eat applesauce or canned fruits.

Today, in homes and restaurants along the Outer Banks, fresh, and when possible, local vegetables and marvelous salads play a starring role on menus.

The Island Farm on Roanoke Island

Peek into the whitewashed rooms of the restored main house at the Island Farm and wander among the reconstructed dairy, corncrib, and outdoor kitchen to get an idea of what life was like for a farm and fishing family during the 1840s on the northern end of Roanoke Island.

The Island Farm was the Etheridge Homeplace, first acquired by the family in 1783, and is typical of other farms on the island. Just before the Civil War, the farm produced corn, peas, Irish potatoes, sweet potatoes, pecans, figs, and grapes. There were sheep, cows, pigs, and chickens for the family's and farm workers' consumption.

Helen Etheridge Daniels, eighty-four, grew up on the property next to the Etheridge Homeplace, which at that time belonged to her uncle. Both are on high ground, all of 17 feet above sea level. And like the Etheridge Homeplace, her farm had sheep, to keep the grass down, and pigs and chickens. They kept barrels of salt in the dairy, one for fish, the other for pickles. Summer gardens yielded tomatoes, snap greens (in the South, green beans are snapped by hand into bite-size pieces), peas, greens, collards, corn, and watermelon. They also had peach, fig, and pear trees and Scuppernong grape arbors. Helen remembers sharing and trading food through all the hard times and storms, with neighbors and fishermen. "There was no welfare system, for everyone shared," she said.

The Island Farm opens to the public during the summer of 2008. They hope to have live animals, gardens growing, and interpretive guides that will offer an authentic look at what life used to be like on Roanoke Island.

Buttered Green Corn

Sweet corn, like Silver Queen or Princess varieties, comes into season during early June and July along North Carolina's coastal plain. You'll find roadside stands open as you approach the Outer Banks, and some local farmer markets once you're there.

Corn is a perfect accompaniment to all seafood, but sweet corn is a particularly good partner with crabmeat. This recipe makes a colorful presentation.

6 ears sweet corn, shucked and cleaned of silk

2 teaspoons salt, divided

1/3 pound asparagus (optional)

1/2 red pepper, roasted

4 tablespoons butter

2 tablespoons minced sweet onion (try North Carolina's Sweet Mattamuskeets)

1 tablespoon chopped fresh chives

1/2 teaspoon freshly ground black pepper

1. Fill a medium saucepan with water to a depth of 3 inches and 1 teaspoon salt, and bring to a boil.

2. Meanwhile, cut kernels from corncobs with a sharp knife.

3. Pour corn into boiling water and cook for 2 minutes. Drain, then refresh under cold running water and drain again. Set aside.

4. Cut asparagus into 2-inch pieces on the diagonal. Place in the saucepan, and barely cover with water. Set on stove on high heat, and bring to a boil. As soon as water boils, remove and drain. Refresh under cold running water to stop asparagus from cooking and to retain a brighter green color. Set aside.

5. If you need to roast the red pepper, place on a hot grill or under the broiler until skin is blackened on all sides. Remove from heat and allow to cool slightly. Peel blackened skin away, and remove core and seeds. Then, slice the 1/2 pepper needed for the recipe into thin slivers.

6. Melt butter in a large sauté pan. Add onion and stir for about 2 minutes, until onion is softened.

7. Add corn, asparagus, and red pepper to the pan, and stir to coat with butter. Sprinkle chives over the mixture, and season with remaining salt and pepper. As soon as vegetables are heated through, it's ready.

YIELD: *about 3 cups, or 4 servings*

Roasted Corn Salsa

Here's a colorful topping for grilled fish or chicken breasts. Roasting makes the corn caramelize, giving it a more intense, sweeter flavor. Pairing it with a vinaigrette makes a nice contrast of flavors.

1. Bring a large pot of water to boil. Add ears of corn, and cook just until tender, about 4 to 5 minutes. Remove from the water and allow ears to cool to your touch.

2. Preheat oven to 375 degrees.

3. Using a very sharp knife, set each ear of corn on its base inside a work bowl, and cut kernels from the cob. Pat dry with towels.

4. Toss cut kernels with olive oil, salt, and pepper. Spread evenly on a baking sheet, and bake until just beginning to brown, about 5 to 10 minutes. Allow corn to cool.

5. In a serving bowl, whisk together the vinegar, oil, and chives for the vinaigrette. Add the cooled corn, onion, and red pepper, and stir to coat the vegetables. Salt and pepper to taste.

YIELD: *about 2 cups*

6 ears corn, shucked and cleaned of silk

¼ cup olive oil

1 teaspoon sea salt

½ teaspoon freshly ground black pepper

2 tablespoons minced sweet onion (try North Carolina's Mattamuskeet Sweet)

2 tablespoons chopped fresh chives

¼ cup finely diced red pepper

FOR THE VINAIGRETTE:

3 tablespoons white wine vinegar

½ cup olive oil

1 tablespoon chopped basil

The Algonquians' Green Corn Celebrations

In the summer, when corn was ripe and abundant, the Algonquians celebrated with a huge feast, a Green Corn Celebration. The "green" or raw corn was roasted on the cob over a fire. However, most of the corn they grew was dried to provide for the winter and to make the meal for their breads.

The Green Corn Celebration was also a time for an annual cleaning ritual, not unlike our idea of spring cleaning. Algonquian women would purge their communal lodge and huts, cleaning out old foods, especially.

Corn Pudding

Corn pudding is a Southern favorite. This recipe adds onions, which are not a traditional ingredient but certainly gives the corn flavor a bit more zing. Try serving corn pudding with crab cakes, especially, or with simply prepared shrimp.

This recipe is similar to those found in old Outer Banks cookbooks, but is my adaptation from several of the women from the country church I grew up in.

2 tablespoons butter

¼ cup finely chopped sweet onion (Vidalia, or North Carolina's Mattamuskeet Sweet)

4 cups sweet white corn, fresh (4–6 ears), or frozen kernel corn, thawed and drained

½ cup sugar

2 tablespoons flour

½ teaspoon salt

½ teaspoon nutmeg

2 eggs, slightly beaten

¾ cup half-and-half

1 teaspoon vanilla

1. Preheat oven to 350 degrees. Butter a 2-quart casserole.

2. In a sauté pan, melt butter, and add onion. Stir over medium heat until onion is softened and translucent, about 3 minutes.

3. Add corn to a mixing bowl, then add onions. In a small bowl, mix together sugar, flour, salt, and nutmeg. Sprinkle over corn and onions.

4. Mix eggs, half-and-half, and vanilla, then pour over corn mixture. Gently stir until blended together.

5. Pour mixture into casserole, and bake for about 45 minutes to 1 hour, or until the middle of the pudding is set and slightly browned.

YIELD: *8 servings*

So Exactly
What Are Grits?

The Croatan tribe taught the early settlers how to grind dried corn kernels by rubbing two stones together, or by pounding huge wooden pestles in a tree stump. The coarser grind was grits, which allowed them to cook a mush that reminded the settlers of home. The finer grind was cornmeal, which gave them a daily bread. (The Italian version of a somewhat coarse grind of cornmeal made into a mush or porridge is known as polenta.)

The Indians also soaked dried corn kernels with lye, water that was run through ashes, to remove the outer coating to make hominy. Hominy was also dried for storage, then either reconstituted with water to make a stew, or ground to make what is called hominy grits. (Unless a package says it contains "hominy grits" you can assume you're getting "corn" grits.)

Cornmeal and grits that have been freshly ground at a local mill between two huge stones are ten times more flavorful than what you usually find on the grocery shelf. That's because the germ, the oily "innard" of the corn kernel, is retained, which gives the meal a more nutty taste and more texture. But because of that oil, stone-ground products can grow rancid, so keep them refrigerated and use within months of purchase. In contrast, commercial steel rollers produce a finer grind because that tasty germ is removed, making for longer shelf life but less taste. Yellow grits and cornmeal retain the outer kernel, which has been removed for the white varieties made from dried hominy. You can find stone-ground cornmeal and grits online if you reside outside of the South.

Classic Grits

Stone-ground grits, like most good things, are best done slow. The classic recipe is 1 part grits to 4 parts water, with salt and butter added to taste, cooked over very low heat with a watchful eye and a bit of stirring.

The coarser the grind, the stronger the corn taste, and those grits are excellent with just a little butter. With the finer grind typical of hominy grits, try milk or cream in place of some of the water. Also, if you are making shrimp and grits, use shrimp broth made from the shells saved from cleaning shrimp, or canned chicken broth to add more flavor.

4 cups water

1 teaspoon salt

1 cup stone-ground grits

4 tablespoons butter

1. Bring water to boil. Toss in the salt.

2. While stirring constantly, add grits slowly, in a steady stream. Lower heat to a simmer and stir occasionally.

3. The grits are ready when most of the water has been absorbed and they are tender, about 12 to 15 minutes. Stir in butter till melted.

YIELD: *4 servings*

Baked Cheese Grits Cakes

Cheese grits are a wonderful side dish for any meal. Instead of making thin "cakes" as below, cook the mixture in a deep, buttered casserole dish for about 40 minutes.

1. Preheat oven to 350 degrees. Line a shallow 10- by 15-inch baking pan with foil, and spray lightly with nonstick cooking spray.

2. Bring water and milk to a boil in a large saucepan. Toss in the salt. While stirring constantly, add grits slowly, in a steady stream. Lower heat to a simmer and stir occasionally.

3. Meanwhile, in a medium bowl, beat eggs, then add cheese and cayenne pepper.

4. After about 10 minutes, when most of water has been absorbed in the grits, add the egg and cheese mixture. Continue to cook over low heat, stirring constantly, until eggs are cooked and cheese is melted.

5. Immediately pour mixture onto prepared baking pan. Spread to about a 1-inch thickness.

6. Place in oven and bake for about 20 to 30 minutes, or until semi-firm to the touch.

7. Cool, then refrigerate for at least 1 hour.

YIELD: *4 servings as side dish*

2 cups water

1 cup milk

1 teaspoon salt

¾ cup stone-ground grits

3 eggs

1 cup grated cheese (Parmesan or Asiago)

¼ teaspoon cayenne pepper

Scraped Potato Pudding

Sweet potatoes grow prolifically in the loamy soil of North Carolina's coastal plain, and have always been a staple in Outer Banks pantries. Mrs. Ivadean Priest, of Manteo, shared this recipe that has earned her compliments over the last six decades. She combines all ingredients except the sweet potatoes first, then grates, or as some Bankers say, "scrapes" the potatoes, so that they are not exposed to the air long enough to turn brown.

1 cup sugar

4 eggs

½ stick (4 tablespoons) butter, melted

1 12-ounce can Carnation evaporated milk

2 tablespoons water

1 cap of vanilla (1 teaspoon)

3 cups scraped (grated) sweet potatoes (about 2 potatoes)

1. Preheat oven to 350 degrees. Butter a shallow brownie pan (8 inches square).

2. Mix together sugar, eggs, melted butter, evaporated milk, water, and vanilla.

3. Grate the potatoes, then quickly add to the milk mixture.

4. Pour into prepared pan, and place in oven. Bake for about 45 minutes to 1 hour, or until pudding is set in the middle.

YIELD: *8 servings*

Ocracoke's Veggies

Surprisingly, vegetables seem to thrive in backyard gardens on Ocracoke in spite of the sandy soil. Asparagus reportedly grows wild, and beets grow large but sweet, as do tomatoes and green beans. But storms and too-hot weather can wreak havoc with Bankers' gardens, and with no grocery stores available, old-time residents of this rather isolated island looked forward to the vegetable truck that used to arrive by ferry every Wednesday morning.

Fresh Tomato and Mozzarella Salad

Annie Davis, owner/chef at The Great Gut Deli in Wanchese, buys her tomatoes fresh from local grower Bubba Livezay. This recipe is best when fresh, juicy summertime tomatoes are available.

1. Cut tomatoes into thick slices. Salt them, then place on paper towels and refrigerate for about 1 hour. (Annie says this will help get the moisture out of the tomatoes so they are not so runny.)

2. Pat mozzarella dry. Cut into thin slices (try for 8).

3. On each serving plate, begin with a slice of tomato, then stack mozzarella between tomatoes, alternating colors.

4. Stack basil leaves, roll together, then thinly slice. Sprinkle the basil over the stack.

5. Sprinkle each plate with olive oil, balsamic vinegar, salt and freshly ground pepper to taste.

YIELD: *4 servings*

2 large yellow tomatoes

2 large red tomatoes

8 ounces fresh mozzarella

Handful of fresh basil leaves

Extra-virgin olive oil

Balsamic vinegar

Salt and pepper to taste

Juicy, red ripe heirloom tomatoes provide summertime delights. E F Wiegand

Fire-and-Ice Cukes

4–5 small pickling cucumbers

2 tablespoons apple cider vinegar

Salt to taste

½ teaspoon freshly ground black pepper

½ teaspoon Tabasco sauce or to taste

6 or so regular-size ice cubes

Cucumber slices in vinegar were served at every meal on most Southern tables during the summer months. Sometimes tomatoes were added. And in some families, onions were not allowed; in others, it was mandatory. This version, from the Basnight family of Manteo, spices up the cool of the cucumbers with a dash of hot sauce. Della Basnight remembers her mother taking a fork to the sides of the cucumber, striating it so that it would absorb more vinegar.

1. Carefully skin the cucumbers, then slice thin.

2. In a medium-size bowl, mix together the vinegar, salt, pepper, and Tabasco sauce.

3. Add cucumbers, and stir to coat. Add ice cubes, and stir. Place in refrigerator until ready to serve. Stir to blend in melted ice, and serve with a serving spoon which allows the liquid to be drained.

YIELD: *4 servings as side dish*

Cilantro-Lime Slaw

1 small head of cabbage, shredded

½ cup chopped fresh cilantro

½ cup olive oil

¼ cup rice wine vinegar

¼ cup honey

Salt and freshly ground pepper to taste

2 limes, juiced

At the Red Sky Café, Chef Wes Stepp pairs this slaw with flounder and other fish.

1. Combine all ingredients except for lime juice. Chill in the refrigerator for 30 minutes.

2. When ready to serve, toss with lime juice.

YIELD: *4 servings as side dish*

Rice Salad

Salads made with rice are great during the heat of the summer, because they can be made ahead and are easily portable for picnics or boat outings. This savory salad was designed by Chef Wes Stepp of the Red Sky Café in Duck.

1. In a large bowl, place rice and separate grains.

2. Meanwhile, if using fresh, hulled peas, place in a small saucepan with just enough water to cover. Bring to a boil, then turn heat down and simmer until peas are tender, about 15 minutes. Drain, and cool slightly before adding to rice. If using canned peas, rinse in a colander and drain before adding to rice.

3. Add onion and peppers to the rice mixture.

4. In a small bowl, whisk together the olive oil, vinegar, salt and ground pepper, and sugar. Pour over rice mixture and gently combine all ingredients. Sprinkle the basil chiffonade over the top of the salad.

5. Serve at room temperature. May also be made ahead, refrigerated, and served chilled.

YIELD: *4 servings*

3 cups cooked white rice, cooled

½ cup fresh or canned black-eyed peas

½ cup canned chickpeas, rinsed

1 small onion, diced

¼ cup each diced yellow and red pepper

¼ cup olive oil

¼ cup rice wine vinegar

Salt and freshly ground pepper to taste

Pinch of sugar

2 tablespoons basil, cut into strips (chiffonade)

Waxed Poetic Potato Salad

With this version of potato salad, you don't have to worry so much about it being exposed to the summer heat, as it does not include mayonnaise but rather a tangy vinaigrette. Make sure you use waxy potatoes, like Yukon Gold or red-skinned potatoes, because they hold their shape better, and you don't really have to peel them.

6 cups chopped red-skinned or Yukon Gold potatoes with skin (about 1-inch cubes)

½ cup finely chopped red or sweet onion, to your taste

2 tablespoons minced fresh parsley

2 tablespoons minced fresh chives

¼ cup chopped and pitted oil-cured black olives

FOR THE VINAIGRETTE:

¼ white wine vinegar

2 tablespoons Dijon mustard

2 teaspoons salt

½–1 teaspoon freshly ground black pepper, to taste

½ cup olive oil

1. Place potatoes in the top of a double boiler, and steam over high heat for about 20 minutes or until potatoes are tender.

2. Place potatoes in a large bowl, and allow to cool for about 10 minutes. Add onion, parsley, chives, and olives to the bowl.

3. Mix vinaigrette in a small bowl by whisking together the vinegar, mustard, salt, and pepper. Then, add the olive oil in a steady stream while constantly whisking. Whisk until mixture is thick (emulsified).

4. Pour vinaigrette over potato mixture and gently stir. Taste for seasoning and add more salt and pepper if desired.

YIELD: *6–8 servings*

Jalapeño Potato Salad

Like a lot of good recipes, this one happened from a mistake. "One of my line cooks accidentally put in jalapeño peppers instead of green bell peppers, and the result was, well, we liked it," says Tom Lozupone, chef and director of operations of Stripers Bar & Grille overlooking Shallowbag Bay in Manteo. It's become a restaurant favorite.

Here's a helpful hint: Chef Lozupone recommends soaking the potatoes overnight covered with water in the refrigerator.

1. Place potatoes in a stock pot and cover with water. Place on high heat and bring to a boil, stirring often. Boil for 5 minutes, then drain potatoes well, and let cool to room temperature.

2. After potatoes have cooled, mix all ingredients in a large mixing bowl.

3. Refrigerate, and serve cold.

YIELD: *2 quarts*

8 cups (2 quarts) red potatoes, chopped into ½-inch dice

4 stalks celery, chopped into ¼-inch dice

¼ cup chopped green onions

½ cup pickle relish

¼ cup Dijon mustard

2 tablespoons minced jalapeño pepper (2–4 jalapeños, depending on size)

1 cup mayonnaise

2 teaspoons kosher salt

2 teaspoons coarsely ground black pepper

Pony Potatoes

The Pony Island Restaurant on Ocracoke is known for its big, Southern-style breakfasts, offering herring roe in season, fish cakes with eggs, and these hashed brown potatoes. Local flounder, drum, green tail shrimp, and salty oysters caught nearby are lunch and nightly features.

Owner and chef Vince O'Neal comes from one of the first families to settle at the port of Ocracoke, many of them known as good cooks. His mother continues to make the crab cakes and pies. Vince got an early start in the restaurant business, working in the dining room of the Island Inn when he was just eleven years old.

4 tablespoons butter

About 4 cups diced and peeled potatoes (thawed, if frozen)

Salt and pepper to taste

½ cup grated mozzarella cheese

½ cup grated American cheese

½–1 cup prepared salsa

½ cup sour cream

1. Melt butter in iron skillet over medium-high heat. Add potatoes, and cook until brown. Salt and pepper to taste.

2. Divide potatoes among four plates. Season with salt and pepper, then sprinkle with cheeses.

3. Place plates either in the microwave or under a broiler to melt cheese. Then top with salsa and sour cream.

YIELD: *4 side servings*

Roasted New Potatoes

This is such an easy way to make an accompaniment for grilled or roasted fish, chicken, or steaks. You may also use any fresh herb to complement your main dish, like rosemary with lamb or steak, chives with grilled fish. Kosher salt, which is more coarse, tends to stick with the potatoes better when they are stirred in the oven. If the baby size is not available, use large red-skinned potatoes cut into bite-size chunks.

1. Preheat oven to 375 degrees.

2. Wash, then dry potatoes.

3. Place in a large mixing bowl, and pour enough olive oil over to coat, stirring the potatoes. Add the herbs, if desired, and stir to combine.

4. Place potatoes in large ceramic baking dish or on foil-lined baking sheet. Sprinkle with kosher salt. Bake for about 45 minutes, or more if you prefer a more browned, crisp skin. During baking time, stir potatoes around. You may need a spatula to help move the potatoes. Serve warm.

YIELD: *1 serving*

PER SERVING:

4–6 baby-size new potatoes or 1 cup chunked red-skinned potatoes

Olive oil

1–2 tablespoons chopped fresh herbs (optional)

Kosher salt

Potato Sheds

In days past, potatoes and sweet potatoes were stored in a potato shed, a cavity dug several feet into the ground where the potatoes were laid, with a roof and maybe three walls built over it. Straw was spread over the potatoes during colder months. Sometimes folks just dug a "potato hill," a hole in the ground where the potatoes would be piled, then covered back with the dirt.

Manteo native Mrs. Natalie Gould Mandell, eighty-nine, recalls when she was a little girl, the potato shed's roof was like a sliding board to her, providing her with some home-grown fun. She grew up within the confines of the old Tranquil House Inn in Manteo, which was self-sustaining with its vegetable garden, chickens, pigs and cows.

Stewed Tomatoes

Here's a recipe that shows how the Bankers always prepared for future meals. Jeanie Williams's father loved tomatoes, and could hardly wait for those in his summer garden in Avon to ripen. There was always an abundance of tomatoes, so she learned early in her cooking days to can, then later freeze, tomatoes for cold winter days. Her husband, a radio operator with the Coast Guard, always went out fishing on Fridays, and requested this dish to help him warm up when he got back. She served it with the fish he caught, or with fried herring roe. At age ninety-four, she still prepares these for her son.

5–7 medium-size ripe tomatoes, chopped, or 1 quart frozen tomatoes with juice, thawed

1 tablespoon sugar

2 cold biscuits, crumbled

1 tablespoon butter

Salt and pepper to taste

1. Put tomatoes and juice into a saucepan. If using fresh tomatoes, softly boil for 5 to 10 minutes. Add sugar, crumbled biscuits, and butter. Season with salt and pepper to taste.

2. Bring mixture slowly back to a boil.

3. Remove from heat and serve warm.

YIELD: *Serves 4*

Freezing Tomatoes

Jeanie Williams freezes tomatoes when they are at their peak during the summer. She makes a cross cut on their bottom half, then places them in boiling water for just a minute to make them easier to peel. She then places them in resealable plastic bags and stows them in the freezer.

For stewed tomatoes, she simmers peeled tomatoes for 5 to 10 minutes, then freezes the mixture in quart-size containers.

The First Outer Banks Inn

The original Tranquil House Inn was built in downtown Manteo and took up an entire city block. It burned and was rebuilt in 1898 as the Roanoke Inn, which also burned in the 1950s. Natalie Gould Mandell, now eighty-nine, remembers how self-sufficient her family's hotel was, with its own garden, chickens, and pigs. She and her three sisters had lots of chores, and even as a very young child, she gathered the eggs daily.

In the 1890s, her father, Nathaniel Gould, fell in love with the area's abundance of waterfowl, as well as a local girl. Together they ran both the inn, bought in 1898, and two hunting lodges near Bodie Island and Pea Island for Mr. Gould's cronies back in Cape Cod, Massachusetts. Which explains the menu served every Saturday night that included clam chowder, baked beans, and brown bread, with ham and apple dumplings.

Winter was the busiest time of the year for them, with hunters from "up North" flocking to the Outer Banks until hunting restrictions were enacted during the late 1920s and '30s. Her father also performed some of the first beach "renourishment," building crude "fences" from driftwood and flotsam from the ocean to build up sand dunes to help stabilize the beach at Bodie Island. When a ridge of dunes formed, he sowed sea oats. He hoped his efforts would keep the ocean from overwashing the ponds he maintained for waterfowl hunting.

Natalie left Manteo when she was nineteen to work and live abroad, but returned at age eighty. Meanwhile, one of her three sisters continued the family tradition, running the Arlington Hotel and the Seafare restaurant in Nags Head. Nephews and nieces continue to own or work in restaurants on the Outer Banks.

Baked Beans

This is a family recipe that was also served at the first hotel on Cape Cod that Nathaniel Gould owned before he migrated south to the Outer Banks.

1 pound smallest-possible pea beans

2 square inches salt pork

½ tablespoon light brown sugar

2 whole onions, sliced

1 cup molasses

Salt and pepper to taste

1 teaspoon Worcestershire sauce

2 tablespoons rum (a little splash)

1 tablespoon ketchup

1. Place beans in a pot and cover with water. Soak for at least 2 hours, then drain.

2. Place beans on burner over medium-high heat. Add enough boiling water to cover. When beans begin to boil, reduce the heat and simmer for 30 minutes.

3. Preheat the oven to 225 degrees.

4. Dredge the salt pork in the brown sugar. Lay in the bottom of a bean pot or casserole dish. Put the onion slices on top of the salt pork. Submerge them in molasses. ("A real old recipe calls for 2 glugs.")

5. Scoop beans from their water and add to the bean pot over the bottom ingredients. Then sprinkle with salt, pepper, Worcestershire sauce, and rum. Add enough of the water in which the beans boiled to fill the pot. Do not stir.

6. Cover the bean pot or casserole with a lid or tightly fitting aluminum foil.

7. Place in oven for 6 hours. Do not stir during this time.

8. After cooking, remove 1 cup of beans, and mash to a paste. Add ketchup, and then stir into bean pot to thicken it. Stir gently to keep from breaking the beans.

9. Remove the onion and throw it away. Remove the salt pork, and thinly slice and then return it to the bean pot. Reheat in the oven for a few minutes, then serve.

YIELD: *8 servings or more*

Mixed Salad with Spiced Peaches and Sugared Pecans

The sweetness of the peaches and pecans—two delicious products available near the Outer Banks—make a delightful pairing with shrimp or fish.

1. To toast pecans, preheat oven to 325 degrees. Line a baking sheet with foil. In a large bowl, combine corn syrup, butter, egg white, and cinnamon. Add pecans and stir until evenly coated. Spread pecans in one layer on baking sheet. Bake for 12 to 16 minutes or until a deep golden brown. Remove from oven and cool.

2. In a medium bowl, whisk together orange juice, vanilla, cinnamon, and cloves. Thinly slice peaches, add to mixture, and gently stir until coated.

3. Make the vinaigrette by whisking together the balsamic vinegar, salt, and pepper in a small bowl. Slowly whisk in the olive oil (or use a small jar with a lid and shake till emulsified.)

4. Arrange the salad by dividing the greens among six plates. Drizzle the vinaigrette over the greens. Sprinkle a handful of pecans over each plate, then arrange the peaches over the salads, leaving space for a mound of steamed shrimp or grilled grouper in the middle.

YIELD: *4–6 servings*

FOR THE PECANS:

2 tablespoons light corn syrup

3 tablespoons butter, melted

1 large egg white

½ teaspoon cinnamon

2 cups pecan halves

FOR THE PEACHES:

2 tablespoons orange juice

1 teaspoon vanilla extract

½ teaspoon cinnamon

$1/8$ teaspoon ground cloves

3–4 peaches, peeled

FOR THE VINAIGRETTE:

2 tablespoons balsamic vinegar

Salt and pepper to taste

¼ cup olive oil

FOR THE SALAD:

5–6 cups mixed baby greens (1 bag)

1½ cups (1 pound) steamed shrimp, or flaked grilled grouper (about 1 pound) seasoned with 1 teaspoon Old Bay seasoning

Tarkington Household Boiled Dinner

½ smoked ham hock

8 pounds green beans, trimmed and washed

15 small new or red potatoes, or larger ones cut into chunks

2 cups white, medium-grind cornmeal

1 teaspoon salt

1 tablespoon sugar

Black pepper to taste (¼ teaspoon)

2–5 tablespoons of ice water

Frank White is a retired professor of marketing who moved back to his native Manteo and is now involved in local theater productions. He remembers how boiled dinners easily and efficiently fed many Southerners and particularly Outer Bankers, who had to make do with what they had because of their isolation. Salt pork, a ham hock, or streak of lean (similar to bacon) offered the meat flavoring for the vegetables simmered or "boiled" together. A seasonal green vegetable, like collards or cabbage during the winter, played the leading role. Frank's family was fond of Kentucky Wonder green beans. Potatoes and carrots stretched the meal even further.

But the best part was the cornmeal dumplings that were floated on top of the broth, says Frank. A staple in older Outer Banks kitchens, they are a bit tricky to produce, but well worth the effort.

1. Wash salt off ham hock in cold water, and trim if necessary. Leave the fat on the ham, if desired, for flavor.

2. "Snap" or cut the beans into 2-inch lengths.

3. Put ham in a very large kettle, and cover with cold, salted water. Place on high heat, and bring to a rapid boil, then reduce heat to low and simmer until ham is almost done and tender.

4. Add the beans to the pot, and continue to simmer for about 45 minutes or until bean are almost tender. Add the potatoes to the pot, and continue to cook until they are knife-tender.

5. Taste the broth and beans and add salt if necessary.

6. Remove the ham, beans, and potatoes from the boiling pot and keep them warm.

7. Make the cornmeal dumplings: In a medium bowl, combine the cornmeal, salt, sugar, and black pepper with a whisk.

8. Add about 2 cups of the hot liquid from the pot of green beans (mixture will not be very moist.) Add enough ice water just until the mixture sticks together. Frank says that when you press the mixture with your finger, your fingerprint should remain.

9. Wet both of your hands. Using a generous $1/2$ to $3/4$ cup of the cornmeal mixture, form patties that are $3/4$ thick. Drop patties into the boiling pot liquid. Cover and cook for about 20 to 25 minutes.

10. To serve, place the warm vegetables into individual, shallow soup bowls, and cover with a little hot liquid. Place dumplings on top.

YIELD: *10–12 servings*

sauces and dressings

SAUCES AND DRESSINGS

The finishing touch to many dishes is a dollop of herbed-flavored mayonnaise, a puddle of buttery sauce, or a zing of spicy salsa. And of course, what really makes a salad is the blend of oil, herbs, and acid used to provide its final dressing. Sometimes, as well, it's the marvelous blend of spices imparted in a marinade that starts a dish well on its delicious way.

Contemporary Outer Banks chefs use their creativity, training, and experience to provide just the right seasonings and flavors to enhance their final products. Here are some recipes they've shared.

Creamy Ginger Dressing

This is a frequently requested recipe from the Red Sky Café. Chef Wes Stepp dresses greens, carrots, Granny Smith apples, and cukes with this simple yet delightful combination of flavors.

Combine all ingredients thoroughly in a food processor. May be stored in the refrigerator for 2 to 3 days.

YIELD: *about 2 cups*

1 cup mayonnaise

½ cup rice wine vinegar

½ cup pickled ginger

2 tablespoons finely chopped cilantro

Salt and freshly ground pepper to taste

Pinch of sugar

Fresh Basil Vinaigrette

At The Great Gut Deli in Wanchese, Annie Mancini Davis uses recipes from her Italian heritage for her fabulous meatball sandwiches, salads, and this vinaigrette. "Extra-virgin olive oil," she says, "makes any food a meal." She grabs a handful of fresh basil from her garden outside the deli at Thicket Lump Marina. The recipe can be easily multiplied for the amount you need.

1. Place red wine vinegar in small mixing bowl or jar with lid. Whisk or mix in salt, pepper, basil, and garlic.
2. If using a bowl, slowly add oil in a small, steady stream while whisking constantly. If using a jar, add oil, then shake vigorously.
3. Taste for seasonings and correct if necessary.

YIELD: *about 1 cup*

¼ cup red wine vinegar

½ teaspoon salt

¼ teaspoon freshly ground pepper

1–2 tablespoons chopped fresh basil, to taste

1 small clove garlic, minced

¾ cup extra-virgin olive oil

Elizabeth's Café
Wine-Friendly Salad Dressing

¼ cup lightly toasted pecans

1 tablespoon honey

$^1/_3$ cup chardonnay

½ cup canola oil

½ cup extra-virgin olive oil

Nothing can mar the taste of wine quicker than a salad's vinaigrette, and that's because of the vinegar, lemon, or salt , says Leonard Logan, owner of Elizabeth's Café. This charming upscale restaurant is nestled among the live oaks at Scarborough Faire in Duck. Years of experience and training enable Logan to pair each course of his fixed price menu with the perfect wine, earning the cafe national accolades and awards.

Instead of vinegar, use a good chardonnay in your vinaigrette, he says. "We use Joseph Drouhin Bourgogne Blanc, a French burgundy, because it is acidic and not very buttery like most California chardonnays. A North Carolina chardonnay may also work. You can pour the same wine to drink as you use in the dressing, but always use a good wine."

Just like water and oil do not mix, neither do wine and oil, says Logan. "You must use something as an emulsification agent, so we use lightly toasted pecans which also contain some oil and thicken the dressing."

Any time you cook with wine or allow the alcohol to evaporate, you must add some sweetener, he advises. "We never use sugar, but rather a little honey. Add any fresh herbs you like." And he warns that you should make only the quantity you need. "Don't hold the dressing in the refrigerator after your party, as nuts tend to go rancid."

The head chef at Elizabeth's Café, Brad Price, gave this practical recipe with proportions for home cooks.

1. Place pecans, honey and chardonnay in blender. Blend until nuts are pulverized.

2. With the top opened while blending, slowly add both oils and continue to process until dressing is thick and emulsified.

3. Dressing should be used immediately.

YIELD: *about 1$^1/_2$ cups*

Chile-Lime Vinaigrette

This vinaigrette is excellent on a salad topped with shrimp or fish, or as a marinade for seafood prior to grilling.

1. Place all ingredients minus the oil in a blender, and pulse several times until mixture is pureed.

2. With blender running, slowly add oil, then blend until mixture is thickened, about 20 seconds.

YIELD: *1¹/₂ cups*

4 tablespoons fresh lime juice

1 tablespoon vinegar, preferably red wine vinegar

½ teaspoon cayenne pepper

1 tablespoon minced fresh garlic

2 tablespoons minced sweet onion (try North Carolina's Mattamuskeet Sweet)

2 tablespoons minced fresh cilantro

1 tablespoon minced jalapeño pepper

½ teaspoon salt

Several grinds fresh black pepper

1 cup canola oil

Cocktail Sauce

It's easy to mix up your own cocktail sauce for shrimp or other shellfish. Be sure to make it ahead so that it will be chilled.

1 cup ketchup

2 tablespoons prepared horseradish (or to taste)

1 tablespoon lemon juice

1 teaspoon Worcestershire sauce

1/8 teaspoon freshly ground black pepper

1. In a small bowl, mix all ingredients thoroughly,
2. Refrigerate until chilled, about 1 hour.

YIELD: *1 cup*

Lynne Foster's Secret Sauce

Lynne Foster of Hatteras is an intuitive cook who seldom measures the spices, oils, or special sauces from her well-stocked pantry. She grows her own herbs year-round in an aeroponics garden, and uses her experiences of traveling around the world to develop her culinary magic. Here is one of her tricks to serve with fish. She keeps a fresh batch ready in her refrigerator all summer.

½ cup mayonnaise

¼ cup Dijon mustard

1 teaspoon fresh tarragon, minced

Mix all together. Store in refrigerator until ready to use.

YIELD: *1/2 cup*

Tomato and Black Olive Salsa

When summer tomatoes start rolling in, it's easy to indulge in a variety of preparations to take care of the bounty as well as satisfy your taste buds.

This colorful combination can top green salads, toasted garlic bruschetta, or grilled scallops or fish.

1. Seed and chop tomatoes, and place in medium-size bowl.
2. Pit and chop olives, then add to tomatoes.
3. Stack basil leaves together, roll into a tube, then thinly slice (chiffonade). Add to the tomato mixture. Add garlic and scallions.
4. In a small bowl or jar, combine oil, vinegar, salt, and pepper. Thoroughly mix until blended. Spread over tomato mixture, then gently stir in.
5. Allow dressing to sit for about 30 minutes at room temperature to allow flavors to meld.

YIELD: *about 1½ cups*

3–4 large, ripe tomatoes

½ cup black olives, preferably kalamata or other oil-cured olives

1 small bunch basil

1 medium clove garlic, minced

2 tablespoons thinly sliced scallions

4 tablespoons olive oil

2 tablespoons red wine vinegar

1 teaspoon salt

½ teaspoon freshly ground black pepper

Green Tomato Salsa

This is a great complement to fish tacos, grilled shrimp, or fried oysters.

Mix all ingredients together. Taste for seasoning. Refrigerate.

YIELD: *1½ cups*

1 cup green tomatoes, chopped (about ½ pound)

¼ cup finely chopped sweet onion

2 tablespoons finely chopped cilantro

½ teaspoon Tabasco sauce, or more to taste

1 tablespoon vinegar

1 teaspoon lime juice

2 tablespoons olive oil

1 teaspoon salt

Freshly ground pepper

Cucumber Vinaigrette

Chef West Stepp of the Red Sky Café in Duck serves this colorful combination as a cooling effect for his Wasabi Sesame Tuna (see page 199). It's good served with any fish or shellfish, or to mix with greens for a tasty salad.

1 cup cubed cucumber (peeled and seeded)

½ red onion, diced

¼ each sweet red and yellow pepper, diced

1 red tomato, diced

1 tablespoon cilantro, chopped

2 tablespoons rice wine vinegar

3 tablespoons olive oil

Pinch of sugar

Salt and freshly ground pepper to taste

Combine all ingredients in a small bowl.

YIELD: *about 2 cups*

Summer Tomato and Sweet Pepper Vinaigrette

Chef Wes Stepp of the Red Sky Café in Duck uses this to top pan-seared rockfish, when in season, or swordfish steaks. And it's especially good with a spinach salad.

3 vine-ripened red tomatoes, cored and diced

½ sweet red pepper, diced

½ sweet or red onion, finely diced

1 jalapeño pepper, seeded and diced

1 tablespoon fresh cilantro

3 tablespoons rice wine vinegar

2 tablespoons olive oil

½ teaspoon sugar

Salt and freshly ground pepper to taste

Combine all ingredients. Taste for seasoning.

YIELD: *about 1½ cups*

Lime-Mustard Aioli

Store-bought mayonnaise can be flavored with a variety of juices and spices. This particular aioli is a good accompaniment to grilled or fried shrimp, scallops, or fish.

Combine all ingredients in a small bowl and mix well. Refrigerate until ready to use.

YIELD: *about 1 1/3 cups*

1 cup mayonnaise

5 tablespoons Dijon mustard

¼ cup lime juice

½ teaspoon salt

½ teaspoon white ground pepper

Wasabi Aioli

This is a great topping for grilled, broiled, or fried fish. Chef Tom Lozupone, of Stripers Bar & Grille on Shallowbag Bay in Manteo, who shared this recipe, suggests pairing this with grilled fresh rockfish.

1. In a large mixing bowl, dissolve the wasabi powder in the rice wine vinegar.
2. Whisk in the oil and mayonnaise, blending until fully incorporated.
3. Serve as a topping on fish. May be stored in the refrigerator for up to 3 weeks.

YIELD: *1 1/2 cups*

¼ cup wasabi powder, high grade

6 tablespoons (3 ounces) rice wine vinegar

¼ cup blended oil (Tom uses 3 parts olive oil blended with 1 part vegetable oil)

1 cup mayonnaise

Chipotle Aioli

This adds a final, extra punch to so many seafood preparations. Drizzle it over crab-stuffed tilefish or flounder, use it on fried soft-shells, or spread it on bread for a kicker of a fish sandwich.

Chipotle can be hot, so be sure not to get it too overpowering for your tastes. You can save the rest of the canned chipotles in the refrigerator.

1 cup mayonnaise

1 tablespoon chopped chipotle chiles packed in adobo sauce

1 teaspoon adobo sauce

1 tablespoon lime juice

Pinch of salt

Grind of black pepper

1 tablespoon finely chopped chives

1. In a small mixing bowl, gently mix all ingredients together.

2. If you would like to be able to drizzle the dressing, put it in a recycled mustard/ketchup squeeze bottle; or pour into a small ziplock bag, make a small diagonal cut off a corner of the bag, and squeeze.

YIELD: *about 1 cup*

Chipotle-Soy Mustard

Some fish tend to need a little something extra to enhance the taste. Tom Lozupone, chef at Stripers Bar & Grille overlooking Shallowbag Bay, developed this recipe to serve with broiled, grilled, or fried fish.

½ cup soy sauce

½ cup Dijon mustard

1 teaspoon minced garlic

2 tablespoons canned chipotle chiles, pureed

½ teaspoon kosher salt

2 cups blended oil (Tom uses 3 parts olive oil blended with 1 part vegetable oil)

1. Place soy sauce, mustard, garlic, chipotle chiles, and salt into a blender. Blend on low until thoroughly mixed.

2. Slowly add 2 cups oil from the top of the blender, while mixing. Blend until thoroughly incorporated.

3. Serve on top of fish, or on the side if preferred.

4. Can be refrigerated for up to 3 weeks.

YIELD: *3 cups*

Chimichurri Marinade

Chef Wes Stepp, of the Red Sky Café, uses this marinade also as a sauce, applied from a squeeze bottle to garnish plates or to add an extra zing to finish fish. Unlike traditional Spanish chimichurri, his recipe adds chopped tomatoes.

This is an excellent marinade for grilling shrimp or any firm white fish.

Place all ingredients in a blender, and pulse until combined. Will keep in refrigerator for several days.

YIELD: *about 2 cups*

1 cup seeded and chopped tomatoes

½ cup packed cilantro

½ cup packed parsley

¾ cup extra-virgin olive oil

¼ cup rice wine vinegar

1 teaspoon salt

½ teaspoon freshly ground black pepper

2 cloves garlic

Pinch of sugar

Blackening Spice

A great addition to grilled fish, chicken, steaks, or pasta dishes, this spice is hot, warns Chef Tom Lozupone of Stripers Bar & Grille. Use caution when mixing.

1. Place all ingredients in a mixing bowl and blend.
2. Store in an airtight container, at room temperature.

YIELD: *1¹/₂ cups*

¼ cup cumin

¼ cup chili powder

1 tablespoon salt

1 tablespoon white pepper

¼ cup cayenne pepper

¼ cup dried thyme

1 tablespoon paprika

Lemon and Herb Butter Sauce

This is a quick and easy "sauce" to serve over the grilled catch of the day. Use a combination of fresh herbs, or stick with just one primary herb flavor. Lemon thyme is especially nice.

4 tablespoons butter, at room temperature, cut into ½-inch cubes

1 tablespoon finely chopped fresh chives or green onions

2 tablespoons fresh lemon juice

½ teaspoon lemon zest

2 tablespoons chopped fresh herbs (dill, parsley, tarragon, thyme)

Pinch of salt

1–2 grinds black pepper

1. In a small saucepan over medium heat, melt 1 tablespoon of the butter. Add the chives or green onions, and stir for 1 minute.

2. Add the lemon juice, and as soon as it begins to simmer, begin whisking in the cubes of butter, one at a time.

3. Remove the pan from the heat, and stir in the lemon zest and herbs. Add a pinch of salt and a grind or two of freshly ground pepper.

4. Use immediately, or set the pan into another pan of hot water.

YIELD: *about ¹/₂ cup, enough for 4 servings*

Tropical Salsa

The Native Americans who lived on the mainland set up summer camp on Colington Island, where they smoked and dried the fish and water-fowl they caught to take back home. The winding road leading through the island, from Kill Devil Hills, follows an old Indian trail that was probably also used by the cattle later allowed to roam free.

Carlen Pearl, of the Colington Café, shared this recipe and recom-mends topping shrimp, scallops, fish, or chicken with this salsa.

1. In a large bowl, combine all ingredients.
2. Let it sit for 30 minutes, at room temperature. Use as a topping on seafood or chicken.

YIELD: *about 2 1/2 cups, enough for 8 servings*

½ red pepper, diced

½ yellow pepper, diced

½ cup canned crushed pineapple, slightly drained

½ cup mandarin oranges

1 medium fresh tomato, diced

¼ cup purple onion, diced

¼ teaspoon crushed garlic

1 tablespoon chopped fresh cilantro

3–4 tablespoons lime juice (Key lime if available)

½ teaspoon red chile sauce or crushed red pepper (or to taste)

Hot and spicy peppers help spice up salsas and other toppings for grilled fish. E F Wiegand

Drunken Peach Glaze

This is a great glaze for grilled grouper or salmon, chicken, or pork chops.

¼ cup whiskey, preferably Jack Daniels

½ cup pure maple syrup

1 peach, peeled, pitted and minced

1 tablespoon butter, room temperature

½ teaspoon crushed red pepper flakes

1. Place whiskey and maple syrup in a small heavy-bottomed saucepan. Bring to a boil over medium heat. Reduce heat, and continue to softly boil until mixture is reduced by half, about 5 to 10 minutes.

2. With a potato masher, macerate the peach, than add to the pot, along with the butter and red pepper flakes. Continue to simmer on low heat until thick and syrupy, about 10 minutes.

YIELD: *coating for 4 pieces of fish or meat*

breads and muffins

BREADS and MUFFINS

Corn provided the South with its daily bread—cornbread, hush puppies, and hoe cakes—as well as grits and hominy. The small size of most North Carolina family farms and the typically poor soil were more amenable to growing corn than wheat. And, corn was a legacy handed to the early settlers from the Native Americans who domesticated the plant over 5,000 years ago.

Not much grew on the Outer Banks itself. Rather, early settlers traded fish for their corn. Cornbread, corn pones (pancake-like hoe cakes), and hush puppies, basically fritters, provided sustenance and comfort when there wasn't much else to eat. Although early European settlers found cornbread inferior to their breads back home made from wheat flour, at least they didn't starve.

Later, when sacks of wheat flour were available, biscuits were a quick bread that did not require a long time to knead and rise. Yeast rolls, such as those produced at early Outer Banks hotels, were considered real treats and only duplicated by skilled home cooks.

Today, even the finer Outer Bank restaurants pride themselves on their crisp, hot hush puppies or squares of sweet cornbread served by the basketful at each table.

Southerners also serve "dressings," dishes made of similar ingredients as those used in traditional stuffings but baked separately. On the Outer Banks, the Oyster Dressing on page 274 is still a marvelous side dish for wild duck, goose, or the holiday turkey.

Sweet potatoes were also a sweet, starchy staple in the Outer Banks, and were used to make biscuits and muffins. They are as delicious today as when they were served on earlier tables. Make sure you try the Sweet Potato Biscuits on page 280.

Windmills

During the eighteenth and nineteenth centuries, there were dozens of windmills located on the Outer Banks that harnessed the power of the wind to grind the corn, traded for "harvests" of fish, into grits or cornmeal. Large catches of "bugs," the unappetizing shrimp that fouled fishermen's nets, were also swapped with farmers on the mainland who used the shrimp for fertilizer. Even leaves from the native yaupon shrubs, which the Indians taught settlers to harvest, dry, and steep for a strong tea, were exchanged, at the rate of two bushels for one of corn.

New corn had to be dried before grinding, sometimes on top of sails stripped from boats and laid over porch roofs so the corn could be dried in the sun. Other Bankers used crude log corncribs.

Skilled boatbuilders were employed to construct the German-style, wooden-post mills that could be turned to face the wind. Sailmakers fashioned sails for each blade that could be reefed or unfurled according to the strength of the wind. The grinding stone could not turn too quickly because it could scorch the corn and meal. Summer brought becalmed winds, when islanders prayed for wind when fresh cornmeal supplies ran low.

Hurricanes, particularly the one in 1899, destroyed most of the Outer Banks' windmills. You can see a fairly authentic replica outside of the Windmill Point Restaurant in Nags Head, at Milepost 16.5 on the 158 Bypass.

Traditional Cornbread

Outer Bankers, especially, made their bread with cornmeal when flour could not be shipped in. This basic recipe was also used to make Oyster Dressing, see page 274.

Cornmeal that is stone-ground has more flavor, because that process retains the inner germ. That also means it needs to be stored in the refrigerator.

1. Preheat oven to 425 degrees. Add corn oil to coat a 9-inch ovenproof skillet, preferably a seasoned iron skillet, and place skillet in oven while mixing cornbread.

2. In a medium bowl, stir together cornmeal, baking powder, baking soda, and salt.

3. Break eggs into a small bowl and beat until yolks and whites are mixed. Add milk and stir, then add melted butter and stir.

4. Slowly add milk mixture to cornmeal mixture, stirring. Mix until well blended.

5. Pour into preheated skillet and bake for 15 to 20 minutes, or until top is golden and a toothpick inserted in the middle comes out clean. Cut into wedges to serve.

YIELD: *8 servings*

1 tablespoon corn oil

2 cups cornmeal, preferably stone-ground

1 tablespoon baking powder

½ teaspoon baking soda

¾ teaspoon salt

2 eggs

1¼ cups milk

¼ cup butter, melted

Hush Puppies

Who can eat but one hush puppy, brought hot to the restaurant table?

Hush puppies are easy enough to make at home, especially if you have an electric fryer or skillet, but a deep, heavy skillet or pot will do.

And who knows if they really got their name from being thrown to the dogs? That's the legend, from fish fries held at the shore of the sound or river with the dogs hanging out. And with other Southerners, you can always get into a debate as to whether or not onions should be added to the batter.

2 cups cornmeal

1 tablespoon flour

½ teaspoon baking soda

1 teaspoon baking powder

1 teaspoon salt

1 cup buttermilk

1 egg

3 tablespoons minced onion (optional)

Vegetable oil for frying

1. In a medium mixing bowl, mix together the cornmeal, flour, baking soda and powder, and salt.

2. In a small bowl or cup, beat the buttermilk and egg together. (Optional: Place the minced onions in the bowl before adding buttermilk and egg.) Stir into the dry ingredients just until the batter is moistened. Set aside.

3. Pour the oil into a deep skillet or pot until it is 2 to 3 inches deep. Heat over medium-high heat until it reaches 350 degrees, or until a drop of the batter begins to "dance" in the oil.

4. Drop the batter by a few spoonfuls at a time into the hot oil without crowding the pot. Fry until golden brown. Drain on paper towels. Serve immediately.

YIELD: *2–3 dozen*

Cornmeal Griddle Cakes

Here is a traditional Outer Banks recipe, adapted from the *Roanoke Island Woman's Club Cookbook*, which was served for breakfast, especially with salt fish. Note the use of molasses, a pantry staple, for sweetening. Butter and syrup are added at the table.

1. Combine cornmeal and shortening, using two forks or a pastry blender, or food processor. "Scald" or pour boiling water over and let stand for 5 minutes.

2. Add milk, and let stand for another 5 minutes. Beat in eggs and molasses.

3. Sift together flour, salt, and baking powder, then add that to the cornmeal mixture.

4. Heat a greased griddle or heavy skillet over medium heat. When hot enough for a drop of batter to sizzle, ladle batter by large spoonfuls onto griddle. When brown, turn on other side.

YIELD: *2 dozen 3-inch cakes*

³/₄ cup cornmeal

3 tablespoons shortening

1½ cups boiling water

1¼ cups milk

3 eggs, beaten

2 tablespoons molasses

1½ cups flour

1 teaspoons salt

1½ tablespoons baking powder

Cornmeal Muffins

These muffins are light and airy, good enough to eat by themselves but even more wonderful smeared with butter. This recipe comes from the Gillam family, who owned one of the oldest cottages on Nags Head. John and Muffin Gillam are now permanent residents.

⅓ cup (5⅓ tablespoons) butter

⅓ cup sugar

1 egg

1¼ cups milk

1 cup flour

½ teaspoon salt

4 teaspoons baking powder

1 cup cornmeal

1. Preheat oven to 425 degrees. Grease a 12-muffin baking pan.

2. In a mixing bowl, cream the butter with the sugar.

3. Mix in remaining ingredients. Spoon batter into prepared muffin pan.

4. Bake for about 25 minutes, or until golden brown and cooked through.

YIELD: *12 muffins*

Spoonbread

An old-fashioned favorite that's almost a soufflé, spoonbread has graced many a Southern table, especially before store-bought bread was available. It's a very soft bread which generally requires a spoon to serve and eat.

This recipe was handed down from Eliza Midgette Gould, who cooked for the original Tranquil House Inn in Manteo, then the Arlington Hotel in Nags Head, plus for two hunting lodges on Bodie and Pea Islands she owned with her husband. Eliza grew up in Rodanthe and was a well-known cook when she married Nathaniel Gould, who owned a hotel in Cape Cod but came to the Outer Banks area to hunt each winter during the 1880s and eventually was "trapped" here himself.

Miss Eliza's recipe notes that the recipe can be divided by thirds for fewer servings.

2 cups water

1 cup yellow cornmeal

1 tablespoon butter

1 teaspoon salt

1 cup milk

3 large eggs, well beaten

1. Preheat oven to 375 degrees. Grease a 1½–2-quart casserole.

2. Bring water to boil in a 1½-quart saucepan. Slowly add the cornmeal, stirring constantly until mixture is thick and smooth, about 5 minutes. Stir in the butter and salt, and remove from heat. Cool until lukewarm.

3. With a wooden spoon, add milk and eggs, and beat well for 2 minutes.

4. Pour mixture into greased casserole dish, and bake for about 35 minutes or until golden brown. Do not overbake.

YIELD: *6–8 servings*

Oyster Dressing

Most wild geese or ducks taken from the marshes that line Pamlico and Currictuck Sounds were too small to stuff with breading, so instead, Outer Banks cooks made "dressings" to be served on the side, using day-old bread or cornbread and the native oysters that were abundant at that time. This dressing recipe is an updated version of a traditional Southern holiday dish that's also good as an accompaniment to turkey or fish.

1 pint shucked oysters with juice

½ cup (1 stick) butter

1 cup finely chopped celery

1 cup finely chopped onions

1 recipe skillet cornbread, crumbled

3 cups bread cubes

2 teaspoons chopped fresh thyme, or
    1 teaspoon dried

2 tablespoons fresh parsley

1 teaspoon salt

½ teaspoon black pepper

1 cup chicken stock (or water),
    if necessary

1. Preheat oven to 350 degrees. Butter a large casserole dish.

2. Drain oysters and reserve the juice. Chop oysters into small pieces. Set aside.

3. Melt butter in a large sauté pan over medium-high heat. Cook celery and onions until tender, about 8 minutes.

4. In a large mixing bowl, place crumbled cornbread, bread cubes, thyme and parsley, salt and pepper. Add oysters and their juice. Mix well. If mixture seems too dry, add enough chicken stock to moisten. It should just be moist enough for ingredients to stick together, not mushy or soupy.

5. Place in prepared casserole dish, cover with foil and bake for about 30 minutes. Remove foil, and continue to cook until top of dressing is browned, about another 10 to 15 minutes.

YIELD: *8 servings as side dish*

Pecan Dressing

The *Roanoke Island Woman's Club Cookbook,* published in the 1960s by members of the Manteo Woman's Club, contains a number of delightful traditional recipes that feature what was readily available to local housewives and their cooks, like pecans, which grow very well there. Mrs. Rennie G. Williamson recommended serving her recipe, which we've adapted, with baked fowl, probably the chickens that roamed backyards and possibly the wild ducks or geese hunted in nearby marshlands.

4 slices bread

1/3 cup milk

2 tablespoons olive oil

2 small onions, finely chopped

1/2 pound ham, finely chopped

2 hard-boiled eggs, chopped

Salt and pepper to taste

2 tablespoons chopped parsley

1/2 teaspoon dried thyme

1 cup chopped pecans

1 raw egg

1/4 cup Scuppernong wine, or another sweet white wine

1. Cut bread into 1/2-inch cubes. Soak bread in milk for about 5 minutes, then squeeze until the bread is almost dry.

2. Heat olive oil in a large sauté pan over medium heat. When oil is hot, add bread, and sauté, stirring frequently, for about 3 minutes. Add onions and cook until onions are tender, about 4 minutes. Stir in ham cubes and cook just until heated, about 3 more minutes. Remove from heat.

3. Add the hard-boiled eggs and stir to blend. Sprinkle with salt and pepper, chopped parsley, dried thyme and pecans.

4. Beat egg with wine, then stir into mixture until well blended. Place in a buttered casserole dish. Bake for about 1 hour at 350 degrees, or until middle is well heated.

YIELD: *6–8 servings as side dish*

Rum Rolls from The Seafare

The Seafare Restaurant, on the Beach Road at Nags Head, had quite a reputation for serving outstanding food. The Goulds, owners of The Arlington Hotel, first built it as an oyster bar, to keep the odor of steaming oysters away from guests. Only a few could sit at the long, curved bar, and such a line would form that a huge dining room was soon added which also served prime rib, steaks, and seafood. Unfortunately, the restaurant burned years ago, but not before other family members, who became the owners and chefs of Kelly's and Penguin Isle, got their training there.

The tastiest memories are not just the oysters but the rum rolls, which were served by the basketful at each table. Mrs. Natalie Gould Mandell, eighty-nine, shared the Gould family recipe for this long-ago favorite.

FOR THE ROLLS:

2 cups sweet milk

1½ cups sugar, divided

½ cup shortening

2½ teaspoons salt

2 packages dry yeast (4½ teaspoons)

2 eggs, beaten

1 tablespoon dark rum

7 cups sifted flour, divided

4 tablespoons butter or margarine, melted

1½ cup seeded raisins, cut fine

FOR THE ICING:

2 cups confectioners' sugar

4 tablespoons hot water

4 tablespoons rum

1. Heat milk in a small saucepan just until it begins to bubble around the edges. (Scald the milk.)

2. In a small bowl, combine ½ cup sugar, the shortening, and salt. Pour the scalded milk over, and stir until mixed thoroughly. Cool to lukewarm.

3. Sprinkle yeast over cooled milk mixture, and beat with whisk or low speed of electric mixer until smooth.

4. Add beaten eggs and rum, and mix well. Add half the flour (3½ cups), and beat until smooth. Cover with a clean towel and let rise in a warm place (80 to 85 degrees) until double in bulk, about 3 hours.

5. Divide dough in two. Roll each half into two strips, each 12 inches long, ½ inch thick, and 4 inches wide. Brush top of strips with melted butter and sprinkle with a cup of sugar and raisins. Roll strips up, pulling the dough out at edges to keep uniform. They should be 15 inches long when rolled.

6. Grease 3 dozen-sized 3-inch muffin tins (for 36 muffins). Cut rolls in crosswise slices $1/2$ inch thick, and place each into individual muffin cups. Cover with a clean towel and let rise in a warm place until doubled in bulk.

7. Preheat oven to 375 degrees. Bake rolls for 15 to 20 minutes.

8. While rolls are baking, mix together confectioners' sugar, hot water, and rum. As soon as rolls are removed from oven, cover with icing.

YIELD: *36 rolls*

Zillie's Rolls

1 cup boiling water

1 cup sugar

1 cup shortening

2 packages yeast

1 cup warm water

2 eggs, slightly beaten

2 teaspoons salt

6 cups flour

½ cup butter, melted

Miss Zillie O'Neal, born in 1859, was just one of Ocracoke's legendary characters and great cooks. A spinster, she lived on the Back Road with her sister and helped raise her nieces and nephews. In response to praise for her famous yeast rolls, she would proclaim, "Don't let your pantry become empty or bare, otherwise the devil will make his home there!" Or so say the owners of Zillie's Pantry, a gourmet shop named in her honor in Spencer's Market just as you come into the village. Owners David Bundy and Roy Reeves stock the store with coffee, wines, beer, fresh bread and cookies, chutneys, prepared sauces, spreads, and salads.

And they shared this recipe for yeast rolls, a close approximation to Miss Zillie's. You can leave the dough in the refrigerator for several days, and use as needed.

1. In a large bread bowl, mix boiling water, sugar, and shortening.

2. In a measuring cup, mix yeast and the warm water. Pour the yeast mixture into the first mixture.

3. Add the beaten eggs and salt, and mix until combined. Add the flour, a cup at a time, and mix well into a soft dough.

4. Cover bowl with a dish towel and set in a warm place. After the dough has risen or doubled in size, about 1 to 2 hours, punch it down.

5. Lightly grease muffin tins. Pinch off dough and form 1-inch balls, placing two balls in each hole of the pan. Cover and let rise until doubled, about 1 to 2 hours.

6. Preheat oven to 400 degrees. Bake rolls for 10 to 12 minutes. Remove from oven and brush each roll with melted butter.

YIELD: *2–3 dozen rolls*

Blueberry Muffins

Blueberries are grown along the middle and southern parts of North Carolina's coastal plain, so you should see more local berries available during the early summer at Outer Banks' markets.

Since everyone in my house seems to love the top crust of muffins the best, I now use the special flat muffin-top pans. What makes these muffins taste even better is the caramelized, final sprinkle of sugar over the top, something Marion Burros suggested several years ago in *The New York Times*. I also hand-place blueberries across the top of the muffins, as I do with blueberry pancakes, to distribute the fruit more evenly. Here is my adaptation.

½ cup (1 stick) butter, softened

1 cup sugar, plus another ¼ cup

2 eggs

½ cup buttermilk

2 cups flour

½ teaspoon salt

2 teaspoons baking powder

1 teaspoon cinnamon

2 cups blueberries, washed, drained, and patted dry

1. Preheat oven to 375 degrees. Grease muffin pan.

2. In a large mixing bowl, using an electric mixer, beat together the butter and 1 cup sugar. Add eggs and mix well. Stir in buttermilk.

3. In a small bowl, mix flour, salt, baking powder, and cinnamon together. Gradually add to mixture while stirring constantly.

4. Gently fold in half of the blueberries.

5. Fill greased muffin cups about ⅔ full. On the top of each muffin, drop more blueberries, filling in the gaps so that blueberries are distributed evenly.

6. Sprinkle the tops of each muffin with the additional sugar.

7. Place in oven and bake for about 20 to 30 minutes, depending on thickness of your muffins.

YIELD: *about 12 muffins, or 8 large muffin tops*

Sweet Potato Biscuits

1 pound sweet potatoes

1 cup light brown sugar (you may prefer to cut that by half)

¼ cup water

2¼ cups Bisquick (or any biscuit mix) (see Note)

Something is always happening at Kelly's Outer Banks Restaurant & Tavern, whether it's the St. Patrick's Day Parade, open mic night, or the hottest bands playing downstairs in the Tavern. That's in keeping with history, for you'll see an impressive array of vintage posters announcing the likes of Fats Domino, Louis Armstrong, or Jerry Lee Lewis who performed during the 1950s and '60s at the famed Casino, which used to be down the Beach Road in Nags Head.

Upstairs, the menu features everything from Gulf Stream fish to top-quality duck, and in another nod to history, these sweet potato biscuits. The recipe was inspired by the biscuits made by an older Outer Banks friend, Martha Kay Helms, who used to cook at the Dews Island Hunt Club on Currituck Sound.

These biscuits are almost like dessert since they use more than twice as much brown sugar as other traditional recipes. Mike Kelly prefers to steam the sweet potatoes, in order to retain more moisture. He says to look for sweet potatoes that are more orange in color, for they will be more moist and sweeter, too. He recommends serving these biscuits buttered with thinly sliced country ham.

1. Cook sweet potatoes by either placing unpeeled potatoes on a steamer over boiling water, or if you prefer, in boiling water for about 20 to 30 minutes or until tender when pierced with a fork. Or, microwave by first pricking the skin with a fork, then cooking on high for about 8 minutes. Or you may bake them for about 1 hour in a 350 degree oven.

2. When you are ready to mix the biscuits, preheat oven to 350 degrees. Grease a baking sheet.

3. Cool and peel sweet potatoes, and mash them slightly. (Should measure about 1½ cups).

4. Mix together sweet potatoes, brown sugar, Bisquick mix, and water. Combine ingredients thoroughly. The mixture will be moister than regular biscuits.

5. Flour work surface. Roll or pat biscuit mix to ½-inch thickness. Cut with a smaller (2½-inch) biscuit cutter.

6. Bake for 16 to 18 minutes. The moist mixture will not allow the biscuits to rise a great deal. As Kelly says, "A mindful eye should be kept on the biscuits so they do not overcook."

NOTE: Instead of Bisquick, substitute 2 cups flour, 2 tablespoons baking powder, 1¾ teaspoons salt mixed together before adding sweet potatoes, then add 4 tablespoons of melted butter, and instead of water, milk.

YIELD: *1½ dozen*

Sweet Potato Muffins

A basket of these warm muffins are as great to serve with dinner as they are with brunch. Use mini-muffin tins to make a one-bite delight. Serve with Honeyed Pecan Butter (recipe follows).

Sweet potatoes grow well in the loamy soil of North Carolina's coastal plain. It's easy to microwave the 1 or 2 sweet potatoes needed for this recipe. Just make sure to pierce the skin with a fork in several places so they won't explode, then heat on high for about 8 minutes or until they are "squeezeable."

½ cup (1 stick) butter, softened

1¼ cups sugar

2 eggs

1¼ cups cooked sweet potatoes

1 cup milk

1½ cups flour

2 teaspoons baking powder

¼ teaspoon salt

1 teaspoon cinnamon

½ teaspoon nutmeg

¼ cup chopped pecans or walnuts

½ cup raisins (optional)

1. Preheat oven to 400 degrees. Grease mini-muffin tins or line with paper cups.

2. In a large mixing bowl, using an electric mixer, cream together the butter, sugar, and eggs.

3. Blend in sweet potatoes and milk.

4. In a small bowl, mix together the flour, baking powder, salt, cinnamon, and nutmeg. Fold into the sweet potato mixture. Do not overmix.

5. Fold in nuts, and if desired, raisins.

6. Fill muffin cups $2/3$ full. Bake for about 10 to 12 minutes if using mini-muffin tins, or about 20 to 25 minutes if using a regular muffin size.

YIELD: *about 18 mini-muffins, or 12 regular muffins*

Honeyed Pecan Butter

¼ cup (½ stick) butter, softened

2 tablespoons honey

2 tablespoons finely chopped pecans

Delicious on toast, biscuits, or with Sweet Potato Muffins.

Combine all ingredients in a food processor or thoroughly mix with a fork. Store in refrigerator.

YIELD: *$1/2$ cup*

desserts

DESSERTS

Desserts were not an everyday occurrence for Outer Bankers. In fact, they were a real treat because of the difficulty to get pantry items such as sugar, flour, or vanilla. It's not like there was a market just blocks away. Even until just recently, there was not a major grocery store in Duck or Hatteras.

But when peaches or blackberries or figs were in season, Outer Bankers were treated to wonderful pies and cakes and ice cream, a rarity in the old days.

Recipes for some of the traditional desserts were shared with me as though they were treasures, which they truly are. Enjoy what delighted the older Bankers, and indulge with some newer, contemporary desserts provided here, too. Leave your dinner guests with a lasting impression.

Blackberry Pie

Each summer, Carlen Pearl, owner of the Colington Café, heads down the Banks to pick blackberries from the thickets near Salvo. These vines have survived many hurricanes and fed Outer Bankers for generations, including the native Croatan tribe, which had a permanent settlement in nearby Buxton.

Helen Daniels, eighty-four, remembers going for picnics at the northern end of Roanoke where it was covered in patches of blackberries, huckleberries, blueberries, and wild grapes before Fort Raleigh was rebuilt. "You had to watch out for snakes, and chiggers, too," she recalls.

Fortunately, farmers are now growing cultivated blackberries which you can find in the markets during the early summer.

I like the convenience of having the rectangular boxes of prepared pastry dough rolled up in a tube on standby in the fridge, waiting for me to unfold the pastry and give it a few turns with my rolling pin before draping it over my own pie plate. And no, I do not pretend it's my own handiwork.

2 piecrusts, uncooked

4 cups fresh blackberries, rinsed, drained, and patted dry

1 cup sugar

3 tablespoons cornstarch

1 teaspoon nutmeg

1. Preheat oven to 400 degrees.

2. Roll out one of the prepared piecrusts and place it in a pie pan.

3. Place blackberries in a large bowl.

4. In a small bowl, mix together the sugar, cornstarch, and nutmeg.

5. Sprinkle the sugar mixture over the blackberries, gently stirring until all berries are coated.

6. Place blackberries in piecrust. Roll out the other piecrust and drape it across the berries. Firmly press down on the edge of the pie pan, then cut excess away and pinch around the edge of piecrust. Make several long slits in the top crust.

7. Place in oven and bake for about 45 to 55 minutes, or until top crust is browned and filling is bubbling through the slits.

8. Serve warm with ice cream. The filling will be quite runny. Or, refrigerate for several hours and serve with whipped cream.

YIELD: *8 or more servings*

Juicy blackberries can still be found in thickets up and down the Outer Banks.
E F Wiegand

Old-fashioned Peach Cobbler

During baking, this cobbler does a flip-flop: the fruit and juice go to the bottom and a cake-like layer forms on top.

1. Preheat oven to 375 degrees. Spray or lightly butter one 10x5x3-inch loaf pan.
2. In a large bowl, cream together butter and sugar until fluffy.
3. Sift flour, baking powder, and salt in alternately with milk, and mix just until smooth. Pour batter into prepared pan.
4. Place fruit over batter, and sprinkle with $1/3$ cup sugar. Pour fruit juice over top.
5. Bake for 45 to 50 minutes, until top is browned.

YIELD: *6 servings*

FOR THE BATTER:

¼ cup (½ stick) butter, softened

$1/3$ cup sugar

1 cup sifted all-purpose flour

2 teaspoons baking powder

¼ teaspoon salt

½ cup milk

FOR THE FRUIT TOPPING:

2½ cups sliced peaches

$1/3$ cup sugar

1 cup fruit juice (I use orange juice; you might want to try peach or apricot nectar)

Peaches Near the Beaches

Knotts Island, a short ferry ride from the mainland and across Currituck Sound from Corolla, is home to beautiful peach orchards. The last full weekend of July is the annual Peach Festival, with a parade, cloggers, and of course, peach ice cream, pie, jams, and cobblers.

You'll also find roadside peach stands along all the sandy plains of North and South Carolina as you make your way to the Outer Banks.

When buying peaches, give them a sniff for that tantalizing peach smell. Look for a peachy glow and less green on the skin. You really should not squeeze the peach to test for ripeness. Most peaches are rather hard while at the market but will ripen when allowed to sit on your countertop, away from direct sunlight, for several days. To speed up the ripening process, you may place them in paper bags.

Peach Gingersnap Tart

I love the extra bite the gingersnaps give this dessert. It's an easy recipe to make while on vacation. Be sure to allow enough time for the pie to chill in the refrigerator. The crust will stay crisp for only one day, but it's still good when gooey with the peach juices.

FOR THE CRUST:

Nonstick spray

1½ cups gingersnap crumbs (about 3 dozen crispy cookies)

6 tablespoons butter, melted

2 teaspoons finely grated lemon rind (from about 1 lemon)

FOR THE FILLING:

6–8 medium-size ripe peaches

3 tablespoons fresh lemon juice (from 1 large lemon)

⅓ cup sugar

3 tablespoons cornstarch

TO MAKE THE CRUST:

1. Preheat oven to 350 degrees.

2. Spray a 9-inch tart pan with removable bottom with nonstick spray.

3. With knife blade in food processor, pulse the cookies until pulverized into a fine crumb.

4. Add melted butter and lemon rind, and pulse until mixture is just moistened.

5. Pour into prepared tart pan, and using fingers, press dough evenly over bottom and up sides of pan.

6. Bake until almost dry, about 8 to 10 minutes (it will become very crisp after it cools, so be careful!).

7. Cool completely before adding filling. Can be made one day ahead. Cover tightly and leave at room temperature.

TO MAKE THE FILLING:

1. Peel the peaches. Coarsely chop about half, until you have 2 cups. Thinly slice the remaining peaches. Splash the peaches with the lemon juice. Retain all peach juice that collects.

2. Mix sugar and cornstarch together in a medium-size heavy saucepan.

3. Add the 2 cups coarsely chopped peaches and any accumulated juices. Drain lemon and peach juices from the sliced peaches into the pot also. With a potato masher, mash into a coarse puree.

4. Simmer puree over medium-low heat, stirring constantly, until mixture is thick, about 5 minutes.

5. Allow mixture to cool, then fold in sliced peaches. Spread filling into prepared crust.

6. Refrigerate until well chilled, at least 3 hours.

7. Slice and serve with a dollop of whipped cream, if desired.

YIELD: *6–8 servings*

Strawberry Shortcake

Developed by Christine Zambito, executive chef of The Sanderling, this dessert is just wonderful when fresh strawberries are in season. It gets its extra boost of flavor from oranges, which complement the strawberries.

NOTE: The components for this recipe include shortcake biscuits, orange-strawberry compote, whipped cream, fresh strawberries, fresh mint and powdered sugar.

10 shortcake biscuits

2 cups orange-strawberry compote

2 cups cream, whipped

1 cup fresh strawberries

Fresh mint

Powdered sugar

FOR THE SHORTCAKE BISCUITS:

1½ cups all-purpose flour

1 cup cake flour

½ teaspoon salt

1 tablespoon baking powder

½ cup granulated sugar

2 tablespoons poppy seeds

6 tablespoons cold, unsalted butter,
    cut into ½-inch dice

⅔ cup buttermilk

1 orange, zest and juice

1 tablespoon granulated sugar
    (for tops of shortcakes)

TO MAKE THE SHORTCAKE BISCUITS:

1. Preheat oven to 375 degrees.

2. In an electric mixer or with a pastry cutter, mix together flour, salt, baking powder, sugar, poppy seeds, and butter to a coarse cornmeal consistency.

3. Slowly add in buttermilk, orange zest, and juice, mixing just until the dough comes together.

4. Turn dough out onto a lightly floured board and knead dough slightly, about 12 folds.

5. Roll out dough to 1 inch thick.

6. With a 2½-inch biscuit cutter, cut 10 biscuits, re-forming the dough once if necessary.

7. Place biscuits on a lightly greased jellyroll pan with about 1 inch spacing between biscuits.

8. Sprinkle granulated sugar on top.

9. Bake for 15 to 20 minutes, or until the biscuits just begin to brown on top.

TO MAKE THE COMPOTE:

1. Heat oil in medium saucepan.

2. Add orange zest and cook for 1 minute.

3. Add strawberries and cook 5 minutes, stirring, frequently.

4. Add brown sugar and orange juice and stir until sugar is dissolved.

5. Simmer over low heat 5 minutes.

6. Add the orange segments and stir well.

7. Return to a simmer and add cornstarch mixed with 2 tablespoons of water if necessary to thicken.

8. Let cool completely before serving.

TO WHIP THE CREAM:

1. In a medium mixing bowl, mix all ingredients together with a wire whip.

2. Continue to whip until soft peaks form.

3. An electric mixer can be used, but be careful not to over-whip.

4. Use immediately or refrigerate for up to 30 minutes.

TO ASSEMBLE THE DESSERT:

1. Split biscuits in half.

2. Place bottom half of each biscuit on individual serving plates or a large platter.

3. Place a dollop of whipped cream on each biscuit bottom.

4. Spoon compote over the whipped cream.

5. Top with biscuit top.

6. Garnish each plate with fresh strawberries, mint, and powdered sugar.

YIELD: *10 servings*

FOR THE ORANGE-STRAWBERRY COMPOTE:

1 teaspoon canola oil

Zest and juice of 2 oranges

3 cups chopped strawberries

½ cup brown sugar

1 cup orange segments

1 tablespoon cornstarch

FOR THE WHIPPED CREAM:

2 cups cold heavy whipping cream

½ cup granulated sugar

½ teaspoon vanilla

Lemon Curd and Blueberry Tart

A beautiful presentation, this tart will cleanse the palate, especially if a heavy seafood was served during the meal. A very "tart" tart, it's best eaten the day it's made. The tart is also good made with sliced strawberries instead.

NOTE: You'll have to assemble the pastry crust first, then make the lemon curd and allow it to cool before adding the blueberries.

1 batch tart pastry

1 batch lemon curd

1½ pint blueberries, rinsed, picked over, and patted dry

FOR THE PASTRY:

½ cup butter, melted

½ teaspoon vanilla

Zest of 1 lemon, finely grated

¼ cup confectioners' sugar

1 teaspoon salt

1–1¼ cups flour

FOR THE LEMON CURD:

3 whole eggs

3 egg yolks

¾ cup sugar

2 tablespoons finely grated lemon zest

¾ cup fresh lemon juice, strained (5 to 6 large lemons)

Pinch of salt

6 tablespoons unsalted butter, cut into ½-inch cubes

TO PREPARE THE PASTRY:

1. Preheat oven to 350 degrees. Butter the bottom and sides of a 9-inch fluted tart pan.

2. In a large bowl, combine butter, vanilla, lemon zest, sugar, and salt. Gradually stir in enough flour to form a soft ball of dough.

3. Place the dough in the center of the prepared tart pan. Press the pastry evenly over the bottom and up the sides, using your fingertips.

4. Place the tart shell in the center of the oven and bake until pastry is lightly browned, about 15 to 18 minutes.

5. Place on a wire rack and cool before adding the lemon curd.

TO PREPARE THE LEMON CURD:

1. In a large saucepan, whisk eggs, yolks, sugar, lemon zest and lemon juice, and pinch of salt.

2. Add butter, and cook over medium-low heat, stirring constantly with a rubber spatula, scraping sides and bottom of pan. Do not boil.

3. Cook for 7 to 10 minutes, until the mixture is the consistency of loosely whipped cream, thick enough to coat the back of the spatula and leave a trail when a finger is drawn through it.

4. Pour mixture through a fine-mesh strainer into the pre-baked pastry crust.

TO FINISH THE TART:

1. Allow the tart to cool to room temperature, about ½ hour.

2. Sprinkle the blueberries evenly over the top.

3. Refrigerate, for up to 1 day.

4. When ready to serve, remove the outside ring from the tart, and let sit at room temperature for 20 to 30 minutes before serving. Best eaten the day it's made.

YIELD: *8–10 servings*

Strawberry-Chocolate Tart

Here are two sensuous flavor combinations and a beautiful presentation that always elicits awe. Each time I serve this tart, the recipe gets tweaked. This rendition is just about perfect.

Eastern North Carolina produces very sweet strawberries along the sandy, coastal plain near the Outer Banks. Make sure you save the prettiest berries for the top of the tart.

6 ounces bittersweet chocolate, coarsely chopped

3 tablespoons butter, cut into pieces

3 tablespoons heavy cream

1 9-inch pie crust, baked (I use a loose-bottomed tart pan)

1 quart (4 cups) whole, fresh strawberries, hulled (large ones halved) rinsed, and dried

2 tablespoons strawberry or red currant jelly

1 teaspoon water

Confectioners' sugar, sifted

Sprigs of lemon verbena or mint

1. In the microwave, or in a double boiler, melt the chocolate and butter together, stirring frequently. When thoroughly melted and mixed, stir in cream and beat with spoon until combined.

2. Spread mixture into the baked tart shell.

3. Immediately place berries, bottoms up, starting in the center, in a patterned circle covering the tart.

4. Melt jelly and water together in the microwave, stir, then brush the tops of each strawberry with that mixture so that berries will glisten.

5. Serve within 2 hours, or refrigerate for up to 6 hours, allowing tart to warm to room temperature before serving so that chocolate layer can be sliced. Sprinkle confectioners' sugar over the top of each slice, and place a sprig of lemon verbena or mint on top.

YIELD: *8 servings*

Lemon Squares

Tart and refreshing on a summer day spent at the beach, these lemon bars are almost addictive.

When you need to both zest and juice a lemon, remove the zest first. Lightly graze a grater across the lemon, or make the job even easier with a Microplane, a kitchen tool adapted from woodworking shops.

TO MAKE THE CRUST:

1. Preheat oven to 350 degrees. Butter a 9x13-inch baking pan.

2. With an electric mixer, beat butter and sugar together until fluffy.

3. Fold in flour. Press mixture evenly into the bottom of the prepared pan.

4. Bake for about 20 minutes or until lightly browned.

TO PREPARE THE FILLING AND BAKE THE SQUARES:

1. Beat the sugar and eggs together until smooth. Add the lemon zest, juice, salt, and flour, and stir until just combined.

2. Pour the filling over the crust and bake for about 20 minutes, or until filling is set. Cool on a wire rack. When cool, sift top with confectioners' sugar.

3. Cut into 2-inch squares.

YIELD: *about 18 squares*

FOR THE CRUST:

1 cup (2 sticks) butter, softened

½ cup sifted confectioners' sugar

2 cups flour

FOR THE FILLING:

1 cup sugar

2 large eggs

1 generous tablespoon lemon zest (about 2 lemons)

$^1/_3$ cup lemon juice (about 2 lemons)

½ teaspoon salt

2 tablespoons flour

¼ cup sifted confectioners' sugar

Wanchese Lemon Pie

Maude Etheridge Daniels was the mother of fifteen—eleven sons and four daughters—and was rightfully considered the matriarch of the Wanchese Fish Company, which her husband and some of their sons have been running for decades. She passed her recipes over to Denise, one of her daughters-in-law, before she recently died.

1 cup sugar, divided

¼ cup cornstarch

1 cup water

⅓ cup fresh lemon juice

2 egg yolks, beaten

½ teaspoon lemon zest

4 ounces cream cheese

2 egg whites

1 9-inch piecrust, baked

1. In a saucepan, mix ¾ cup of the sugar, cornstarch, water, and lemon juice. Add beaten egg yolks and lemon zest.

2. Bring to a boil, slowly stirring until thick.

3. Remove from heat, and stir in cream cheese until well blended.

4. In a medium bowl, beat egg whites, add remaining ¼ cup sugar, and continue beating until egg whites are stiff. Fold into lemon mixture.

5. Pour filling into baked, cooled piecrust.

6. Refrigerate about 2 hours before serving.

YIELD: *8 servings*

Lemon Souffle Cheesecake

A retreat at The Sanderling Resort & Spa is a sensuous experience, from walks along isolated beaches to massages and facials. Here is another way to indulge yourself with this sensuous, cool creation from Pastry Chef Kevin Wirt.

1. Preheat oven to 325 degrees.

2. Spray a 9-inch cake pan or springform pan with nonstick cooking spray and line the bottom with a piece of parchment or waxed paper.

3. In a small bowl mix together graham cracker crumbs and butter.

4. Press crumbs into bottom of prepared cake pan and freeze 10 minutes.

5. In a mixer blend together cream cheese, sour cream, and sugar until smooth, frequently wiping down the sides of the bowl to avoid lumps.

6. Slowly add egg yolks. Wipe down sides.

7. Add lemon zest, juice, and vanilla.

8. In a separate bowl, whip egg whites and cream of tartar until stiff but not dry peaks.

9. Gently fold egg whites into cream cheese mixture using a rubber spatula.

10. Fill the cake pan with the batter (about ¾ of the way full).

11. Place filled cake pan into a larger baking pan. Fill with hot water to a depth that's halfway to the top of the larger pan. Place in oven, and bake for about 40 minutes.

12. Remove from heat and let cool to room temperature, then refrigerate until completely cooled.

13. Serve cold with fresh fruit or sorbet.

YIELD: *8 to 10 servings*

1 cup graham cracker crumbs

2 tablespoons melted butter

1 pound cream cheese (2 8-ounce packages)

¼ cup sour cream

¾ cup granulated sugar

2 egg yolks

2 teaspoons grated lemon zest

2 tablespoons lemon juice

1 tablespoon vanilla extract

3 egg whites

1 pinch cream of tartar

Traditional Key Lime Pie

You'll find Key Lime Pie served in many restaurants and homes along the Outer Banks. Here is a standard, traditional recipe that many like to serve topped with whipped cream and garnished with lime slices.

³/₄ cup Key lime juice

1 tablespoon finely grated lime zest

4 large egg yolks, beaten

1 14-ounce can sweetened
    condensed milk

9-inch graham cracker crust,
    baked till golden brown

1. Preheat oven to 325 degrees.

2. In a large bowl, whisk together lime juice and zest with egg yolks until mixture is creamy. Slowly whisk in condensed milk, and mix until well blended.

3. Pour filling mixture into prepared piecrust, and bake for about 10 to 12 minutes, until the filling is set like a soft custard.

4. Cool on a rack, then refrigerate for at least one hour. If desired, serve with whipped cream and lime slices.

YIELD: *8 servings*

Basnight's Lone Cedar Café's Key Lime Pie

This is a creamier and thicker version than the traditional Key lime pie recipe. Make sure you use the real Key lime juice, for it does make a difference.

Pastry chef Janie Midgett sent this recipe the day after the restaurant burned to the ground in May 2007. Sharing this recipe developed by Head Chef Bud Gruninger was their way of making sure the restaurant's reputation would continue.

1. Preheat oven to 325 degrees.

2. Prepare crust and bake for 5 to 7 minutes.

3. Meanwhile, whisk condensed milk and Key lime juice together.

4. When crust is beginning to brown, remove from oven. Pour Key lime mixture into crust and bake for another 10 minutes, or until mixture is somewhat set.

5. Cool, then refrigerate.

6. This pie is best when baked the day before you serve it so it is nice and firm.

YIELD: *8 to 10 servings*

1 graham cracker crust prepared in a 9½-inch pie plate

3 14-ounce cans sweetened condensed milk (Janie prefers Eagle Brand)

1 16-ounce bottle Key lime juice (Janie uses Nellie and Joe's brand)

Pineapple Cake

Jeanie Williams still loves to bake, at age ninety-four, in her Manteo kitchen. Before global transportation, Manteo, like many of America's small towns and villages, did not have access to fresh fruits year round, so canned fruits, and recipes to use them, were welcome to Outer Bankers. This recipe is one of Jeanie's favorites.

FOR THE CAKE:

1¾ sticks of butter

³/₄ cup milk

4 eggs

2 cups sugar

1 teaspoon vanilla

2½ cups flour

2 teaspoons baking powder

1 teaspoon salt

FOR THE FROSTING:

1 tall can (12 or 16 ounces) crushed pineapple

2 tablespoons sugar

2 tablespoons cornstarch

1 14-ounce can sweetened condensed milk

TO MAKE THE CAKE:

1. Grease and flour three 8- or 9-inch cake pans. Preheat oven to 350 degrees.

2. In a small saucepan, combine butter and milk, and bring to a boil over medium heat. Set aside to cool.

3. In a large mixing bowl, using an electric mixer, beat eggs and sugar together until fluffy. Add vanilla and beat in.

4. Add flour, baking powder, and salt, and mix well. Slowly pour in hot milk while mixer is running, and beat until well mixed. Pour into prepared cake pans. Bake for about 15 minutes, or until the middle of each layer is done, springing back when lightly touched or when an inserted toothpick comes out clean.

5. Set cake pans on racks to cool.

TO MAKE THE FROSTING AND ASSEMBLE THE CAKE:

1. In a small saucepan, combine pineapple with juice and sugar. Over medium heat, bring to a boil.

2. Add cornstarch, and allow mixture to boil for just 1 minute. Refrigerate mixture until cool.

3. Add sweetened condensed milk to the pineapple mixture and stir until thoroughly mixed.

4. Divide the mixture evenly between each layer and the top of the cake. Cool in the refrigerator before serving.

YIELD: *about 12 servings*

Pineapple Ice Cream

Pineapple ice cream, made every Sunday at The Arlington Hotel in Nags Head, was churned by Mr. Mel Bowser, one of the elegantly dressed black men who served the hotel guests in the dining room. Mrs. Natalie Gould Mandell, now eighty-nine, remembers as a child standing on top of the churn to weigh it down while Mr. Bowser turned the crank. She also remembers shivering with anticipation of the cool ice cream.

Down the Banks, Tom Angell was Hatteras Island's only African-American during the turn of the last century, and he died in 1937. He, too, churned pineapple ice cream each Sunday, inviting neighbors to join him at his home for such a rare cool treat.

The recipe shared by Mrs. Mandell did not cook the eggs, so to avoid problems with salmonella I have substituted one made for years by my mother. It also includes sweetened condensed milk, a staple found in Outer Banks pantries due to the lack of fresh milk and cream.

1 quart (4 cups) heavy cream, divided

1 pint (2 cups) whole milk

4 eggs

1 14-ounce can sweetened condensed milk

1 cup sugar

¼ teaspoon salt

1 teaspoon vanilla

2 large 12-ounce cans pineapple, drained

1. Place 2 cups of the heavy cream and the milk in a heavy saucepan. Scald (bring to a simmer, just when bubbles are beginning to around the edges). Remove from heat.

2. In a large bowl, beat eggs, then add sweetened condensed milk, sugar, and salt.

3. Very slowly beat in the scalded cream and milk. Pour mixture back into the heavy saucepan or the top of a double boiler. Cook over low heat, stirring constantly, for about 5 minutes, or until mixture is thick enough to coat a spoon.

4. Remove from heat and cool.

5. When cool, stir in vanilla and remaining cream and mix well.

6. Add the drained pineapple, and refrigerate mixture until thoroughly chilled, about 2 hours.

7. Place in an ice cream maker and follow manufacturer's directions for freezing.

8. Serve immediately, especially if it's a Sunday afternoon.

YIELD: *about 2 quarts*

Pound Cake

A pound of sugar, a pound of butter, and a pound of flour, plus a dozen eggs: That's what was in most old-fashioned recipes for "pound" cake, and it was a labor of love. The recipe included staples most old-timers had in their larders, like evaporated milk rather than fresh. This one, from my own grandmother, is typical of most found in old Outer Banks cookbooks.

Delicious by itself, it also is wonderful when served with fresh berries and whipped cream. You'll be proud to take it to the church supper or on a picnic to the beach.

3 cups flour, sifted

Pinch of salt

1 teaspoon baking powder

3 cups sugar

½ pound (2 sticks) butter, softened

½ cup Crisco or vegetable shortening, softened

5 large eggs, at room temperature

1 small (6-ounce) can evaporated milk

1 teaspoon vanilla

1 teaspoon lemon flavoring

1. Grease and flour a round tube baking pan.

2. Sift flour, salt, and baking powder together and set aside.

3. In a large bowl, cream sugar, butter, and Crisco together. Beat in eggs, one at a time. Pour evaporated milk into a 1-cup measuring cup; fill empty milk can with water, swirl to rinse sides, and add that to measuring cup until you have a total of 1 cup liquid.

4. Alternately add flour mixture and milk and water, and when blended add vanilla and lemon flavoring. Pour into prepared tube pan.

5. Place in a cold oven, set oven temperature at 300 degrees, and bake for 1½ hours. Do not open the oven door until that time; then check to see if cake is pulling away from sides of pan, which means the cake is done. If not, allow to bake longer.

6. Cool on wire rack for 30 minutes.

YIELD: *about 12 servings*

Chocolate Pound Cake

The age of a chocoholic doesn't matter. Jeanie Williams of Manteo is ninety-four, and she still likes to serve this cake because it includes cocoa. It's particularly good with fresh strawberries and a dollop of whipped cream.

1. Preheat oven to 325 degrees. Grease and flour a tube pan.

2. Sift together flour, cocoa, baking powder, and salt.

3. In a large mixing bowl, using an electric mixer, cream butter, shortening, and sugar until fluffy.

4. Add eggs one at a time, beating well after each one.

5. Add sifted ingredients alternately with milk, mixing on low. Stir in vanilla.

6. Pour batter into prepared pan, and place in oven. Bake for about 50 minutes, then test cake with a toothpick to see if it comes out clean; it might need an additional 10 to 20 minutes' baking time. Do not overbake

YIELD: *about 12 servings*

3 cups plain flour

½ cup unsweetened cocoa

½ teaspoon baking powder

½ teaspoon salt

1 cup (2 sticks) butter

½ cup shortening

3 cups sugar

5 eggs

1¼ cups milk

1 teaspoon vanilla

Hummingbird Cake

Ruth Toth makes all the desserts served at the charming Café Atlantic, which she owns with her husband, Bob, in Ocracoke. Ruth is known as Mrs. Toth to most of the younger generation, for she taught history at the island's only high school for years while her husband worked with a dredging system that kept channels to the port open. During summer breaks, Ruth worked in restaurants. When both were ready for a career change, they opened a restaurant. That was in 1989, and Café Atlantic continues to open its doors to crowds of tourists and locals alike.

Hummingbird cake is an old Southern standby. Ruth's version has always been on the menu, and she says it is foolproof.

2 ½ cups all-purpose flour

2¼ cups sugar

1 teaspoon salt

1 teaspoon baking soda

1 teaspoon cinnamon

1½ cups oil

3 eggs, beaten

1½ teaspoons vanilla

1 8-ounce can crushed pineapple, undrained

2 cups mashed fully ripened bananas

1. Preheat oven to 350 degrees. Line three 9-inch cake pans with parchment or waxed paper, then grease and flour paper.

2. In a large bowl, mix dry ingredients with a whisk.

3. Stir in oil and eggs. Add vanilla, pineapple with juice, and bananas. Pour into prepared pans.

4. Bake for 30 minutes or until cake is evenly browned, and springs back and pulls away from sides of pan.

5. Cool and frost with cream cheese frosting.

YIELD: *at least 12 servings*

Cream Cheese Frosting

8 ounces cream cheese, room temperature

½ cup softened butter

1 pound (box) confectioners' sugar

1 teaspoon vanilla

About 2 tablespoons milk

1. With a mixer, beat cream cheese and butter until well blended.

2. Add confectioners' sugar and mix.

3. Add vanilla and milk a little at a time, until desired consistency for spreading.

Fig Preserves

Dale Mutro mowed yards in Ocracoke when he was growing up, and since just about every backyard in Ocracoke then (and now) has a fig tree, he helped tend to them as well. He ticks off the names of the varieties found here: Celeste, Turkey, Lemon, and the Pound fig (so named because it weighs a pound, he says). Dale harvests figs when they are not all the way ripe, to keep the birds, bees, and wasps from getting them. When they start coming in fast during the summer, he makes huge batches of preserves, which he sells at the old Albert Styron General Store, owned by his cousin and located near the lighthouse.

Fig preserves are the necessary ingredient for making the famed Ocracoke Fig Cake (see page 306). Some cooks on Ocracoke add thin slices of seeded lemon.

1 peck (8 quarts) fresh ripe figs

5 pounds sugar

1. Place figs in a sink full of water and wash them well.

2. Cut stems off figs, then halve or quarter them, depending on size.

3. Place figs in large kettle, pour the sugar over the top, and shake the kettle and/or gently stir to mix in the sugar and to start the syrup forming.

4. Place on low heat, and cook gently, stirring occasionally to make sure the figs are under the juices. Cook at a very low simmer until the juice has caramelized and figs are golden brown. The mixture should be very thick. This may take several hours or all day.

5. When syrup is thick and dark, ladle mixture into clean and sterilized jars. Fasten lids while hot to seal.

YIELD: *about 6 pints*

Ocracoke Fig Cake

Figs grow profusely in Ocracoke village, perhaps due to the moist, salty air. Residents tend to place oyster shells around the base of their trees, or add a fish to the soil around them. Although figs were grown on most Southern homesteads, they are not native to the New World but rather to Asia Minor. They probably migrated with the Spanish via the West Indies, but perhaps it was a pirate, like Blackbeard, who frequented the port of Ocracoke and left this treasure.

The ladies of Ocracoke are known for their fig cakes, using the preserves they "put up" from all the figs that ripen during the summer. Some use a cream cheese frosting between layers, others make a tube cake.

Dale Mutro's grandmother, Mrs. Ollie Styron Mutro, taught him how to make this version, which uses twice as much fig preserves as the standard Ocracoke recipe. Dale claims this one is so moist it needs no frosting.

2 cups flour

1 teaspoon cinnamon

1 teaspoon nutmeg

1 teaspoon allspice

1 teaspoon salt

3 eggs

1 cup sugar

1 cup vegetable oil

1 cup buttermilk

1 teaspoon vanilla

1 teaspoon baking soda dissolved in 2 teaspoons hot water

1 cup nuts, preferably pecans

1 pint (2 cups) fig preserves (see previous recipe)

1. Preheat oven to 350 degrees. Grease a 10-inch tube pan.

2. In a small bowl, sift together the flour, cinnamon, nutmeg, allspice, and salt. Set aside.

3. In a large mixing bowl, beat the eggs. Add the sugar and oil.

4. Alternately add the dry ingredients with the buttermilk. Add vanilla, then soda dissolved in hot water.

5. Gently stir in nuts and fig preserves.

6. Pour in prepared pan, and bake for about 1 hour, or until toothpick comes out clean.

YIELD: *10–12 servings*

Ocracoke and Hatteras Islands are famous for their figs and the marvelously moist fig cakes made from recipes passed down generations. E F Wiegand

Hatteras Fig and Whiskey Cake

"Miss Edith" Stowe Oden swears whiskey is the key to what makes her cake so moist. It's also redolent with spices and this exotic, yet local, fruit. Her friend and fellow resident of Hatteras, Lynne Foster, shared her adaptation of this traditional Outer Banks recipe, and notes that figs are the island's only home-grown fruit, and that's why they have always been "put up" as preserves or baked into cakes. They're best planted against a sunny wall or heat trap with clamshells added to their base for more warmth and to enrich the soil, says Lynne. Birds keep a fig watch, too, so pick the fruits as soon as they begin to ripen.

1. Preheat oven to 325 degrees. Grease and flour a 10-inch tube pan.

2. In a large bowl, cream together the sugar, eggs, and oil. Stir in vanilla.

3. Into a small bowl, sift together the flour, salt, soda, and spices.

4. Alternately add dry ingredients with buttermilk to egg mixture, mixing well.

5. Beat in the fig preserves, nuts, and whiskey.

6. Pour into the prepared pan, and bake for about 50 minutes to 1 hour, or until an inserted toothpick comes out clean.

7. Cool on a rack, then remove from pan. Delicious served warm.

YIELD: *12 servings*

1½ cups sugar

3 eggs

1 cup oil

1 teaspoon vanilla

2 cups flour

1 teaspoon salt

1 teaspoon baking soda

1 teaspoon nutmeg

½ cup buttermilk

1 teaspoon allspice

1 cup fig preserves

1 cup nuts, preferably pecans or walnuts, finely chopped

½ cup whiskey

Tiny Layer Cake

There is an Outer Banks saying that a woman is not ready to get married until she masters the 15-layer cake that graces the lucky dessert tables on these islands. This incredible cake typically features 14 or 15 crepe-thin layers melded together with a very rich chocolate frosting.

Peggy Snead of Manteo shared this recipe for the Tiny Layer Cake she makes for Basnight's Lone Cedar Café on the Nags Head Causeway. But she learned how to create this scrumptious dessert from her mother, Mildred Stanley Langdon, who lived inland near Smithfield. Although she has lived in Manteo since 1962, Peggy still considers herself an "off-islander."

Peggy remembers her mother serving the chocolate frosting many mornings as a "sopping" sauce over hot homemade biscuits.

Her hints: Use a cake plate that will accommodate an overflow of frosting; put frosting on layers as soon as they come out of oven; cook 4 layers at a time on two racks in oven; and plan on 15 or 16 layers so you have extra in case of a goof. She says this cake keeps well for several days (actually gets better) and freezes well.

Peggy says that you can use the same cake batter with a pineapple, coconut, lemon, or caramel frosting instead of chocolate. She is fond of the caramel alternative (recipe follows), and notes that because it is a bit heavier, she makes only 12 cake layers instead of at least 14.

FOR THE CAKE:

2 cups sugar

1 cup (2 sticks) butter or margarine (Peggy uses I Can't Believe It's Not Butter brand)

5 eggs

3 cups self-rising flour, sifted (or plain flour with 1 teaspoon salt, 1 teaspoon baking soda, and 1 teaspoon baking powder, sifted)

1 cup milk

1 teaspoon vanilla

FOR THE CHOCOLATE FROSTING:

5 cups sugar

2/3 cup cocoa

½ cup water (approximately)

2 12-ounce cans evaporated milk (or equal parts evaporated and regular milk

1 cup (2 sticks) butter or margarine

1 teaspoon vanilla

14 regular-size marshmallows (if doubling recipe, use only 25 maximum)

TO MAKE THE CAKE:

1. Preheat oven to 500 degrees. Spray four 9-inch cake pans with a non-stick cooking spray. Prepare frosting as detailed below.

2. In a large mixing bowl, using an electric mixer, cream together the sugar and butter or margarine.

3. Add eggs one at a time, and beat until well incorporated.

4. Add sifted flour alternately with milk and vanilla and mix well.

5. Using a large cooking spoon, ladle one large spoonful of batter into each prepared pan. (If you prefer thicker layers, you can add two spoonfuls.) For thin layers, swirl the pan to make batter barely cover the bottom.

6. Place pans on two racks in oven so that they are not on top of one another, and bake for approximately 3 to 4 minutes, or until layer is completely cooked. (Ovens vary, so keep an eye on the cakes.) Remove cakes from pans immediately and place on a board or parchment paper.

7. Clean pans with a paper towel, reapply cooking spray, and ladle more batter into the four pans and place in oven. Begin frosting the cooked layers.

8. Continue this procedure until batter is finished.

TO MAKE THE CHOCOLATE FROSTING:

1. In a large (6-quart) saucepan, mix together sugar and cocoa, leaving no lumps.

2. Add approximately 1/2 cup water, and stir with large cooking spoon until dissolved thoroughly.

3. Add milk, mixing well.

4. Add butter, and over low heat let mixture come to a boil, stirring often.

5. Add vanilla and marshmallows, and continue cooking over low heat until marshmallows are melted and mixture begins to bubble and thicken, approximately 10 to 15 minutes. Do not overcook, but mixture needs to be thick enough to spread well.

6. Frosting can be used warm or cool.

Fourteen layers with chocolate frosting make a rich dessert that is a tradition in the Outer Banks. It is said that you are not ready to marry until you master this cake. E F Wiegand

TO ASSEMBLE CAKE:

1. Place one layer in bottom of deep cake pan or plate. Coat with a thin layer of frosting. Place another layer on top, spread frosting, and continue until all layers are used.

2. Coat top layer with frosting, then sides.

3. Let cake cool before covering and especially before cutting. Cake does not need to be refrigerated, but may be stored in the refrigerator after it is cooled.

4. Tip on how to cut: Make a cut to the center of cake, then another at right angles so that cake is divided into a quarter. Then slice that quarter into 1/2-inch slices. Continue to slice in a similar manner.

YIELD: *about 20–22 thin slices*

Caramel Frosting

1½ cups white sugar

2 cups firmly packed dark brown sugar

18 ounces (1½ 12-ounce cans) evaporated milk

6 tablespoons butter

½ teaspooon salt

30 marshmallows

6 cups confectioners' sugar, sifted

2½–3 cups finely chopped nuts

1. In a large saucepan, mix together both sugars. Add evaporated milk and stir.

2. Add butter and pinch of salt, and bring to a boil over low heat. Boil slowly for 2 minutes.

3. Add marshmallows and stir until melted.

4. Cool mixture until lukewarm.

5. Add sifted confectioners' sugar, and beat until smooth.

6. Add nuts and stir until incorporated.

7. Spread over cake layers and sides.

Crustless Coconut Pie

Somehow this pie miraculously makes its own crust when baking, says Mrs. Ivadean Priest, a native of Manteo. She remembers that this pie was also served by Gertrude Rogallo. Gertrude helped her husband Francis, a NASA scientist, invent the flexible wing, the prototype crafted from their kitchen curtains, in 1948, which led to today's sport of hang gliding. Hang gliding is a renowned activity at Jockey's Ridge State Park, where the Rogallos' test flights occurred. Every Mother's Day there's a Fly-In, with demonstrations and competitions.

1. Preheat oven to 400 degrees. Butter a large pie pan.

2. Cream sugar and butter. Add eggs, milk, flour, and coconut. Stir in vanilla.

3. Pour into buttered pie pan and place in oven. Bake for 5 minutes, then reduce heat to 300 degrees and bake for about 30 minutes or until doubled.

YIELD: *6 servings*

1 cup sugar

1 stick (8 tablespoons) butter or margarine

3 eggs, well beaten

1 cup milk

2 teaspoons flour

1 cup flaked coconut

1 teaspoon vanilla

A mirrored Winged Horse overlooks the hang gliders and climbers of Jockey's Ridge State Park. E F Wiegand

Outer Banks Bread Pudding

With no grocery stores available, early Bankers used leftovers whenever they could. There was no such thing as store-bought bread, so biscuits, loaf bread, or cornbread were made daily. Leftover bread became the next night's welcomed dessert.

Helen Daniels, who grew up on the North End of Roanoke, remembers her mother using up day-old biscuits or bread as a pudding base. Variations of this recipe appear in several old Outer Banks cookbooks. I've added a bourbon cream sauce to top it with.

1-pound French bread loaf or leftover bread cut into 1-inch cubes, about 6 cups

3¼ cups milk

3 eggs

¾ cup sugar

¼ cup (½ stick) butter, melted

2 teaspoons vanilla

½ teaspoon cinnamon

½ cup raisins

½ cup chopped pecans

1. Preheat oven to 350 degrees. Butter a 2-quart casserole or 9x13-inch baking pan (depending on whether you want a thicker, moist pudding consistency or more like a cake).

2. Place bread cubes in a mixing bowl, and pour milk over. Mix with your hands, then let sit for 5 minutes.

3. Beat eggs lightly with sugar. Add melted butter, vanilla, and cinnamon and mix well, then add to bread crumb mixture. Stir in raisins and pecans.

4. Pour into buttered pan and bake for 40 to 50 minutes, or until pudding is slightly browned and dry enough for an inserted toothpick to come out clean.

5. To serve, place spoonfuls of warm pudding in each bowl. Pour Bourbon Sauce over. Serve immediately.

YIELD: *10 servings*

Bourbon Sauce

Decadent as this sauce is, chopped pecans may also be added at the end.
If you prefer non-dairy, simply leave out the cream.

1. Place butter and sugar in a medium saucepan over medium heat.
   Stir until mixture melts, then continue to cook for another 10 minutes,
   or until mixture is browned and thick.

2. Remove pan from heat, and stir in cream, vanilla, and bourbon.

YIELD: *1¹/₂ cups*

1 cup (2 sticks) butter

1¹/₃ cups brown sugar

1 cup heavy cream

2 teaspoons vanilla

¼ cup bourbon, or to taste

Chocolate Surprise Bread Pudding

5 cups whole milk

8 eggs

12 "old" dinner rolls

1 8-ounce can unsweetened cocoa powder

2 sticks unsalted butter, melted

4 cups sugar

1 tablespoon vanilla

1 18-ounce bottle Hershey's Chocolate syrup

Whipped cream, optional

Bread pudding was a frequent dessert served on the Outer Banks in days past because cooks were able to use leftovers and pantry stock. This recipe came about in much the same way, says John Gillam, a longtime resident of Nags Head, who spent his summers at the Outlaw Cottage, the oldest cottage on the beach and one of the Unpainted Aristocracy. He now is an event planner and professionally stages weddings, a needed service with so many wedding nuptials planned on the Outer Banks by those who have had romantic vacations here.

"We were without a dessert for a Nags Head dinner honoring the Secretary of the Commonwealth of Virginia," says John. He pulled out bread from the freezer, chocolate syrup and cocoa from the pantry, eggs from the fridge, and concocted this version of a bread pudding. "It turned out to be a delicious surprise." He now makes it in huge quantities for the large parties he and wife Muffin host at their lovely beachfront home. His neighbors appreciated his efforts to get the measurements written down for this recipe, going through four delicious tries.

He says this dessert freezes exceptionally well, especially in individual serving sizes.

1. Preheat oven to 350 degrees. Grease a very large casserole dish or deep baking pan.

2. In a very large mixing bowl, combine the milk and eggs together. Crumble rolls into large pieces, then mix into egg mixture, turning rolls over and over until thoroughly saturated. Your hands may do the best job.

3. Add the cocoa, butter, sugar, and vanilla, and stir all together until everything is mixed in well. Again, your hands may work better.

4. Place mixture in prepared baking dish, then in oven. Bake for 30 minutes.

5. Open oven and pour one-third of the bottle of Hershey's syrup over the pudding. Slide back into the oven for 30 more minutes.

6. At that time, turn oven down to 300 degrees, and continue to bake for another 30 minutes, or until there is little batter on a knife when inserted in the pudding.

7. When pudding is done, remove from oven, and pour another one-third bottle of Hershey's syrup over the top. Allow to sit for about 30 minutes.

8. Serve pudding warm with the rest of the Hershey's syrup and if desired, whipped cream.

YIELD: *12 servings*

Traditional Pecan Pie

This very Southern recipe takes advantage of the many pecans that Roanoke Island provides. Keep a stock of purchased unbaked piecrusts, rolled in a box, available in the refrigerated section of your grocery. You can place them in your own pie pan, and no one will ever know they weren't made from scratch!

4 eggs

½ cup sugar

1 cup light corn syrup

1 tablespoon flour

⅛ teaspoon salt

1 teaspoon vanilla

4 tablespoons butter, melted

2 cups pecan halves or pieces

1 unbaked 9-inch piecrust

1. Preheat oven to 350 degrees.

2. In a large mixing bowl, beat eggs until frothy.

3. Add sugar, corn syrup, flour, salt, vanilla, and butter, and beat until well combined. Stir in pecans. Smooth the pecans into the top of the pie.

4. Bake until filling is set on the outer edges but soft in the center and crust is lightly browned, about 30 to 35 minutes. You may need to wrap foil around the outer edge to keep it from burning.

5. Cool on a wire rack, and serve at room temperature.

YIELD: *6–8 servings*

Chocolate Pecan Pie

This is one of the most decadent pies, almost fudge-like, featuring two favorite ingredients—chocolate and pecans.

1. Preheat oven to 350 degrees.

2. Place corn syrup and sugar in small saucepan. Stir together, then bring to a boil without stirring further. Remove from heat, and add butter and chocolate, and stir until both are melted and mixture is smooth.

3. In a large mixing bowl, whisk eggs until frothy, then add salt. Slowly whisk chocolate mixture into eggs, and stir until well blended. Add pecans, and stir.

4. Pour mixture into unbaked pie shell, smoothing pecans into filling.

5. Bake at 350 degrees for 30 to 35 minutes, or until filling is set in center.

YIELD: *6–8 servings*

1 cup corn syrup (light or dark)

¾ cup sugar

6 tablespoons butter

4–6 ounces bittersweet chocolate, chopped

3 large eggs

¼ teaspoon salt

2½ cups raw pecans

1 unbaked 9-inch piecrust

Chocolate Cream Pie

"The White family on Roanoke Island is known to be addicted to most anything chocolate," says Frank White, Jr. This favorite was developed by his mother, Donis White. Frank keeps baked pie crusts in the freezer so that he can turn out these pies in record time and number for the neighborhood.

Here's a hint: After you bring the chocolate mixture to a boil and beat it with a mixer, "you will wonder what you have done wrong, but suddenly magic happens," Frank says. He suggests serving the pie topped with sweetened whipped cream, although a baked meringue is good, too (recipe follows).

1 cup sugar

Pinch of salt

2 tablespoons plain flour

1 14-ounce can sweetened
   condensed milk

¾ cup whole milk or half-and-half

2 ounces unsweetened chocolate

2 tablespoons butter

2 large egg yolks

1 baked 8- or 9-inch pie crust

¾ cup extra-heavy whipping cream

3 tablespoons confectioners' sugar

MERINGUE TOPPING

2 egg whites (left over from pie),
   at room temperature

½ cup sugar

1. In a small bowl, combine the sugar, salt, and flour. Set aside.

2. In a large heavy saucepan, combine milk, chocolate, and butter, and stir continuously over low heat until melted.

3. Stir in the dry ingredients.

4. In a small bowl, stir the egg yolks until they are completely broken up. Add 1 tablespoon of the chocolate mixture to the eggs, then 4 more tablespoons, and stir. (This is called tempering the eggs, and prevents the eggs from turning into scrambled eggs when added to a hot mixture.) Turn the heat to medium, and pour the egg mixture into the chocolate.

5. Stir continuously until the mixture comes to a bubbling boil. (Frank says to stir from the bottom, "or you will have a scorched mess which is not even fit for pig slop.")

6. As soon as the mixture boils, remove from heat. Beat with an electric mixer on high until the mixture is smooth, about 2½ minutes.

7. Pour the mixture (it will seem thin) into the baked pie shell, and refrigerate overnight or until completely cooled and set. (Or, for an optional meringue topping, follow the recipe below, spreading the topping on the warm pie.)

8. Whip cream with confectioners' sugar until very thick, then spread on top of chilled pie. Refrigerate until ready to serve.

MERINGUE TOPPING:

1. In a large bowl and using an electric mixer, begin to whip egg whites.

2. When they begin to foam, gradually add sugar. Continue to beat, until soft peaks form when beaters are lifted.

3. Spread topping over warm pie, then bake at 325 degrees for 20 to 30 minutes, or until meringue is golden brown. Remove from oven, and cool before refrigerating.

YIELD: *8 servings*

Chocolate Chess Pie

Jeanie Williams, who shares this classic Southern recipe, says not to overcook this pie. You want the middle to just seem set when you jiggle the pie.

1. Preheat oven to 350 degrees.

2. In a medium saucepan, melt margarine or butter over medium heat. Add cocoa and sugar, eggs, vanilla, nuts, and milk, stirring until well combined.

3. Pour mixture into unbaked pie shell and bake for about 40 minutes, or until center is set.

4. Allow to cool to room temperature before serving.

YIELD: *6–8 servings*

½ stick margarine or butter

3½ tablespoons unsweetened cocoa

1½ cups sugar

2 eggs beaten

1 teaspoon vanilla

1 cup crushed, raw pecans or walnuts

1 5-ounce can evaporated milk

1 unbaked 9-inch pie shell

Raw Apple Cake

Jeanie Williams, ninety-four, lived most of her adult life in Manteo while her husband worked as a radio operator in the Coast Guard. She likes this recipe because she could use apples, pecans, and figs that were grown on Roanoke Island, if not in her own backyard.

FOR THE CAKE:

1½ cups salad oil

2 cups sugar

3 eggs

3 cups unsifted flour

1 teaspoon baking soda

1 teaspoon salt

1 teaspoon grated orange peel

3 cups diced and peeled cooking apples (4–5 medium apples)

1 cup chopped pecans

½–1 cup fig preserves

½ cup candied pineapple, raisins, or dried cranberries (optional)

FOR THE GLAZE:

1 cup confectioners' sugar

1½ tablespoons margarine, softened

1 teaspoon grated orange peel

2–3 tablespoons orange juice

1 tablespoon light syrup

1. Preheat oven to 350 degrees. Grease and flour a 12-cup Bundt pan. Set aside.

2. In a large mixing bowl, using an electric mixer, beat oil and sugar for 1 minute. Add eggs and beat another minute.

3. In a medium bowl, combine flour, baking soda, and salt. Add to oil mixture and beat until well combined.

4. Add remaining ingredients and stir until blended. Mixture will be very thick.

5. Spoon batter evenly into pan and smooth top.

6. Bake 1 hour 15 minutes, or until toothpick inserted in center of cake comes out clean. Cool on a wire rack for 20 minutes. Remove from pan and cool completely.

7. In small bowl, combine ingredients for glaze.

8. Prick top of cake with toothpick or fork and pour glaze over.

YIELD: *about 12–14 servings*

Pecan Icebox Cookies

Inger Lewis, Frank White's grandmother, was the cookie maven of Manteo. She was Norwegian, and Frank remembers the sideboard in the dining room laden in her native tradition with a variety of cookies. Mrs. Lewis encouraged young and old alike to sample all of them and take home some of the ones they preferred. This cookie was one of Frank's favorites, and he often doubles the recipe.

1. In a large bowl, with an electric mixer, cream butter and sugars. Add egg, milk, and vanilla.

2. In a medium bowl, sift together the flour, baking powder, and salt. With the mixer on low speed, gradually add the flour mixture to the creamed mixture. Stir in the pecans.

3. Flour a dough board or countertop. Flour your hands. Place the cookie dough on the floured top, and shape into two rolls approximately 2 inches in diameter. Wrap each roll in waxed paper, and refrigerate until chilled thoroughly, about 1 hour. At this point, the rolls of dough can be put into resealable plastic freezer bags and frozen until ready to bake.

4. Preheat oven to 375 degrees. Line baking sheets with parchment paper or grease the sheets with butter.

5. Using a floured surface and a sharp knife, slice the dough into $\frac{1}{4}$-inch slices. Place on prepared baking sheets.

6. Bake for about 7 minutes, or until delicately browned on the edges.

YIELD: *about 4 dozen cookies*

1 cup butter, softened

½ cup white sugar

½ cup brown sugar, packed

1 large egg

2 tablespoons condensed milk or cream

1 teaspoon vanilla extract

2¼ cups plain flour

½ teaspoon baking powder

½ teaspoon salt

1 cup chopped pecans

Blondie Brownies

This is a popular dessert that Tom Lozupone adapted for Stripers Bar & Grille which overlooks Shallowbag Bay in Manteo. You may top these brownies with ice cream and chocolate sauce, or try to eat just one!

½ cup (4 ounces) shortening

1¾ cups dark brown sugar

2½ cups all-purpose flour

1 tablespoon baking powder

½ teaspoon salt

5 eggs

2 teaspoons vanilla

2 cups dark (semisweet or bittersweet) chocolate chips

2 cups white chocolate chips

¾ cup water, room temperature

1. Preheat oven to 325 degrees. Spray a 10x15-inch jelly-roll pan with cooking spray.

2. In a small saucepan, melt shortening and brown sugar over low heat, stirring until fully incorporated. Pour mixture into a large bowl and let it cool to room temperature.

3. In a medium bowl, sift together the flour, baking powder, and salt. Set aside.

4. When the brown sugar mixture is cool, beat in the eggs, one at a time, scraping down the sides of the bowl periodically. Beat in vanilla.

5. Fold in flour mixture, gently stirring until incorporated.

6. Stir in both kinds of chocolate chips, then gently fold in water.

7. Spread batter evenly on prepared pan.

8. Bake for 45 minutes or until tester comes out clean.

9. Let cool to room temperature before cutting. Cut into 2x3-inch squares, and store wrapped in plastic or in an airtight container.

YIELD: *15 squares*

METRIC CONVERSION TABLES

APPROXIMATE U.S.–METRIC EQUIVALENTS

LIQUID INGREDIENTS

U.S. MEASURES	METRIC	U.S. MEASURES	METRIC
¼ TSP.	1.23 ML	2 TBSP.	29.57 ML
½ TSP.	2.36 ML	3 TBSP.	44.36 ML
¾ TSP.	3.70 ML	¼ CUP	59.15 ML
1 TSP.	4.93 ML	½ CUP	118.30 ML
1 ¼ TSP.	6.16 ML	1 CUP	236.59 ML
1 ½ TSP.	7.39 ML	2 CUPS OR 1 PT.	473.18 ML
1 ¾ TSP.	8.63 ML	3 CUPS	709.77 ML
2 TSP.	9.86 ML	4 CUPS OR 1 QT.	946.36 ML
1 TBSP.	14.79 ML	4 QTS. OR 1 GAL.	3.79 LT

DRY INGREDIENTS

U.S. MEASURES		METRIC	U.S. MEASURES	METRIC
17⅗ OZ.	1 LIVRE	500 G	2 OZ.	60 (56.6) G
16 OZ.	1 LB.	454 G	1 ¾ OZ.	50 G
8⅞ OZ.		250 G	1 OZ.	30 (28.3) G
5¼ OZ.		150 G	⅞ OZ.	25 G
4½ OZ.		125 G	¾ OZ.	21 (21.3) G
4 OZ.		115 (113.2) G	½ OZ.	15 (14.2) G
3 ½ OZ.		100 G	¼ OZ.	7 (7.1) G
3 OZ.		85 (84.9) G	⅛ OZ.	3½ (3.5) G
2 ⅘ OZ.		80 G	1/16 OZ.	2 (1.8) G

Index

About the Author

Elizabeth Wiegand, who grew up landlocked on a tobacco farm, fell head over heels in love during her honeymoon, a six-week long feast of fresh fish, clams, and crabs she and her new husband caught while at the coast of North Carolina. That was over thirty years ago, and her love affair with her state's barrier islands—and the seafood treasures they provide—has continued.

While attending cooking classes in the heartland of France, she recognized that the foods of North Carolina deserved accolades, too. So she began focusing her feature writing for regional and national publications on North Carolina's culinary specialties and the hard-working folks who bring them to the table. She's also been a special education teacher and raised three daughters. She lives in Raleigh with her husband, and spends as much time as possible at the beach, or traveling the world, sailing, scuba diving, fishing, and cooking the local seafood she loves.